POSTMODERN SOPHISTRY

Stanley Eugene Fish

Photo by Barney Cokeliss

POSTMODERN SOPHISTRY

Stanley Fish and the Critical Enterprise

Edited by
Gary A. Olson
and
Lynn Worsham

Afterword by
Stanley Fish

State University of New York Press

Published by
State University of New York Press, Albany

Printed in the United States of America

For information, address State University of New York Press, 90
State Street, Suite 700, Albany, NY, 12207

Production by Diane Ganeles
Marketing by Fran Keneston

Library of Congress Cataloging-in-Publication Data

Postmodern sophistry : Stanley Fish and the critical enterprise /
edited by Gary A. Olson and Lynn Worsham; afterword by Stanley Fish
    p. cm.
Includes bibliographical references and index.
ISBN 0-7914-6213-7 (alk. paper)—
  1. Fish, Stanley Eugene. 2. Criticism—United States—History—20th
century. 3. Postmodernism (Literature)—United States.
4. Postmodernism—United States. I. Olson, Gary A., date.
II. Worsham, Lynn, date.

PE64.F57P67 2004   2004041688
801'.95'092—dc22
    CIP

10   9   8   7   6   5   4   3   2   1

For Debra Jacobs

Contents

Acknowledgments

We are grateful to several scholars who helped in the production of this text, especially Allison Brimmer, Teresa Grettano, and Deepa Sitaraman. Eric Mason deserves special credit for his editorial expertise and for producing the index. Fran Keneston and Diane Ganeles lent their usual search for perfection to this project, and Priscilla Ross provided inspiration and good judgment.

Introduction

Postmodern Sophistry: Stanley Fish and the Critical Enterprise offers an intensive examination of the theoretical writings of cultural and literary critic Stanley Fish. Fourteen prominent scholars representing a range of academic disciplines—including legal studies, critical legal studies, political science, Jewish studies, rhetoric, and literary studies—explore various aspects of Fish's work on critical and legal issues. Despite Fish's stature as one of the world's preeminent critics, few studies have focused on his theoretical writings. *Postmodern Sophistry* begins a long-overdue dialogue on this work.

Part one, Interpretive Authorities, examines Fish's understanding of how interpretation functions. This section begins with Michael Bérubé's analysis of how Fish almost single-handedly "killed" reader-response criticism. He posits that Fish's turn in the late 1970s from "affective stylistics" to the theory of "interpretive communities" seemed to resolve the critical dilemma of whether the reader or the text is the source of interpretive authority. In his devastating 1981 review of the work of Wolfgang Iser, Fish demonstrated beyond question that the idea of the "gap," so crucial to Iser's work, was in fact incoherent, since "gaps" could not become available for analysis unless an interpretive paradigm were already at work designating certain textual features and/or implications *as* gaps. Fish's turn—in that review and in the latter essays of *Is There a Text in this Class?*—marked the decisive break from formalism in reader-response criticism and an important step toward a sociology of literary criticism in which "interpretive communities" themselves became the objects of analysis. However, this turn also managed to steer criticism away from textual specificity, thereby losing any sense that there is a

1

textual "object" of analysis. Fish ended up adopting a Kuhnian account of interpretive authority but without Kuhn's sense that paradigm shifts are driven by anomalies produced by mature paradigms.

Gerald Graff discusses his initial strong objections to Fish's notion of interpretation, particularly as expressed in *Is There a Text in This Class*, where Fish argues that interpretive communities "create" or "produce" texts rather than take their cues from them. Graff goes on to describe how he came to understand the heuristic usefulness of this argument for his own teaching—and even the argument's truth and validity when understood properly. He came to realize, and still believes, that Fish's arguments are a needed corrective to the still widespread belief that great texts essentially tell us how to read them—a belief that has disastrous consequences in teaching, such as the failure to expose students to literary criticism on the assumption that critical discourse comes between the student and the text. Graff develops this argument by pointing out that our reading of any text is strongly influenced by the information we receive about it before we have read it: through dust jackets, reviews, word of mouth, and so on—what Graff calls "the unofficial interpretive culture"—and he makes a case for bringing this culture more prominently into our teaching.

Legal scholar Martin Stone critiques the "interpretivist" thesis: the thesis that the meaning of a text is available only by way of some interpretation. Fish's work advances this thesis (in various versions) in opposition to a metaphysically suspect notion of meaning; it then introduces the idea of "interpretive communities" as a way of heading off the apparently skeptical consequences of this thesis. The social-pragmatic story Fish tells about meaning cannot, Stone argues, satisfy us as an account of meaning; in fact, it can be seen to be part and parcel of the metaphysically suspect notion it was meant to oppose, once the problem with that suspect notion is understood at the right level of depth. For Stone, there is a more satisfying way of freeing ourselves from that suspect notion, one that does not incur any commitment to the interpretivist thesis. Rather than choosing between the suspect notion and the interpretivist community story, argues Stone, we need to understand what goes wrong in our thinking about meaning to make it look as if these were our only options.

Gary S. Wihl examines the famous debate between Fish and Ronald Dworkin on the use of interpretation in legal reasoning. Dworkin attaches great value to interpretation in order for the law to be fulfilled as social justice. Every element of law, from specific statutes up to constitutional issues, must be actively interpreted to achieve the best expression of justice. Dworkin compares that task to producing the best possible aesthetic interpretation of a literary work. Writing from the perspective of literary studies, Fish's counter-argument is that Dworkin's aesthetic treatment of the law fails to recognize the true depth of constraint in any interpretive activity. In failing to account for interpretive constraint, Dworkin proposes an unattainable, ideal expression of justice. Wihl argues that Fish and Dworkin have constructed a false opposition about insights into interpretative activity that bear on matters of law. Fish's arguments bring to light a deeper set of assumptions in Dworkin's writings that advocate a specifically liberal doctrine of human autonomy and a specifically liberal structure of beliefs. Definitions of autonomy and liberal belief need be carefully sifted out of Dworkin's aesthetic vocabulary. Fish is right to uncover deeper political premises about liberalism in Dworkin's use of literary terms about the nature of law. But, by the same token, Dworkin's liberalism is not reducible to radical constraint of interpretation or simple neutrality of interpretation. Liberalism offers a robust concept of justice that is the focus of interpretive activity. United, rather than opposed, Fish and Dworkin push the discussion of interpretive action to a level of inquiry about the role of law as the primary articulation of social justice.

Part two, Philosophical Interventions, explores various philosophical issues that Fish has addressed (or fails to) in his work. Michael Robertson maintains that many of Fish's contentious positions become less startling when they are shown to be the logical consequences of his commitment to a particular conception of the self. For Fish, the self is constituted by being embedded within interpretive communities, and this means not only that strong forms of context-transcendence are impossible, but also that many of the key organizing categories in our culture need to be rethought. After developing this general claim, Robertson moves to a detailed consideration of the freedom/constraint dichotomy. He analyzes Fish's novel arguments for the claim that freedom always requires constraint, rather than being defined by the absence of constraint, and he examines Fish's application of this insight to the context of academic freedom within the university.

A former student of Fish's, Reed Way Dasenbrock, critiques Fish's neo-pragmatism. In *The Trouble with Principle* and elsewhere, Fish argues against the attempt to systematize our judgments beyond our own community and location by arguing that we never in fact have a coherent pattern of values despite our continual reference to such a pattern. This is in short an argument against ethical discourse. Dasenbrock's counter-argument takes several forms. First, this is not a good descriptive account of what we do, since we in fact do invoke non-situation-specific norms all the time. The attempt to claim that this is not what we should do confronts a fork in the road: if the argument is that we shouldn't do this because there are no such norms, the argument founders on self-contradiction. A more consistent argument, claims Dasenbrock, is that we shouldn't do this because it doesn't work—but this pragmatic advice seems not well founded if we are attempting to influence the world beyond the academy, which believes strongly in non-situation-specific norms. Thus, Fish's new pragmatism seems strikingly unpragmatic. This chapter asks where Fish is grounding his argument. Among the intellectual sources for Fish's position are post-structuralist critiques of ethical discourse and logical positivism, but Dasenbrock believes that Machiavelli is the ultimate source of the position; he argues, however, that Fish is not a very good Machiavellian, precisely because he wears this Machiavellianism on his sleeve, contradicting the advice given in *Il Principe* about rhetorical presentation.

Rhetorical theorists Gary Olson and Lynn Worsham examine Fish's understanding of the role of rhetoric in epistemology. What unites Fish's interventions in so many disparate areas of inquiry is his belief in the centrality of rhetoric. He consistently turns to the specific local, contingent context—to the rhetorical situation at play—to explain how something works. A primary task of rhetoric is to justify our beliefs. For Fish, beliefs are constitutive of consciousness; that is, in many ways we are what we believe. People "understand" or are "persuaded" by a position or belief because it fits into the structure of beliefs already in play, not because they have been swayed by the "reasonableness" of someone's argument; they then pursue the available means of support to justify that belief rhetorically, both to themselves and to others. For Fish, beliefs are the content of rationality, in the sense that rationality arises from beliefs and not the other way around. We justify a belief, then, by turning to the structure of beliefs from which the belief derives its intelligibility and within which it is coherent, and we then seek to express that intelligibility and coherence rhetorically, establishing a case for the belief. While Fish consistently claims that people have beliefs not because of rational arguments but because those beliefs arise from "heartfelt convictions," absent from Fish's work is any discussion of where in fact these heartfelt convictions originate. The authors argue that at the foundation of Fish's philosophy of epistemology—even though he never acknowledges it—

is the role of emotion. Implicit, unstated, but nonetheless central to Fish's position is the role of emotions, affect, in the constitution of convictions. That is, while rationality may in fact arise from a person's structure of beliefs, it is a person's affective relation to those beliefs that determines whether a person adopts the beliefs in the first place and how strongly he or she will adhere to them. Thus, the authors argue that a strong component of Fish's theory (though he never mentions it) is the constitutive role of affect.

Using the September 11 terrorist attacks as a backdrop, Steven Mailloux analyzes the difficult question of universalism versus postmodern contingency. He agrees with Fish in general on the theoretical and practical points he makes; that is, he is persuaded by Fish's rhetorical pragmatist account of postmodernism and the rhetorical strategies he advocates. But Mailloux believes that Fish overlooks something crucial: the full rhetorical force of the ideas associated with the term *postmodernism* for some modernist academics and for many nonacademic commentators. In this thinking, recognition, toleration, and acceptance are always contingently limited; the question is necessarily where do the limits end? And that is an empirical, historical question depending on the other beliefs and practices in place. Mailloux agrees with Fish that no single metabelief (belief about beliefs), no antimodernist, modernist, or postmodernist theory can trump all the other beliefs in the communal set, loosening them up so radically that just anything goes, including the toleration of fundamentalist ideologies inspiring acts of international terrorism. But he believes that Fish fails to appreciate two things: first, that there are emotional or attitudinal effects resulting from the acceptance of even this conservative postmodernism for anyone who converts to it; and second, whatever the logical (non)connection between postmodernism (as he defines it) and other beliefs and practices, there may be rhetorical effects of advocating this or that philosophical theory in the public sphere—for example, more or less toleration of competing ideas. Mailloux offers Alain Badiou's "evental philosophy" as a useful corrective to Fish's postmodernist thought.

Part three, Political Prospects, addresses the political consequences (or lack thereof) of Fish's thought. Fish has argued that central to liberal political philosophy is the notion that a just society is based on such principles as "fairness," principles that supposedly exist in the abstract, independent of any specific situation or context. Fish argues that although such abstractions are thought to be capable of being defined in ways that allow them to remain free from partisan agendas and, thus, are thought to be capable of serving as the foundation of legal and political policies that favor no one person or group in particular but that respect all people and groups in general, such efforts are doomed to fail. In a devastating critique of Fish's argument, Marxist theorist Terry Eagleton contends that while many people characterize Fish as a representative of the political Left, he is in fact an old-style, free-booting captain of industry; in fact, he has hijacked an apparently radical epistemology for tamely conservative ends. Focusing specifically on *The Trouble with Principle*, Eagleton asserts that in effect there are two Fishes: a sabre-rattling polemicist given to scandalously provocative pronouncements, and the respectable dean and academic who will instantly undercut the force of these utterances by insisting that they are descriptive rather than normative.

Political scientist Margaret Kohn also takes issue with Fish's well-known dismissal of theory as irrelevant to matters of practical concern. Fish has consistently claimed that metacritical insights in general, and his own antifoundationalist conclusions in particular, have no political implications. Kohn insists that it is impossible to make political arguments and judgments without relying on the language of principle. If substantive, embedded norms are a fundamental part of politics, then they must be challenged, defended, transformed, and reimagined. She argues that critical theory, a mode of conceptual analysis that is anchored in and contributes to particular historical processes, provides a way of approaching this task.

H. Aram Veeser examines Fish's role as a celebrity intellectual. Once known chiefly among English professors specializing in seventeenth-century studies, Fish today has the public's attention. Whenever the public worries about political correctness, moral relativism, or academic freedom, Fish is available for comment. His identification with one or two issues means that he now ranks among those whom he calls "rent for a day" or "cameo" intellectuals. For example, in a high-profile series of public debates, the conservative author Dinesh D'Souza attacked political correctness while Fish defended it. Of course, one may also observe that Fish has attempted to broaden his range. In a series of *New York Times* op-ed articles, he analyzed the fallacies of popular biography, and he examined the trial procedures at the first Rodney King hearing. Yet, by and large, he has stayed with his specialties: he attacked devotion to principles and values; savaged words like *fairness*, *equality*, and *merit*; and condemned freedom of speech. As he elaborated his illiberal positions, Fish cited his love of Milton, who, as Latin Secretary and publicist to the regicide Oliver Cromwell, advocated silencing—indeed, extirpating—the political opposition. Contrasting himself to one contemporary philosopher, Fish writes that "[Richard] Rorty wants to continue the conversation of humankind. I want to end it." Fish's ideas can hardly be popular among libel-suit-sensitive media gatekeepers, for whom freedom of speech is gospel. Yet, in Veeser's view, Fish gambled that his unpopular views would catapult him to media celebrity. The outsider's road to cultural centrality has been trod before, and it is paved with gold. Regis Debray went to the jungles of Bolivia as a guerrilla soldier with Che Guevara, serving part of a thirty-year Bolivian prison term before returning to become a government minister under French Premier François Mitterand. Edward Said was a Columbia professor who entered the public consciousness only when he returned to his Palestinian loyalties and began to defend the Palestinian liberation movement at its most hated stage: just after the Munich Olympics and the Klinghoffer killing. As Said is to the Palestinians, Fish is to postmodernism. Veeser argues that by championing postmodernism, political correctness, moral relativism, and the silencing of others, Fish has attained the influential celebrity that he has long pursued. Whether Fish will transcend the limited status of cameo intellectual and become a public intellectual, a commentator who is sought for his general wisdom on every issue, remains to be seen.

Evan Watkins examines why Fish's attention to the conditions of disciplinarity and professionalism offers a salutary corrective to a great many forms of "free floating" politics whose imaginaries of political action take no account of actual institutional location. At the same time, Fish's sense of English studies remains organized around a familiar idealism of distinction. Hence, like most idealisms, it functions best as this kind of regulatory warning rather than as a nuanced understanding of the complexities of location in the institution. Watkins takes issue with Fish's assumption that the only direct and necessary effect of interpreting literary texts is to establish the disciplinary distinctiveness of literary studies. For Fish interpretive constructions of meaning and the effects that actually follow are connected only within a contingent circularity— in this case, the differential institutional process by which disciplines realize a certain distinctive "immanent intelligibility." Watkins argues that just as disciplinary distinctiveness only emerges in the context of surrounding disciplines, so too do material resources. At the limit of Fish's epistemological inquiry, however, these considerations disappear into something we might think of as the psychological consolations of epistemology. That is, all the emphasis on conditions of knowledge, on how we know that we know what discipline we're in, is finally suspended at the moments when for Fish it seems most necessary to deliver the subjective incentive for engaging in that inquiry in the first place as well as the reward for having engaged it: do what you do and take pleasure in it; stop trying to be something completely different from what you are.

Recently, Fish has entered into a theoretical minefield: Holocaust denial. Taking on campus newspaper advertisements that question the occurrence of the Shoah, as well as Deborah Lipstadt's defense in David Irving's libel suit against her, Fish makes the same point: that Lipstadt's appeals to the inherent validity of evidence and the deniers' (as well as the historians') appeals to free speech are equally flawed because each rests on a notion that there is such a thing as unmediated reality and that narrative accounts of it are stronger or weaker depending on their ability to hew close to that reality. In this chapter, Michael Bernard-Donals makes a case both for and against Fish in his public pronouncements about the Holocaust. Fish is right to suggest that "academic freedom" and the "self-evidentness of evidence" are naive notions, but he's wrong to suggest that there are no consequences to this position. There are at least two. The first is that even his limited sense of "academic freedom" fails to account for the strong link between disciplinary work and the reality that underpins it (and in this case it is the historical reality of the Holocaust that, like it or not, exerts a certain pressure on any narrative accounting of it). The second is that despite his very lucid and accessible arguments, his positions are infuriating both to deniers and to survivors and their families alike, who see very clear consequences to the arguments and who—in the case of the survivors and their families—have scars (both psychological and physical) to show for them. Finally, Bernard-Donals extends Fish's public argument in such a way that it effectively responds to the deniers while not minimizing the materiality of the Holocaust and its very real contemporary effects.

Together, these fourteen scholars provide a penetrating and at times provocative examination of one of this century's most celebrated (by some) and reviled (by others) intellectuals. We hope this collection opens up a productive discussion and debate about Stanley Fish's contributions to recent intellectual history.

PART ONE

INTERPRETIVE AUTHORITIES

There is Nothing Inside the Text, or, Why No One's Heard of Wolfgang Iser

Michael Bérubé

In 1980, reader-response criticism was considered a major school of contemporary literary criticism. Two important collections were published that year: Susan Suleiman and Inge Crosman's *The Reader in the Text: Essays on Audience and Interpretation*, which consisted of essays commissioned specifically for the volume and which suggested strong connections between reader-response criticism and French narratology, and Jane Tompkins' *Reader-Response Criticism: From Formalism to Post-Structuralism*, which consisted of previously published work and which explicitly set out to construct a developmental narrative of recent reader-response work (moving from Michael Riffaterre and Georges Poulet through Gerald Prince, Norman Holland, David Bleich, and Jonathan Culler, with Stanley Fish threading his way through the volume early and late), the conclusion of which was Tompkins' magisterial history of theories of affect and literary response since Plato. Fish, of course, published the landmark *Is There a Text in This Class?* in the same year. But 1980 was no *annus mirabilis*; the momentum behind reader-response had been building for over a decade—indeed, arguably from Fish's own *Surprised by Sin* (1967). Both in *Structuralist Poetics* (1975) and *On Deconstruction* (1982), theories of reading were integral to Jonathan Culler's account of contemporary theory. Wolfgang Iser's work was everywhere throughout the 1970s, and *Critical Inquiry* staged debate after debate on the determinacy of meaning. It seemed to some observers at the time that reader-response had engaged if not assimilated every other major form of criticism—from narratology to structuralism to psychoanalysis to feminism—and was poised to take on deconstruction and Marxism on matters concerning *différance* and determination.

By 1990, however, any informed observer of the academic scene would have to have wondered where in the world reader-response criticism had gone. Yes, Steven Mailloux had done notable work in the decade with *Interpretive Conventions* (1982), an explicitly Cullerian book, and *Rhetorical Power* (1989), a book seasoned by a few more rounds of *Critical Inquiry* debates; Peter Rabinowitz's *Before Reading* (1987) and Jon Klancher's *The Making of English Reading Audiences* (1987) had made valuable efforts to negotiate reader-response and reception theory; and Janice Radway's *Reading the Romance* (1984) had set a new standard for feminist readings of women's readings of popular cultural forms. But by 1990, reader-response had fallen off the Major Theoretical Positions chart, obliterated by new schools associated with figures such as Stephen Greenblatt, Catherine Gallagher, Nancy Armstrong, Eve Sedgwick, and Judith Butler; postcolonial theory had achieved critical mass; and Radway, for her part, was associated more with the emergent field of cultural studies than with theories of readership, even though, as she notes in her new edition of *Reading the Romance* (1991), the work of the Birmingham School was unknown to her when she was pursuing her doctorate in the University of Pennsylvania's American Studies program in the late 1970s (2). As for Wolfgang Iser, poor Iser had disappeared so completely that some worried theorists of reading wondered if he would ever be seen again save on milk cartons.

To some extent (and I do not have the space to argue this point in detail), reader-response criticism expired of its own success, particularly those branches of it that involved hypotheses of what it might mean to read "like" or "as" a woman; at some point in the past three decades, clearly, the women of the profession stopped hypothesizing about what their readings might be like and simply set about doing them. And to some extent the "success" of reader-response criticism should be measured not by reference to the Major Theoretical Positions chart but by reference to the practical and pedagogical influence it has had throughout the wider K–16 system, in precincts where Louise Rosenblatt is a justly renowned figure and where professors in rhetoric and composition have been talking about "transactional" reading processes regardless of whether the police ever find that Iser fellow. But the fact remains nonetheless that in the annals of critical theory, reader-response criticism was once a major player, a contender, and now it is not. One of the reasons it is not, I will argue, is that one of its most important American exponents, Stanley Fish, killed it the day he published his *diacritics* review of Iser's *The Act of Reading: A Theory of Aesthetic Response*, under the title, "Why No One's Afraid of Wolfgang Iser."

The Fish-Iser Debate

I do not mean this literally, of course. But in retrospect, I think it is hard to overstate the importance of this review, both to the trajectory of Iser's career and, to a lesser extent, to Fish's. Indeed, Fish opens the review by remarking on Iser's exceptional status in the profession; and for readers who do not remember a time when Iser was considered a leading figure in literary theory, Fish's initial assessment might sound a bit odd, even hyperbolic:

> *The Implied Reader* and *The Act of Reading* outsell all other books on the prestigious list of the Johns Hopkins Press with the exception of *Grammatology* [sic] (a book that is, I suspect, more purchased than read). Iser is, in short, a phenomenon: he is influential without being controversial, and at a moment when everyone is choosing up sides, he seems to be on no side at all or (it amounts to the same thing) on every side at once. (2)

Fish comes not to praise but to bury, of course, and before I explain the details of Iser's interment, I should note that even the circumstances of Fish's review deserve comment. "Why No One's Afraid of Wolfgang Iser" appeared as the lead essay in *diacritics* volume 11 number 1 (March 1981), but *diacritics* had in fact already reviewed Iser's *The Act of Reading* in issue 10.2 (June 1980). That review, written by Rudolf Kuenzli, was highly laudatory, closing with no uncertain praise of Iser's project:

> The unquestionable merit of *The Act of Reading* consists precisely in its making us aware of our own reading process. In focusing our attention on our own act of producing the meaning of a text we will become more aware of the textual strategies, of our own dynamic relations to those strategies, and thus of the importance of analyzing the reading process for the study of literature and literary theory. Iser's working model of the interaction between the reader

> and norm-breaking literature presents us with a compelling outline
> of the intersubjective structure of such a reading process—an
> outline to which we can appeal for contextual support as we pursue
> the analysis of our own reading experiences. (56)

Historians of recent literary theory will be able to place this praise
squarely in the context of the debates of the 1970s, in which theorists such
as Culler and Iser forwarded both of the claims Kuenzli presses here:
reader-response criticism makes us more self-aware about the processes
by which readers (including ourselves) construct patterns of meaning,
and it serves especially well as a means of reading the avant-garde or
experimental ("norm-breaking") narrative works of the past one
hundred and fifty years, since these works require readers to engage
in explicitly self-reflexive deliberation about textual patterns of
meaning.

Fish, however, will have none of it. The June 1980 issue of *diacritics*
was supposed to follow Kuenzli's review with an extended (twenty-seven
pages) interview with Iser, conducted by Kuenzli, Norman Holland,
Wayne Booth, and Stanley Fish. But Fish pulled out of the interview, as
Kuenzli notes in his introduction: "Stanley Fish, who had complied with
my original request for concise, pointed questions, was dissatisfied with
the form that the interview—with the extended questions elaborated by
Holland and Booth—had taken; he indicated that he would prefer to
withdraw" (57). The result was *diacritics'* second full-dress review essay
on *The Act of Reading* within two years, a review essay that refused all the
assumptions common to Kuenzli, Holland, Booth, and Iser and that, in
retrospect, helped to change the direction of Anglo-American literary
theory. After the Fish-Iser exchange, it became possible for professional
literary critics to operate as if there were nothing inside the text, and as
if this were a good thing, too.

Fish spends the first four pages of his review faithfully summarizing
Iser's work to date, and then comes the devastating pivot paragraph:

> And yet, in the end [Iser's theory] falls apart, and it falls apart
> because the distinction on which it finally depends—the distinc-
> tion between the determinate and the indeterminate—will not
> hold. The distinction is crucial because it provides both the
> stability and flexibility of Iser's formulations. Without it he would
> not be able to say that the reader's activities are constrained by
> something they do not produce; he would not be able at once to
> honor and to bypass history by stabilizing the set of directions the

text contains; he would not be able to define the aesthetic object in opposition to the world of fact, but tie its production securely to that world; he would have no basis (independent of interpretation) for the thesis that since the end of the eighteenth century literature has been characterized by more and more gaps; he would not be able to free the text from the constraints of referential meaning and yet say that the meanings produced by innumerable readers are part of its potential. (6)

Fish is right to argue that Iser's work depends on the distinction between determinacy and indeterminacy, and he's right—though I will qualify this point below—to argue that the distinction will not hold. The problem with Iser's account of reading, in other words, is that it presumes that some features of texts exist prior to or beyond any scheme of interpretation, while other features are variable and therefore susceptible to interpretation. "Iser insists on the brute-fact status of the text," writes Fish, "at least insofar as it provides directions for the assembling of the 'virtual object.' Thus he declares in one place, 'the stars in a literary text are fixed; the lines that join them are variable'" (6). Readers are thereby assigned the tasks of filling in the "gaps" between the fixed points, and Iser accommodates or licenses a certain degree of critical pluralism by acknowledging that different readers will fill those gaps in different ways. But what counts as a "gap" worth filling? Iser's own work answers this question by examining textual phenomena as disparate as "stylistic patterns" in *Ulysses* and "the nondescription of Lady Booby's surprise" in *Joseph Andrews* (*Reader* 224, 38). A theory of "gaps" that can include everything from the presentation of moral hypocrisy in *Tom Jones* (which the reader must perceive by filling the "gaps" in Squire Allworthy's perception of Captain Blifil) to the paradoxes of "unmasked fiction" in Beckett's *The Unnamable* (in which the reader is led to realize that "the usefulness of fiction cannot be dispensed with") to the facial expressions of individual characters is a remarkably capacious theory, so much so that one is led to suspect that when it comes to texts, everything's a gap, and when it comes to gaps, *pace* Iser's attempt to provide a firm foundation for distinguishing literary from nonliterary texts, there are finally no important distinctions between fiction and nonfiction (268).

Fish makes this point as well, not by questioning the embarrassing shapelessness of Iser's examples but by forwarding a condensed version of the argument he'd advanced in the final four chapters of *Is There a Text in This Class?* Hypothesizing a reader of *Tom Jones* for whom "perfection in humankind" is not "incompatible with being taken in by a hypocrite," and who therefore sees "no disparity between the original description of Allworthy and his subsequent behavior," Fish drives home the point that the very perception of "gaps" in a text depends on what Thomas Kuhn called the priority of paradigms:

> If the "textual signs" do not announce their shape but appear in a variety of shapes according to the differing expectations and assumptions of different readers, and if gaps are not built into the text, but appear (or do not appear) as a consequence of particular interpretive strategies, then there is no distinction between what the text gives and what the reader supplies; he supplies *everything*; the stars in a literary text are not fixed; they are just as variable as the lines that join them. (7)

For Fish, what follows from the possibility that "gaps" are everywhere is the conclusion that "gaps" are only where you—that is, where your interpretive assumptions—find them. But (and by 1981 Fish had already practiced and perfected this closing gymnastic sequence) this does not mean that textual interpretation is a chaotic and hopelessly subjective enterprise; on the contrary, "there is no subjectivist element of reading, because the observer is never individual in the sense of unique or private, but is always the product of the categories of understanding that are his by virtue of his membership in a community of interpretation" (11).

Iser, for his part, did not help his cause by severely misconstruing Fish's challenge to his position. Apparently believing that Fish did not grasp the determinate meaning of what he, Iser, had meant by "determinate meaning," Iser, in his September 1981 *diacritics* reply to Fish's review essay ("Talk Like Whales"), patiently explains that

> Professor Fish's confusion is caused by the fact that he has telescoped three ideas into two. I draw a distinction between the given, the determinate, and the indeterminate. I maintain that the literary world differs from the real world because it is only accessible to the imagination, whereas the real world is also accessible to the senses and exists outside any description of it. The words of a text are given, the interpretation of the words is determinate, and the gaps between given elements and/or interpretations are the indeterminacies. The real world is given, our interpretation of the world is determinate, the gaps between given elements and/or our interpretations are the indeterminacies. (83)

This is a string of terrible, terrible arguments. As if it were not bad enough that Iser insists on *two* kinds of determinacies, the given and the determinate, he further insists that interpretation is determinate (where one might have thought, in the most naively realist terms, that the text was determinate and the interpretations were variable) *and* that the "the words of the text" have the same ontological status as "the real world"—namely, that of the "given," the brute-fact raw material for interpretation (where one might have thought, in the most naively realist terms, that the words of texts were themselves interpretations of a real world). It is not a pretty moment for Iser, who had opened his reply by praising Fish's précis of his work but condemning Fish's critique, clearly failing to see that Fish's précis was every bit as damning as the critique.

Let it not be said that Fish booted Iser off the top of the Johns Hopkins University Press bestseller list all by himself. Still, Fish's readers—and I imagine that the readers of this book are likely to belong to a loose-knit interpretive community designated by the term "Fish's readers"—are no doubt familiar with all these aspects of Fish's modus operandi. The denial of determinate meaning, the insistence on the ubiquity of interpretation, and the antivoluntarist, strong-constructionist account of "communities" that constrain any individual's activity of interpretation: these are features of nearly everything Fish has written after "Interpreting the Variorium," the 1976 essay in which Fish announced his turn to the fully Kuhnian position that every ostensibly obvious "feature" of texts is actually produced by interpretation (the turn comes, appropriately, in the subsection of the essay titled, "Undoing the Case for Reader-Response Analysis"). I am aware, by the way, that I have used the word *feature* twice in the previous sentence, the first time to suggest brute-fact attributes of Fish's texts that are familiar to the loose-knit interpretive community designated by the term "Fish's readers," the second time (in quotation marks) to suggest that the first usage is, in Fish's terms, problematic. I do so in order to suggest another path down the antiformalist road (the road not taken by Iser's reply), for the way to debate Fish on textual "features," it seems to me, is not to claim that some aspects of texts precede interpretation and others are produced by interpretation; rather, the counterargument should be that Fish uses "interpretation" in two different senses, just as Kuhn used "paradigm" (as Kuhn admitted, distinguishing between "the entire constellation of beliefs, values, techniques, and so on shared by the members of a given community," and "the concrete puzzle-solutions which, employed as models or examples, can replace explicit rules as a basis for the solution of the remaining puzzles of normal science"), with appropriately obfuscatory effects (175). Yes, every feature of a text is interpretive and indeterminate—not just with regard to what Molly's final "Yes" means, but even with regard to apparently neutral or submeaningful items such as line endings, chapter headings, and book titles; but as any practicing member of any interpretive community knows, some interpretations are so widely agreed upon as to be indistinguishable from brute facts: "facts," on this reading, are simply interpretations that have won nearly unanimous consensus. Interpretations that designate certain textual features as "characters," "line breaks," "dangling modifiers," and even "scare quotes" are therefore qualitatively and pragmatically quite different from elaborate literary-critical interpretations that see *Paradise Lost* as a poem whose object is to bring the reader "to the realization that his inability to read the poem with any confidence in his own perception is its focus" (*Text* 21), or that render the Trueblood episode in *Invisible Man* as an exemplum of the relation between commerce and the performance of blackness. To put this another way, I know of no reader who is willing to dispute that the title of *Is There a Text in This Class?* is *Is There a Text in This Class?* but I know of many readers who are willing to dispute Fish's claim that he has repudiated the sentence (in "Interpreting 'Interpreting the *Variorum*'") in which he claimed that his form of criticism "relieves me of the obligation to be right (a standard that simply drops out) and demands only that I be interesting (a standard that can be met without any reference at all to an illusory objectivity)" (180). Such readers are perfectly willing to grant that the line breaks in *Paradise Lost* or *Lycidas* or *Il Penseroso* are where Fish says they are, but they persist in reading Fish's ostensibly "repudiated" sentence as a useful gloss on his career since publishing *Is There a Text in This Class?*

It would have been possible, in other words, to contest Fish's reading of Iser not by stubbornly insisting on the determinacy of the determinate, and not, good Lord, by insisting on two separate varieties of determinacy and assigning "interpretation" to one of them, but by acknowledging that all forms of reading are interpretive but that some involve the kind of low-level, relatively uncontestable cognitive acts that we engage in whenever we interpret the letter "e" as the letter "e," and some involve the kind of high-level, exceptionally specific and complex textual manipulations, transformations, and reconfigurations involved whenever someone publishes something like *S/Z*—or *Surprised by Sin*. (And, of course, by acknowledging that there are any number of "interpretations" that fall between these extremes, and that the status of each of them is—what else?—both open to and dependent on interpretation.) But the Fish-Iser exchange did not take this form, and no plausible "interpretation" of it can claim that it did. As a result, Fish's interpretive modus operandi is as familiar to us as it is: interpretation is the only game in town, yadda yadda; but there is no such thing as interpretive self-consciousness, yadda yadda; and, what's more, interpretive theory has no consequences, yadda yadda yadda. The very familiarity of Fish's antiformalism, and of Fish's deliberately counterintuitive declarations thereof, makes my point: because the Fish-Iser exchange took the form that it did, we (and by "we" I mean the even more loose-knit interpretive community designated by the term "Fish's readers and everyone who knows anything about Fish's readers") have long regarded these questions as definitively settled. Interpretive communities determine what's determinate and what's not, so clearly the focus of critical theory should be on the workings of those interpretive communities and not on "texts themselves"; there is no such thing as the "text itself," anyway, and even if there were, there would be nothing inside the text.

I concentrate on Fish's *diacritics* exchange with Iser, then, because I look upon it as the last time Fish would bother to concern himself with people who made claims about the grainy details of literary texts. After this point, Fish devoted himself increasingly to the critical metaproblems produced by his own work, as in the essay "Change," which opens by asserting—or simply recognizing—that interpretive communities are now the only game in town:

> The notion of "interpretive communities" was originally introduced as an answer to a question that had long seemed crucial to literary studies. What is the source of interpretive authority: the text or the reader? Those who answered "the text" were embarrassed by the fact of disagreement. Why, if the text contains its own meaning and constrains its own interpretation, do so many interpreters disagree about that meaning? Those who answered "the reader" were embarrassed by the fact of agreement. Why, if meaning is created by the individual reader from the perspective of his own experience and interpretive desires, is there so much that interpreters agree about? What was required was an explanation that could account for both agreement and disagreement and that explanation was found in the idea of an interpretive community. (*Doing* 141)

Very well, then, now that *that's* settled, we can move on to the question of how these seemingly monadic interpretive communities manage to change, and once we've asked that question, we can move briskly to Fish's answer—namely, that an interpretive community is in fact "an engine of change" (146). But these engines are more complicated than they seem, for "to put the matter in what only seems to be a paradox, when a community is provoked to change by something outside it, that something will already have been inside," and thus "no theory can compel a change that has not in some sense already occurred" (147, 154). On, then, to the metametaproposition that "the question of change is therefore one that cannot be posed independently of some such self-description which gives a shape to the very facts and events to which the question is put" (158). Q.E.D. Onward, then, to law and legal theory.

Perhaps Fish's career always contained the seeds of its own change, or perhaps he was induced to change by antagonists, influences, and interlocutors whose outsideness to him was always already inside. But I feel safe in suggesting that there was, at some point in the 1970s, a significant change between the *enfant terrible* Fish who published jawdroppingly brilliant and original close readings of brilliant writers (from Milton to Donne to Pater) who had been closely read by generations of the most brilliant readers in the English-speaking world, and the *agent provocateur* Fish who abandoned dense analyses of the temporal element in reading in favor of high-flying, high-stakes rhetorical performances in legal theory and campus politics, undertaken solo or in tandem with Ronald Dworkin, Roberto Unger, or Dinesh D'Souza. The Later Fish is not a theorist of the reading process; the Later Fish is a purveyor of provocative paradoxes (or of propositions that only seem to be paradoxes), a Fish who would have you believe—or not, it really doesn't matter—that "anti-professionalism is professionalism itself in its purest form" (*Doing* 245) and that there's no such thing as free speech and it's a good thing, too.

The Limits of Interpretation

I do not want to ask whether the arguments of the Later Fish are right or wrong. Rather, in pragmatist fashion, I want to ask what they have done, and whether they are good in the way of belief. The turn from texts to "interpretive communities" has had some salutary effects on the study of literature, insofar as it has licensed greater inquiry into the sociology of literary reception and the actual mechanics of literary production and transmission. On theoretical grounds, the term "interpretive communi-

try to understand the physical phenomena of the universe *precisely* as phenomena that live and function independently of interpretive activity (see Bérubé). It does not admit that most responsible theorists who try to devise distinctions between brute fact and social fact rely on blurry distinctions rather than "absolute" ones, as John Searle does in *The Construction of Social Reality* when he passes on the question of whether colors "really" exist in nature. And it gives short shrift to the forms of interpretive activity that have so far managed to establish (and make available for further interpretation) those features of our world that do "live and function" independently of the forms of interpretive activity that have disclosed them. Most astrophysicists do not speak of how the cosmic microwave background radiation "lives" or "functions," but all agree that it exists, and that it existed well before, and will exist well after, the interpretive activity undertaken by the small handful of conscious beings who have been debating the size, age, properties, and fate of the universe since our detection of the radiation in 1965.

For all the problems with the word *paradigm*, Kuhn offered an account of how ordinary science produces anomalies that challenge paradigms, and Fish has not; and in the terms he has offered so far, Fish cannot. In the ordinary course of literary study, perhaps, this would not matter, since no one worth attending to believes that literary texts, like rocks and stars, precede interpretive activity. (The day Fish chased the last lingering textual positivists out of the debate club was a good day.) But when Fish tried to defuse the scandal that grew out of Alan Sokal's hoax essay in *Social Text* in May 1996, it did matter; it mattered most obviously the day Fish published a *New York Times* op-ed reply to Sokal ("Professor Sokal's Bad Joke") that relied in part on a comparison of the laws of baseball (which clearly do not exist apart from interpretive activity) with the laws of physics (which so clearly do exist apart from interpretive activity that it is a mild anthropomorphism even to call them "laws"). That this argumentative strategy was a mistake is a truth almost universally acknowledged, or at least acknowledged by sufficient numbers of Fish's admirers (including myself) as to make it "true" in a pragmatist sense. To many observers, Fish's reply had the baleful effect of confirming Sokal's complaint that humanists tend to regard the natural world—not our understanding of the natural world, but the thing itself, with all its carbon and hydrogen and magnetic fields and strong and weak forces—as a "social construction." But it has less often been acknowledged that in denying our capacity to make "any distinction" (or, perhaps, any "absolute" distinction) between the worlds of brute fact and social fact, Fish was, back in 1981 when Alan Sokal was known only to his family and friends, countering one of Iser's worst arguments with one of his own worst arguments.

Just as Iser botched the question of determinacy and indeterminacy, arguing that interpretations were determinate where he should have pointed out the differences between the low-level interpretation by which we perceive the letter "e" and the high-level interpretation by which we produce the book *S/Z*, so too did he botch the question of how interpretations can attempt to distinguish between social fact and brute fact. The most expeditious way of addressing this point, I suggest, is to argue that interpretations are indeterminate *but* that all interpretations produce "objects." The objects themselves depend, just as Fish (and Kuhn and Rorty) would have it, on the workings of the interpretive communities that produce them. The interpretive communities that are known as "low-temperature physicists" or "oral surgeons" operate by different protocols of knowledge production than do the interpretive communities known as "readers of Stanley Fish who specialize in law or literature," and the different protocols of different communities exist in part to produce different kinds of objects. Some of those objects may go by the name "solar wind," some of them may be theories about the solar wind, some of them may be readings of X-rays of impacted wisdom teeth, some of them may be readings of hypocrisy in *Tom Jones*, some of them may be review essays in *diacritics*, and some of them may be analyses of Fish's career as a theorist of interpretation. But they are all objects, and a small but important set of them must be understood as objects that exist independently of anyone's perception of them, *if* they are to be understood properly as the kinds of objects they are. Those are the objects that belong to the world of brute fact, and because brute fact never gets up and speaks for itself in a language that precedes or exceeds all human interpretive paradigms, humans have to keep redrawing the distinction between brute fact and social fact and keep interpreting it anew by way of the protocols of those social facts we now call "interpretive communities."

Iser did not make this argument, and that's one of the reasons why no one hears very much about him anymore. Nonetheless, the terms in which Fish won his argument with Iser, and the very decisiveness of his success, have had lasting effects not only on the careers of both men but on the profession of literary study as a whole. Some of those effects, as Stanley Fish was (characteristically, and perhaps opportunistically) among the first to realize, are now worth trying to undo.

Works Cited

Bérubé, Michael. "The Return of Realism and the Future of Contingency." *What's Left of Theory? New Work on the Politics of Literary Theory.* Ed. Judith Butler, John Guillory, and Kendall Thomas. New York: Routledge, 2000. 137–56.

Culler, Jonathan. *On Deconstruction: Theory and Criticism after Structuralism.* Ithaca: Cornell UP, 1982.

————. *Structuralist Poetics: Structuralism, Linguistics, and the Study of Literature.* Ithaca: Cornell UP, 1975.

Fish, Stanley. *Doing What Comes Naturally: Change, Rhetoric, and the Practice of Theory in Literary and Legal Studies.* Durham: Duke UP, 1989.

————. *Is There a Text in This Class?* The Authority of Interpretive Communities Cambridge: Harvard UP, 1980.

————. *Professional Correctness: Literary Studies and Political Change.* Oxford: Clarendon, 1995.

————. "Professor Sokal's Bad Joke." *New York Times* 21 May 1996 A23+.

————. *Surprised By Sin: The Reader in Paradise Lost.* Cambridge: Harvard UP, 1967.

————. "Why No One's Afraid of Wolfgang Iser." *diacritics* 11.1 (1981): 2–13.

Iser, Wolfgang. *The Act of Reading: A Theory of Aesthetic Response.* Baltimore: Johns Hopkins UP, 1978.

————. *The Implied Reader: Patterns of Communication in Prose Fiction from Bunyan to Beckett.* Baltimore: Johns Hopkins UP, 1974.

————. Interview with Wayne Booth, Norman Holland, and Rudolf Kuenzli. *diacritics* 10.2 (1980): 57–74.

————. "Talk Like Whales: A Reply to Stanley Fish." *diacritics* 11.3 (1981): 82–87.

Klancher, Jon P. *The Making of English Reading Audiences, 1790–1832.* Madison: U of Wisconsin P, 1987.

Kuenzli, Rudolf E. "The Intersubjective Structure of the Reading Process: A Communication-Oriented Theory of Literature." *diacritics* 10.2 (1980): 47–56.

Kuhn, Thomas S. *The Structure of Scientific Revolutions*. 2nd ed. Chicago: U of Chicago P, 1970.

Mailloux, Steven. *Interpretive Conventions: The Reader in the Study of American Fiction*. Ithaca: Cornell UP, 1982.

————. *Rhetorical Power*. Ithaca: Cornell UP, 1989.

Rabinowitz, Peter J. *Before Reading: Narrative Conventions and the Politics of Interpretation*. Ithaca: Cornell UP, 1987.

Radway, Janice A. *Reading the Romance: Women, Patriarchy, and Popular Literature*. 1984. Chapel Hill: U of North Carolina P, 1991.

————. *A Feeling for Books: The Book-of-the-Month Club, Literary Taste, and Middle-Class Desire*. Chapel Hill: U of North Carolina P, 1997.

Smith, Barbara Herrnstein. *Contingencies of Value: Alternative Perspectives for Critical Theory*. Cambridge: Harvard UP, 1988.

Suleiman, Susan R., and Inge Crosman, ed. *The Reader in the Text: Essays on Audience and Interpretation*. Princeton: Princeton UP, 1980.

Tompkins, Jane P., ed. *Reader-Response Criticism: From Formalism to Post-Structuralism*. Baltimore: Johns Hopkins UP, 1980.

How I Learned to Stop Worrying and Love Stanley

Gerald Graff

Stanley Fish has often wryly observed that critics who fulminate against his ideas on first encountering them have a way of meekly coming around and embracing them years later. I may be a case of this syndrome. I published several polemics against Fish's work in the eighties and early nineties, during which time the two of us went at each other frequently at conferences and in print.[1] Fish's arguments still seem to me to need some amending, but I've come to see some major areas in which what he says about interpretation now seems to me right, important, and enormously useful in ways that have been completely missed by his critics, me included. This is especially true of critics who see Fish as a postmodern relativist/solipsist and a cynical operator who cares only for money and academic stardom rather than for truth, students, and education. It's true that Fish himself likes to feed this bad-boy image, but that doesn't mean one should accept it at face value.

Even in the days when I was attacking Fish's work, I was dimly aware that he was changing how I thought. Perhaps this is not surprising, and not just because Fish is such a seductive writer. We are of the same generation and come from similar backgrounds, both having grown up as Jewish city kids (Fish is from Providence, I from Chicago) who cared more for sports than for books (we recently discovered our mutual adolescent worship of the late Ted Williams). Being roughly the same age (at this writing, he's 64 and I'm 65), we went through graduate school in the days when English

27

studies was still dominated (though it would not be for much longer) by a WASP aristocracy that shared an unspoken consensus about what "the profession" was, how "gentlemen" and scholars comported themselves, and how the game of literary studies was played.

One of the unspoken rules of this game was that if you had to ask how it was played you presumably didn't belong in it. That is, the assumption was that if you were any good, you already *knew* what the game was and why it was being played—if you didn't, why were you there? Given our lack of genteel breeding, it's probably no coincidence that Fish and I both developed aggressively polemical stances that aimed to provoke dis-agreements rather than smother them, and that we developed intellectual positions that aimed, in different ways, to make trouble for unspoken consensus—Fish in the fields of interpretive, legal, and social theory, I in those of literary theory and later educational philosophy.

That being said, I confess that I have no idea if Fish will agree that our positions are more alike than different. He has published two critiques of my work on "teaching the conflicts" that I'll return to at the end of this essay. It may be that the spirit of contrariness that we both cultivated in our struggle to make it in "the profession" is stronger than our impulse to agree. Part of my reason for writing this essay is to find out.

Fish on Interpretive Consensus

Let me start by reviewing the criticism of Fish's ideas that I made before realizing that I was of Stanley's party without knowing it. The context was the debate that Fish provoked in the 1980s with his book, *Is There a Text in This Class? The Authority of Interpretive Communities*, over whether texts determine readings or readings determine texts. In that book, Fish argued that the meanings we ascribe to texts are made by us rather than found or discovered in the texts themselves. Interpretations are not interpretations "of" any prior or independent "text itself," but actively bring that text into being. Readers, then, create the textual meanings that they naively think they discover "out there" in the works themselves. But lest we conclude that Fish had reduced interpretation to subjective whim, he argued that readers create these meanings not by imposing their idiosyncratic personalities on texts, but by reflecting the culturally transmitted expectations, predispositions, and biases that produce readers themselves and program them to read one way rather than another.

When Fish's book appeared, I lined up with the opposition, including, among others, M.H. Abrams, E.D. Hirsch, John Reichert, Reed Way Dasenbrock, and Robert Scholes. We all argued that reducing interpretations to products of institutional determination in the way Fish had done deprived interpretation of any cognitive leg to stand on. Fish's theory, we said, regardless of his frequent attempts to deny it, leads to a relativism that releases readers from responsibility to the text, for such a theory can't coherently explain why one interpretation should be chosen over others, or why interpretive paradigms themselves often change in response to new texts and kinds of texts.

In an essay published in *New Literary History* in 1985, I argued that if one accepted Fish's strongest version of his theory of reader determination, readers would always necessarily find the same meanings in texts that their interpretive communities had preprogrammed them to expect. (Scholes, arguing along similar lines, said that Fish's argument was like "saying that bluejays and robins can never be seen by the same person because any person will be either in the bluejay community or the robin community and therefore will see only one or the other" [159]). And indeed, in at least one place in *Is There a Text in This Class?* Fish argues that "theories (interpretive frameworks) always work, and they will always produce exactly the results they predict, results that will be immediately compelling to those for whom the theory's assumptions and enabling principles are self-evident. Indeed, the trick would be to find a theory that didn't work" (274). Here, as I read him, Fish pretty unequivocally says that whatever your theory leads you to expect is always "exactly" what you are destined to find. Elsewhere, however, Fish seemed imperceptibly to slide over to a weaker version of the argument, one that acknowledged that the world is full of theories that don't work. One example was Fish's own earlier theory of "affective stylistics," which he repudiated in *Is There a Text in This Class?*

In the weak version of his theory, I argued, Fish seemed to reverse himself by minimizing the causal force that the strong version had ascribed to prior theories, assumptions, and "enabling principles." But this reversal seemed to get Fish out of one difficulty only to invite another, for if you weaken the causal force of the reader's expectations (that is, the reader's agency in causing the text to mean whatever it means), you rob the theory of reader determination of its explanatory power. I speculated that this equivocation might help explain why Fish ends up so diluting the sense in which interpretive communities "create" or "produce" texts that he admits that his theory (like all theory) has no practical consequences.

I still think that as it is stated the argument of *Is There a Text in This Class?* has problems. When Fish, for example, writes that whereas "skilled reading is usually thought to be a matter of discerning what is there," it is really "a matter of knowing how to *produce* what can thereafter be said to be there," or that "all objects are made and not found" (327, 331), I still have to blink and reply, "Say what?" At the very least, some rewriting seems necessary in order to avoid the either-or binary that Fish invites. I would put the point this way: "Skilled reading makes no sense unless we assume that it's a matter of discerning what is there, though the meanings that readers discern have to be actively constructed by them." And, "All objects are *both* found and made; the finding already involves making."

I'd like to think that there's a way to reconcile social constructionists like Fish with objectivists like Hirsch and Bloom. Richard Rorty improved on Fish's formulations, I think, in a critique of Allan Bloom's *Closing of the American Mind.* Bloom had argued that

> A liberal education means reading certain generally recognized classic texts, just reading them, letting them dictate what the questions are and the method of approaching them—not forcing them into categories we make up, not treating them as historical products, but trying to read them as their authors wished them to be read. (344)

Unlike Fish, Rorty conceded that readers are indeed obliged to read an author on his or her own terms, "trying to put ourselves in her shoes," implying that it can be done. But he went on to make the Fish-like argument that we inevitably bring to books "categories we make up." We come to books, that is, "with questions in mind—questions not dictated by the books—but questions we have previously, if vaguely, formulated" (5).

Rorty's point, as I would restate it, is that reading is not subjective but selective. Readers can't pay equal attention to everything in a text, but must notice some things more than others; and what different readers notice will be influenced not just by the text, but also by the diverse interests they bring to the text before reading it. Some of these interests will reflect readers' social conditioning in the way Fish's interpretive communities do. Rorty might have noted that when Bloom invokes Dante, he himself doesn't try to treat the poet as he might have "wished" to be read, but appropriates him for Bloom's own contemporary polemical purposes. The point, however, is not that the properties of texts are subjective or "socially constructed" rather than objective; unless we assume the properties we attribute to texts are independent of us, reading makes no sense. But *which* of a text's objective properties readers notice or remember (or teachers and students choose to emphasize or ignore in class) will depend on interests and purposes that come from readers and their interpretive communities rather than from the text. Whereas texts in themselves *limit* what we can legitimately say about them, no text can tell us what we should *say* about it (or how we should teach it), something that is shaped by the cultural and critical conversation going on around us as well as by the needs and interests of our students.

I don't know what Fish may think of my rewriting of his argument, but I suspect he would at least now concede, as he seemed unwilling to do earlier, that as readers we have to *assume* that textual meanings exist objectively "out there" in the world, independent of us, that without such an assumption of the exterior independence of texts the practice of interpretation would make no sense. He might also concede that it makes no sense to claim to challenge this assumption of the exterior independence of texts (as he seemingly claimed to challenge it), since to make such a challenge we would have to step outside our own epistemological skin in the very way that Fish has always denied we can.

All this being said, I now think that I and other critics of *Is There a Text in This Class?* missed Fish's key point. When he denied the validity of appeals to objective reality or to "the text itself" independent of interpretation, he did not mean to deny the need to assume the existence of an objective world prior to our interpretations; rather, he was pointing out that, however necessary it might be, this assumption of an independent objective reality becomes useless and question-begging when there is disagreement about what that objective reality is. Fish makes a similar point in his later argument about "the trouble with principle." Invoking supposedly neutral principles to adjudicate social conflicts is as question-begging as invoking a neutral "text itself" to adjudicate interpretive disagreements. Just as the allegedly neutral text turns out itself to support conflicting interpretations, the allegedly neutral principles will end up justifying conflicting behavior. You and I may oppose terrorism in principle, but if you see a certain act as terroristic (a suicide bombing, say) and I see it as a legitimate means of resisting oppression, our agreement in principle won't help us resolve our differences.

As Fish himself put it in *Is There a Text in This Class?* "the question of what is in the text cannot be settled by appealing to the evidence since the evidence will have become available only because some determination of what is in the text will already have been made" (274). I adduced this sentence in my 1985 critique as a glaring instance of where Fish goes astray, but now I think he was right. Appealing to "the evidence" to settle disputes about "what is in the text" works only if there is a consensus about what that evidence is. Once the evidence (including how it should be described) is disputed, appealing to the evidence becomes question-begging, since I don't see the same evidence that you do. Even if we agree on the brute facts—a certain number of people killed by a suicide bomb—one of us calls it "terrorism" and the other "heroic martyrdom."

What I take Fish to be saying, then, is something like this:

> *Of course* we always assume and have no choice but to assume that when we refer to the text or the reality of things out there, whatever we refer to exists independent of our interpretive apparatus and in some sense invites us to describe it the way we do. You'd be talking nonesense if you said, "I think this text is a poem by Milton, but, in saying that, I in no way claim that it *really is* a poem by Milton independent of my description of it." It's constitutive of the idea of "describing" that you think there is something you describe and that really *is* out there and in a way that is answerable to your description. A description that assumed there was no object independent of itself to be described is not properly called a description.

The trouble arises, however, when two or more interpretations or descriptions disagree, when one interpretive community, say, regards suicide bombings as terrorist acts while another regards them as a legitimate form of self-defense against an oppressor. Fish argues that when interpretations are contested, invoking reality or the objective fact of the matter is question-begging—which is to say that they are useless in adjudicating the disagreements. It begs the question to say "but let's look at the facts to see if suicide bombings are terrorist acts or legitimate forms of self-defense," because it's precisely how the facts are to be construed in the first place that is in dispute.

This doesn't mean that reasoned debate necessarily shuts down at such a point: we can and do bring our reasons and evidence to bear on such disputes to try to persuade opponents (and uncommitted third parties) that the facts should be construed our way rather than our opponent's way. But once we enter this process of reasoning and evidence-giving, we have entered the field of rhetoric and persuasion, where how "reality" or "the facts" are construed is acknowledged to be open to debate and therefore not objectively given.

If I have summarized Fish accurately, I think he is dead right, as are Wittgenstein, Rorty, and other pragmatists who argue that we are spinning our philosophical wheels in the mud when we appeal to objective truth as a way of settling disputes—just examine the facts and you'll agree with our side. The mistake, however, is not in believing in truth or the possibility of objectivity, but in invoking truth and objectivity to resolve a dispute when what a true or objective position *is* is itself disputed.

Fish on the Teaching of Academic Discourse

A second area in which the implications of Fish's ideas have been overlooked by critics is that of teaching and learning. Fish's argument that texts and objects are never experienced directly, but only through the filter of interpretation, has crucial implications for teaching, for it shifts attention from the subject matter of education to students' understanding of the subject matter. That is, the "linguistic turn" that Fish's work represents reveals the wide and often educationally disabling gap between the languages in which academic subject matter is couched and the languages of many students.

To put it in terms closer to Fish's own, students and teachers often belong to such different interpretive communities that the process of education breaks down. By calling attention to this gap and its systematic nature, Fish's thinking encourages us as teachers to put ourselves in our students' shoes, to see our often mystifying academic practices as our students see them—or fail to see them. Bad teaching is often the result of our mistaken assumption that we are operating in the same linguistic and conceptual universe as that of our students, that our students understand not only what we are saying but why we are saying it. In literature courses, we rattle on in the foreign language of literary criticism and theory on the premise that most of our students are getting it, and if they aren't that it's their problem, not ours. Even as we spin our complicated webs of textual analysis in class, many students are wondering (but are afraid to ask), "Why do we have to hunt for 'hidden meaning' (or 'symbolism') in these works? Isn't the point of reading literature just to enjoy it?" When we fail to make clear the rationale for the interpretive game we play (and the point holds for the teaching of other subjects besides literature), students take away the message that I got from my graduate school teachers: if you have to ask how and why the game is played, you probably don't belong in it.

I recently heard Fish observe at a college faculty meeting at our university, "We tend to think that the language in which we conduct the business of our academic disciplines is a secondary accompaniment of the subject; but this language *is* the subject." In other words, academic discourse about literature or mathematics or social science is part of the discipline of literary study, mathematics, and social science. Unless students can become socialized into these academic languages, they will continue to struggle with the subject matter in these fields.

This argument poses a sharp challenge to standard practices in the undergraduate curriculum, where students often concentrate on primary texts and are discouraged from consulting "secondary sources." Thus, literature students generally read literature but not criticism, even though what those students are expected to *produce* are critical essays, not tragedies and poems. As the British critic Chris Baldick has noted, "It is a fact too often forgotten that the real content of the school and college subject which goes under the name 'English literature' is not literature in the primary sense, but *criticism*. Every school student in British education is required to compose, not tragic dramas, but essays in criticism" (4–5). Even creative writing courses are conducted for the most part in critical discourse; that is, in writing courses instructors and student talk *about* poetry rather than *in* poetry.

In most fields, undergraduate majors are asked to study the supposed basics of the subject matter apart from the conversation of scholars and commentators, even though that conversation, as Fish reminds us, is inseparable from the subject matter. As a result, many students never move beyond the preliminary stages and would not be able to give an account of the central issues and debates of their major field as it is practiced. (In the same fashion, high school teaching candidates are largely excluded from the cutting-edge debates in their primary content areas.)

Fish has recently begun to apply his arguments more explicitly to issues of teaching and learning. In one of his online columns in the *Chronicle of Higher Education*, he recently argued that teaching "writing and argument" need to take precedence over teaching "ideas" and "opinions," especially in the general education curriculum. As he put it, "Every dean should forthwith insist that all composition courses teach grammar and rhetoric and nothing else. No composition course should have a theme, especially not one the instructor is interested in. Ideas should be introduced not for their own sake, but for the sake of the syntactical and rhetorical points they help illustrate. . . ." ("Say"). Fish's point, I think, is not to banish "ideas" and other intellectual content, but to emphasize that discussions of ideas already presuppose familiarity with the game of "writing and argument," of "grammar and rhetoric." If students are not at home in the game of written persuasive argument, as many undergraduates are not, the game itself and its moves need to be foregrounded in the curriculum.

Here Fish's critiques of "anti-professionalism" and the self-loathing of academics become relevant: instructors who shield undergraduates from criticism and theory, for example, and insist that they concentrate on the primary texts of literature, tend to be motivated by the misguided fear that students will be prematurely professionalized—that is, that they will (horror of horrors!) become like us.[2] When we fail to teach criticism, theory, and other kinds of academic discourse out of a desire to protect students from the corruptions of professionalism, we in effect hide the secrets of our game from students and then punish them at grading time for their inability to play it. In the aim of "empowering" students by refusing to socialize them into our presumably arid professional practices, we actually prevent them from succeeding, from mastering the discourses that we ourselves take for granted and continue to control.

Fish on Teaching the Conflicts

So far, then, I have described how, after years of disagreeing with Fish, I have become a convert to his doctrines (or have realized that I had been one without knowing it). But here my argument runs into an embarrassing problem: I may now agree with Fish, but he evidently doesn't agree with me. If, as I've suggested here, Fish and I are not all that far apart, then Fish *should* agree with my "teach the conflicts" argument, but he has published a couple of strong criticisms of it. I want to conclude this essay by considering these criticisms.

In a 1992 essay, Fish writes that if conflict is made into "a structural principle" of the curriculum, as I had urged, "its very nature is domesticated; rather than being the manifestation of difference, conflict becomes the theatre in which difference is displayed and stage-managed. . . ." In other words, organizing the curriculum around conflict trivializes real conflict by reducing it to "just another topic in the syllabus" (*There's* 36). He further elaborates on the criticism in a second essay published four years later. Quoting my statement that the curriculum should "thematize its own political conflicts," Fish replies that "when you thematize political conflicts, you in effect have washed them in talk, smothered them in discourse. You have thrown a tablecloth of conversation over them and muffled them. . . ." While he concedes that at times "smothering" conflicts in this way "may be a very good thing to do," in the end, teaching the conflicts for him is a manifestation of the liberal "escape into conversation, into the life of the mind," an escape from real conflict into safe and protected academic talk ("Them" 171).

According to Fish, the liberal glorification of "conversation" masks what is really at stake: "Not conversation but war, violence, force, conflicts, fights to the death, or at least (and this is my favorite mode) to the silencing of one's adversary. That is the danger—violence, war, conflicts to the death—that Graff would avoid, and who of us would not join him at times . . ." (172). Again, despite the partial concession, Fish ultimately finds me guilty of wishy-washy liberal pluralism:

> What liberal projects [like Graff's] are designed to stigmatize and evade is conviction—whether the project is called historicism, political criticism, interdisciplinarity, or "teach the conflicts." "Conviction" means believing that something is at stake and that the highest priority is not keeping the conversation going or expanding its horizons or filling it with endless self-qualifications, but turning it in the direction you think good and right—which means silencing the voices of those you think bad and wrong. ("Them" 172)

Unable to face the fact that real conflicts lead to violence and the silencing of opponents, I, then, would domesticate those conflicts, according to Fish, by turning them into "just another topic in the syllabus," another genteel academic conversation in which we politely agree to disagree, to respect all parties, and to keep the conversation going.

So, faced with a clash between those who see suicide bombing as terrorism and those who see it as liberatory martyrdom, the Graffian pedagogue, according to Fish, would presumably say, "Let's respect both sides and treat the conflict itself as a teachable moment." As Fish puts it, echoing John Milton's readiness to persecute heretics, "What I'm saying is that if conviction is not simply a component of an endless liberal debating society, there is always going to be some point at which you are going to say 'Not X: them we burn'" (172). Fish here offers an argument he would make familiar in *There's No Such Thing as Free Speech, and It's a Good Thing, Too*: that the idea of a completely uncoerced free speech is a liberal delusion, since in any community who gets to speak and be heard will already have been enforced by unrationalizable exclusions. The supposedly free marketplace of ideas has already been constituted by the violent exclusion of some positions and voices.

There is something odd to me about Fish's charge that in urging that we teach the conflicts I hope to muffle or disguise real conflict, the Hobbesian war of all against all. For Fish's wife, Jane Tompkins, has charged me with the very opposite sin, that of promoting this same Hobbesian war of all against all (29–35). (Some couples are hard to please!) As it happens, however, I agree with Fish that some degree of Hobbesian coercion prestructures any debate by ruling out some positions in advance. In urging that the curriculum more clearly reflect the cultural conversation, I never suggested that every conceivable viewpoint could or should be represented. On the contrary, I noted in *Beyond the Culture Wars* that some positions and proposed debates are *rightly* silenced and excluded. As I put it, we are right to reject proposals to debate questions like "Did the Holocaust Really Happen?" or "Is Homosexuality a Disease?" though if those who want to debate those questions gain enough power they may succeed in getting their issues on the agenda and excluding my issues. On the other hand, if a student raises these questions in class, teachers may find themselves forced to open them to debate whether they want to or not.

What about Fish's charge that my proposal to organize the curriculum around conflicts would "domesticate" those conflicts? Here, I can only ask what Fish means by such a categorical statement. I'm sure that he and I can think of academics who, through ineptitude or obfuscation, would be able to make even the Israeli/Palestinian conflict seem academic in the worst sense. But Fish's suggestion that this outcome is inevitable, that merely to incorporate such a conflict into an academic syllabus would necessarily "domesticate" it or make it "stage-managed" rather than real, seems inconsistent with his own usual thinking. In fact, his suggestion that academia inevitably domesticates conflicts sounds strangely like the anti-institutional self-loathing on the cultural left that he so frequently rejects. It's almost as if Fish, who has always argued that there is no pure position that stands outside of institutionalization, wants to protect conflicts from institutionalization. Then, too, his argument that teaching the conflicts would necessarily domesticate them smacks of another idea that he generally rejects: that the practical consequences of a theory or practice can be deduced from the theory or practice *itself* independent of its context.

But where Fish seems to me to miss my point most is in listing teaching the conflicts as among those projects that are "designed to stigmatize and evade . . . conviction." On the contrary, for me the whole point of teaching the conflicts is not to stigmatize or evade conviction but to energize conviction by getting it out of the closet. The point is to flush us out of our self-protective classrooms into public spaces in which we would have to engage one another. The point is not to muffle conviction, but to bring it out into the open where as students and teachers we can better decide where our own convictions lie. So the real opposition here is not the one Fish proposes between supposedly authentic conflicts and the domesticating effect of academic institutions, but between conflicts that are privatized by one form of curricular organization and conflicts that other forms of curricular organization can render public.

In short, Fish has things precisely backwards. If anything causes conviction to be muffled and evaded, it is the curriculum as it is, which allows feuding professors to hide out from their critical colleagues, reduces intellectual differences to personal vendettas and backbiting, and keeps students in the dark about the contested issues and what is at stake in them. In this respect, the pedagogical goal of teaching the conflicts is the same as Fish's recently declared program for teaching grammar, rhetoric, and argument: to demystify and clarify academic discourse. To Fish's statement that the language in which we conduct the business of our academic disciplines is not "a secondary accompaniment of the subject" but "*is* the subject," I would add a corollary that I would expect Fish to agree with: the controversies that roil the academic disciplines are not a secondary accompaniment of the subject; they *are* the subject. Arguably, it is only when we gain a sense of what scholars disagree about (as well as agree about) that we begin to become insiders to a field. But even this understates the point, for conflict and opposition are intrinsic to thinking itself; that is, there exists a cognitive connection between controversy and intelligibility. John Stuart Mill pointed out the connection when he observed that we do not understand our own ideas until we know what can be said against them. In Mill's words, those who "have never thrown themselves into the mental position of those who think differently from them . . . do not, in any proper sense of the word, know the doctrine which they themselves profess" (129). In other words, our very ability to think depends on contrast—on asking "as opposed to what?" The best argument for teaching the conflicts is ultimately peda- gogical: because all thinking is structured by contrast, it's at moments of controversy that issues clarify themselves for students.

Here, however, I would think that in lecturing Fish on the pedagogical value of controversy I must be preaching to the converted. Few have done as much as Stanley Fish to teach and model the art of controversy to a generation of students and colleagues. Even more to the point, few academics have done as much as Fish to deprivatize academic contro- versy, to move it from the confines of the classroom, the specialized journal, and the academic conference room into the wider public sphere. He has done this in several capacities, first as a leading scholar and teacher, then as a well-known public intellectual, an op-ed writer and media figure, and finally as an administrator. These different roles came together in the spring of 2002 at the University of Illinois at Chicago in a course, "Public Intellectuals and Their Social Influ- ence," that Fish initiated and co-taught, and for which he secured funding from a new Center for Public Intellectuals that he brought to our campus.

The course syllabus, which was organized around visits from UIC colleagues and national public intellectuals, was a kind of running daily debate (my debate with Fish on my own visit to the class was for me at any rate one of the high points of the semester). This debate, moreover, was extended beyond the course meetings through a number of symposia and visiting lectures that were integrated into the syllabus, thereby making intracurricular events out of what are usually extracurricular add-ons. I'd like to think that these discussions proved that, contrary to Fish, intellec- tual debate *can* be structured into a syllabus without being "stage- managed" in some sterile way.

The course fittingly culminated in a large and well-attended public debate involving Fish, Richard Rorty, and Richard Posner (whose book criticizing the record of public intellectuals had recently appeared). The three principals were all in top form that day, the audience joined in with many provocative questions and comments, and the event generally gave one a taste of what intellectual life can be like when it doesn't have to stop because the class bell has rung but continues in a wider public forum. My own thought as I watched the debate was that this is what academic institutions could be like all the time, every day, not just on rare special occasions, and what they could be like for all students and teachers, not just the featured performers. This, I hope, is another of the things that Fish and I agree on—but that, as I say, is what I've written this essay to find out.

Notes

1. See, for example, our exchange in *New Literary History* (Graff "Interpretation"; Fish "Resistance").

2. See "Profession," "Anti-Professionalism," and "Unbearable."

Works Cited

Baldick, Chris. *The Social Mission of English Criticism, 1848–1932*. Oxford: Clarendon, 1987.

Bloom, Allan. *The Closing of the American Mind: How Higher Education Has Failed Democracy and Impoverished the Souls of Today's Students*. New York: Simon, 1987.

Fish, Stanley. "Anti-Professionalism." *Doing* 215–46.

———. *Doing What Comes Naturally: Change, Rhetoric, and the Practice of Theory in Literary and Legal Studies*. Durham: Duke UP, 1989.

———. *Is There a Text in This Class?: The Authority of Interpretive Communities*. Cambridge: Harvard UP, 1980.

———. "Profession, Despise Thyself." *Doing* 197–214.

———. "Resistance and Independence: A Reply to Gerald Graff." *New Literary History* 17 (1985): 119–27.

———. "Say It Ain't So." *Chronicle of Higher Education* 21 June 2002.

———. "Them We Burn: Violence and Conviction in the English Department." *English as a Discipline; Or, Is There a Plot in This Play?* Ed. James C. Raymond. Tuscaloosa: U of Alabama P, 1996. 160–73.

———. *There's No Such Thing as Free Speech, and It's a Good Thing, Too*. New York: Oxford UP, 1994.

———. *The Trouble with Principle*. Cambridge: Harvard UP, 1999.

———. "The Unbearable Ugliness of Volvos." *There's* 273–79.

Graff, Gerald. *Beyond the Culture Wars: How Teaching the Conflicts Can Revitalize American Education*. New York: Norton, 1992.

————. "Interpretation on Tlön: A Response to Stanley Fish." *New Literary History* 17 (1985): 109–17.

Mill, John Stuart. *On Liberty.* In *Utilitarianism, Liberty, and Representative Government.* New York: Dutton, 1951. 81–229.

Rorty, Richard. "That Old Time Philosophy." *New Republic* 198.4 (1988): 28–33.

Scholes, Robert. *Textual Power: Literary Theory and the Teaching of English.* New Haven: Yale UP, 1985.

Tompkins, Jane, and Gerald Graff. "Can We Talk." *Professions: Conversations on the Future of Literary and Cultural Studies.* Ed. Donald E. Hall. Urbana: U of Illinois P, 2001. 21–36.

Theory, Practice, and Ubiquitous Interpretation: The Basics

Martin Stone

Throughout his work, whatever the topic, Stanley Fish is preoccupied with a question concerning the basis of our entitlement, in various domains of discourse, to the notions of correctness and objectivity in judgment. Literary criticism and legal analysis supply his main examples. In virtue of what, he often asks, is one reading of a literary text or one application of a legal rule correct, and not another? This question is already present (though outside the main focus) in *Surprised by Sin*, with its perception of Milton as a writer concerned with severe disagreements: cases where someone's access to how things are, or to what is a reason for what, appears to depend on his or her acceptance of a premise that is undemonstrable (since the compellingness of any demonstration seems to depend on it).[1] Next, *Self-Consuming Artifacts* argues for the role of the reader in determining the meaning of a literary text—and this in something more than the trivial sense that insofar as there are works of literature there must be readers of them. (The idea, rather, is that something about the reader or the reader's situation *explains* why a literary text means what it does.) This view gets articulated in *Is There a Text in this Class?* as a kind of "conventionalism," according to which communal accreditation determines what counts as correct in judgments about literary texts. And this thesis is extended to other subjects (especially law) in *Doing What Comes Naturally*, where Fish portrays a number of otherwise diverse theorists (Unger, Dworkin, Hart, Posner) as seeking—often against their own declared intentions—an Archimedean standpoint for judgment. Doubting the availability of such a standpoint, Fish proposes a "pragmatic" alternative in which the notions of interpretation and community again help to secure the notion that a text sometimes means one thing rather than another.[2]

In this essay, I sketch the main argument running through these works, address a few misunderstandings, and indicate, somewhat programmatically, how the argument deserves to be criticized.[3] The grounds for my criticism are not exactly foreign to Fish's work. In fact, my main premise might be described as "the priority of the practical point of view," something Fish himself seems to favor in his criticism of the theorists mentioned above. Thus, my hope is that Fish will be able to see my critique as a friendly one: as clarifying and extending a valuable line of his thought, notwithstanding that the theory to be exorcized, in this case, is his own. Otherwise put, my criticism finds a conflict within Fish's work; and the part of a friend, in such a case, is naturally to be an ally— giving reinforcement or resolution—to the better side.

The Skeptical Argument

To start things off, we might remember that Milton writes in a historical moment of crises having the form of a perceived gap between the desire for a just order of society and historical experience, or between moral value and social fact—a gap figured by Milton as the relation between God and man.[4] The project of *Paradise Lost*—"to justifie the ways of God to men"—is motivated by a sense of the apparent failure of God, and hence implies the need for human speech and judgment to bring moral intelligibility to historical experience. Thus, what attracts Fish to Milton is that Milton treats poetry's religious theme as a *secular*, not a religious poet. That is, unlike his predecessors in this theme, Milton's focus is not the difficulties man encounters in keeping to the demands of God but the potentially false surmise—the idolatry, as it were—involved in talk of the specific content of divine imperatives.[5]

Two ideas may be extracted from this general picture of Milton— ideas that structure a great deal of Fish's subsequent work: the idea of correct judgment or right social order as that judgment or order that is in accord with God's will; and the idea that what makes a particular judgment one that accords with (keeps faith with) God's will is itself a question that calls for human judgment. The first of these ideas expresses what a "judgment" is for the human being laboring in history, a creature capable of departing—through responsible exercises of his or her conceptual capacities—from the divine will. The second idea might be thought of as a form of "antinomianism." Putting these together, we have the thought: Although correct judgment is judgment in accord with God's will, there is no means of externally validating (that is, from a point external to our judgments) whether one has got things right. In Fish's words, "The doctrine of the inner light marks out the area of interpretive labour; the doctrine of the single Truth names the goal of that labour, but withholds explicit directions for attaining it" (*Surprised* xliv). In saying that a thought along these lines structures Fish's work, I mean that Fish is concerned to respond to a certain *felt difficulty* with this thought. The difficulty is characteristic of modern philosophy. People are apt to feel that, in the absence of "directions" for certifying disputed judgments as correct, the very idea of correctness in judgment—of their being something to "get right"—must come under threat. The difficulty arises in the assumption that our entitlement to regard one of two conflicting judgments as "objectively correct" requires that there be some means of *demonstrating* its correctness through premises that do not presuppose either of the positions in question.

It appears questionable, to say the least, whether this requirement can be satisfied in such contest-laden domains as law or literary criticism, where judgment nonetheless has objective purport. So someone working in these domains might come to feel the pinch of the present difficulty. And they might then naturally move in one of two opposing intellectual directions:

> (a) They might attempt to vindicate the objectivizing view of discursive participants by supplying a theory of what makes judgments in the relevant domain correct. That is, they might construct a theory of validity for the discourse in question. (Or, if we call different judgments—that is, about literature or law— different "interpretations," then we may speak here of a theory of validity in interpretation.)

> (b) Alternatively, they might come to deny that talk of correctness has the substance that discursive participants are inclined to credit it with. In its extreme versions, this view says that we are not really entitled to talk about "getting things right," only about what people *take* to be right. This means that engaged participants are prone to an illusion of some kind, for they take their judgments to be not

merely their way of "taking" things, they take them—this *defines* the participant perspective—to be true; whereas according to the theorist, such claims need to be accounted for in other terms, for example, as ideology or the rhetorical camouflage of power, and so on.

Since (b) evidently expresses a form of skepticism, it is tempting to think of those embracing (a) as *anti-skeptics*. This is right in one way, but misleading in another. It accurately records the way (a) and (b) are interlocked voices in a single argument, as well as the intellectual derivativeness of (a): proponents of (a) are often defending certain commonplaces of the practice against the threat of skepticism. However, in a somewhat broader sense, one might regard both positions as "skeptical" ones. That is, "skepticism" might be taken to refer not just to arguments that deny that correctness in judgment is possible, but also to attempts to refute those arguments. Why speak this way? The point is to mark an alternative point of view from which (a) and (b) look intellectually intimate with each other, from which it appears that what these views share in common is larger than the point over which they disagree. What these views share in common is the premise:

> (P) Our entitlement to see one of two conflicting judgments as objectively correct requires some means, independent of those judgments, for validating one or another of them as correct.

The intimacy between positions (a) and (b) is that neither so much as sees a question to be asked about (P). That is, for each of them, (P) is invisible as a premise. Thus, each position takes itself to be the only alternative to the other.

Where in this landscape does Fish belong? The answer is: Fish wishes to reject both (a) and (b). So, he is essentially an *anti-skeptic* in the broad sense of the term: "Various characterizations of me as a skeptic—as someone who disbelieves in truth or relatives value . . . or is unconfident in his judgments, follow from the confusion between a very limited denial of a universal mechanism of validation and the denial, which I do not and never would make, of just about everything"—of just about everything (I take this to say) about which people judge and, often enough, agree ("Reply" 65).

As this makes clear, Fish's intended target is not the possibility of true or confident judgment *as such*, but only what he regards as one mistaken defense of this possibility—one that seeks a "universal mechanism." Fish sometimes calls the mistaken defense a "foundationalist" one. His continuous theme is that the options described by (a) and (b)—the Scylla of foundationalism and the Charybdis of skepticism, as it were—are not exhaustive; and that we can locate another possibility if we allow ourselves to question (P), the premise that the skeptic and his or her traditional opponent share in common.

Now it should be noted that "questioning (P)" evidently means *for Fish* constructing an alternative explanation of the basis of our entitlement to the notion of correctness in judgment. This means giving an alternative account, as we shall see, of how there could sometimes be "plain meanings"—obvious cases that no one disputes (see "Force" 513). But I shall suggest below that this misses a more radical possibility.

One doesn't need to read *Milton*, of course, in order to feel that (P) is not an innocuous premise. Indeed, one might see (Fish's) Milton's central thought—that we endeavor to judge the "single Truth" without anything standing surety for our judgments—as a variation on a point of Aristotle's: that the practically wise person doesn't have a recipe (or a set of deductively applicable instructions) for living well, but rather is able to *see* the significance of the details of practical situations in light of a correct grasp of the relevant ethical concepts. Aristotle's remarks trace a circle that never leaves the domain of ethical thinking, for if we ask, "What makes a grasp of the relevant ethical concepts a correct one?" Aristotle is apt merely to refer us to the judgments of the practically wise person, just where a more modern (and in the broad sense, skeptical) line of thought would expect to find an attempt at external validation (see McDowell, *Mind*).

At this point, however, someone might wish to object: "Surely, Fish is a skeptic. Doesn't he everywhere say that every judgment is contestable and that there may be no means, independent of the dispute, for settling the matter, that what will count as evidence in favor of one or another judgment, for example, may itself be a function of the position one holds? What is this if not a skeptical challenge to our notion that some judgments are objectively correct?"

This is a misunderstanding of Fish's aim, though it may not be one, I'm inclined to think, of his achievement. As I will later explain, there are genuine difficulties in Fish's argument, difficulties that understandably lead his readers to take him for a skeptic. (Thus, disclaimers like the one quoted above need to be continually reissued.) This recurrent mistake on the part of Fish's readers needs a more careful account, however, for the present objection merely records the fact that Fish does indeed set his face

against attempts to defend "objective correctness" along the lines of (a).
The objection thus testifies to the tenacious hold of premise (P). For *if* one
unquestioningly accepts (P), then one is bound to hear Fish's opposition
to (a) as incurring a commitment to the skepticism of (b). This misses the
general alternative Fish has in mind: the failure of foundationalism, rather
than affording a reason for embracing skepticism, should, given the
practical intolerability of the skeptic's position, provide a reason for
questioning (P), the premise that makes it appear as if these were the
only options.

"Theory"

Fish sometimes calls (a) "theory hope" and (b) "theory fear." (What I call
(P), therefore, exhibits the common genus.) These labels imply that
someone questioning (P) is seeking freedom from a way of thinking that
makes having a "theory" a prerequisite to our entitlement to take up the
participant or objectivizing point of view. That, of course, is how Fish
often presents himself: as being against "theory" in some sense of the
word (see "Consequences" and Dennis").

This way of talking won't do any harm if one bears in mind what
"theory" stands for—the requirement expressed by (P). Yet, it is not
especially perspicuous either, if only because the word "theory" is so
beloved by academics today as to be almost devoid of significant contrast:
it seems that to think or reason about anything at all is to "theorize"
("Dennis" 378). (This emptiness is, I think, significant: it expresses the
difficulties we have with the thought that certain forms of reasoning
are distinctively "practical.") Here, the following points ought to be
kept in view.

First, "theory/practice" is not to be construed as a contrast between
what we should ordinarily call "doing something," on the one hand, and
reasoning or reflecting, even very abstractly, on the other. Fish's anti-
theoreticism is not the view—which might describe certain spiritual
exercises like Zen or Pyrrhonism[6]—that it is useless to reason or ponder.
It is true that in some activities—playing basketball, for example—one's
performance is apt to be hindered if one reflects on what one is doing
while doing it. This shows up in forms of training: one learns basketball
by playing it, not (as one first learns, say, law) by studying it. Nonetheless,
this is simply a special feature of certain activities, related to the kinds of
performances and skills they require. (For this reason, Fish's use of the

game of baseball as an analogy for legal "practice" is as obscuring as it is clarifying.)[7] In the case of other activities—legal argumentation, for example—to perform successfully is to reason at a high level of abstraction; it is to advance, as lawyers say, a "legal theory." Being a plumber is perhaps an intermediate case, somewhere between basketball and law. Much of what a competent plumber does he could do "in his sleep." Yet, a competent plumber ought also to be capable, when the occasion demands, of posing alternative hypotheses about the source of a problem and considering different ways of proceeding. (The best course may not be the one that "comes naturally" or prior to deliberation.) The general point here is twofold: first, it does not make sense to contrast doing something and reasoning or reflecting *in general*; second, where such a contrast can be drawn (for example, in describing two aspects of the plumber's job), the contrast will clearly be seen to be beside Fish's point.

Why should premise (P) be associated with a kind of "theoreticism"? The idea calls for a contrast, as I have hinted, not between doing something ("practice") and reasoning about it ("theory"), but between two forms of reasoning—namely, theoretical and practical.

Consider a judge who endeavors to apply a legal rule—say, one requiring good faith in one's dealings with others. The judge must think about what this concept requires and must determine what, in particular cases, would be in accord with the rule. Now, we might wish to call this movement from the abstract to the concrete "practical" reasoning because it involves capacities of thought that are distinct from drawing logical inferences and from thinking about what will lead to what.[8] This will be true if, as here, the rule in question cannot be expected to function as part of a premise from which, given the facts, one could simply deduce the desired conclusion. Of course, there may be room for explanations of "good faith dealing"—explanations that might even be called (in an anodyne sense) a "theory" of it. But it may also be that to grasp the concept of "good faith" correctly—or some concept used to explain it—just is, in part, to be able to see that *this* and not *that* is required in circumstances like *these*. Applications of theoretical rationality cannot in general tell one what it is to get things right in such applicative judgments, or how to recognize particular acts or circumstances as instances of general classifications. Nor can correct judgment be generally explained by means of rules for making those judgments, for then we should need rules for correctly applying those rules, and so on, in a hopeless regress.[9]

Now, suppose that a dispute breaks out about what the rule requires. Premise (P) says we are not entitled to think of either view as being genuinely "correct" unless we have a validating argument from the outside. Applied quite generally (that is, not just to "good faith" but to every concept that can be used to explain it), this can only be a demand that "correct" judgment be made deductively accessible: the correct resolution of the issue would be expressible as the conclusion of an argument that would be compelling to anyone who can draw logical inferences and recognize what the facts are.[10] (If someone still persisted in not "getting it," that person could be convicted of irrationality by established standards of theoretical rationality, so this would comprise a "universal mechanism.") To be "against theory," in this context, is to allow that there may be useful explanations of "good faith," but it is to reject the thought that no applicative judgment can be regarded as "objectively correct" without an explanation of this sort: one that makes judgment available in a way that, in principle, obviates the need for practical discernment.[11]

"Interpretive Communities"

The example of applying a legal rule brings out the fact that any account of how correct judgment is possible (and that is Fish's general question) must explain also how it is that certain actions or events can be "in accord" with a rule, or indeed with any bit of intentionality. Meaning has a normative aspect: we could not speak about texts (or correct judgments about them) if we couldn't make use of such notions as "accord." The difficulties we get into over such normative notions are thus at the core of Fish's argument.

To illustrate, consider a simple statement describing how things are in the world—for example, "There is a vehicle parked on Elm Street." This sorts the world into states of affairs that are in accord with it and those that are not; it makes a demand, one may say, on how the world must be if the judgment is to be correct. A similar point applies to any item— for example, a rule, judgment, wish, order, thought, expectation, belief, and so on—that carries meaning: generally speaking, meanings sort things out.

One important bit of the world that meanings sort out is, of course, human linguistic behavior itself. For example, if someone grasps the meaning of the word "vehicle," then that person is required, if he or she is to act "in accord" with what he or she has grasped, to reach certain determinate verdicts when the world presents him or her with circumstances that bring this concept into play. Naturally, there may be border-line cases (Is it still a "vehicle" even though it lacks a motor? Is it "on Elm" when it is abutting the corner?), but insofar as these words can be used to communicate anything at all, there must also be plain cases, cases in which no classificatory hesitation arises. This commonplace idea—that is, that meaning has a normative bearing on linguistic performances—is related to other commonplaces concerning truth and objectivity: for example, that the world can be such as to make it correct or incorrect to *say* certain things about it. The very idea of "something that can correctly be said about the world" presupposes that there is a normative pattern in our use of words, a pattern that a particular use can (or can fail) to keep faith with. If that weren't the case, then anything could be said about anything—so nothing could be said at all.

The upshot is that should we begin to loosen our grip on normative notions like "accord," then our notions of meaning, objectivity, and truth will come under threat as well. And this is just what is happening in the skeptical currents in which Fish is swimming. Keeping a grip on the notion of "accord" (or related normative notions: "misuse," "misunderstanding," "misapplication") turns out to be a difficult thing to do, for there is a tempting line of thought that seems precisely to unhinge us here. And this line of thought provides the right context in which to understand the general work that Fish sees "interpretive communities" as doing.

The unhinging line of thought begins with the notion of a "sign" or a "text." A sign or a text is anything that carries linguistic meaning.[12] Thus, the first line of Milton's Paradise Lost—"Of Mans First Disobedience . . . ."—comprises a sign or text, as does a road sign pointing out the direction in which one is to go (——>). It will be useful to take the latter as our example because it makes immediately perspicuous that a sign carrying meaning sorts behavior into that which accords with it and that which does not. (This, in fact, is the chief difference between signs carrying meaning and mere doodles or noises: signs are "alive" in that they have such normative reach. But this is also the thought on which we seem, under theoretical pressure, to loosen our grip.)

Before proceeding, two comments may help to set things up more clearly. First, concerning exemplification. Fish initially introduced the notion of "interpretive community" to address a set of questions arising within literary studies: the relevance of authorial intentions, the distinctive "literariness" (if there be any) of literary texts, the semantic multiplicity or univocity of such texts, the reasons for interpretive disagreement, the status of appeals to the "text itself" in resolving disagreement, the possible innovativeness of literary interpretation, and so on. Our board (———>) would be a poor example for discussing such issues (at least without some further details). But it becomes clear, in the evolution of Fish's work, that insofar as literary texts always require interpretation, they are to be regarded as merely exemplary of how it is with discourse in general: "Communications of every kind are characterized by exactly the same conditions—the necessity of interpretive work . . . and the construction by acts of interpretation" ("Compliments" 43–44). I find this development disappointing because, for reasons that will soon appear, I think the necessity of interpretation could *only* have been plausible as a restricted thesis about the meaning of literary texts. (In this role—as opposed to the perfectly general role Fish gives it—the necessity of interpretation might also have told us something genuinely informative about "literature," or about the nature of our interest in it.)[13] In any case, given the generality of Fish's thesis, a basic example (———>) is just what is wanted for discussing it; the more basic the better.

     Second, concerning skepticism. The line of thought to be considered may be called "skeptical," though it doesn't *aim* toward a skeptical conclusion. It does not aim to deny, for example, that it is sometimes perfectly plain what road signs or other texts mean. The question is merely how such "plainness" is possible. What Fish (and others today) wish to deny is not that there are perfectly plain meanings (that would make them not just skeptical but mad),[14] but only a purportedly suspect conception—naive or metaphysical—of such phenomena or of their conditions of possibility. Provisionally, we may say that on the suspect conception, a case of plain meaning is apt to be considered "inherently plain, plain in and of itself," or plain as a simple fact-of-the-matter ("Force" 513).[15]

     Briefly, then, the "skeptical" line of thought unfolds like this:[16]

> 1. Considered just "in and of itself" (say, as an inscribed piece of wood), the sign (———>) does not determine what is in accord with it and what is not; it does not determine, say, whether one is to go in the direction of the arrow or in the opposite direction. (This is true of any text: just in itself, it is dead matter, powerless to determine its own meaning or how we are to understand it; powerless, as Fish sometimes likes to say, to "execute" its own meaning.)
>
> 2. To animate the sign into meaning something—that is, to get the normative notion of "accord," and hence of "meaning" into play—

we need to consider the sign not "in itself" but under some interpretation that has been put on it. That is, we need to interpret it—for example, as a road sign saying that one is to go in a certain direction. Signs mean what they do only by way of some interpretation.

3. This seems clear enough. But is it? If a sign or text cannot "in itself" determine what accords with it, how does it manage to do so when considered under an interpretation? In fact, it looks like there's a problem here.

4. Suppose that an "interpretation" involves some further sign or text. For example, one might "interpret" the sign (———>) by using the spoken words "this way," accompanied by a pointing gesture. Surely, the original sign is now alive with meaning, no? Well, no, for according to step (1), this new text cannot "in itself" determine how *it* is to be followed. It too seems dead—a bit of sound and fury. It seems that if the interpretation ("this way") is really to animate our original sign into meaning something, we shall first need an *interpretation* of this interpretation, and so on. A hopeless regress—not to mention an hysteria of gesticulation (*"this* way, I mean *THIS* way")—looms before us.

5. We had better back up. Why did we think—in step (2)—that an interpretation could help bring "meaning" into the picture? The answer seems clear. There was a doubt about how the sign was to be followed, and we know that "interpretations" do sometimes successfully function to remove or avert such doubts. "Interpretations" in a familiar, sense are a kind of explanation: they come into play when the meaning of a text isn't fully clear.[17] Thus, it was hoped that we could get "meaning" into our picture by making a quite *general* use of this familiar function of interpretation. But it appears now that the notion of "interpretation" is unsuited for this general role. Rather than animating our original sign, the requirement of interpretation seems only to redouble the problem of its impotence.

6. But wait, someone will say. When we put someone pointing and saying "this way" into the picture, we didn't just introduce another inert block of wood, or even (comically) any number of inert items, each one standing behind the next; nor did we just introduce some noises, such as a person might make. Instead, we put a person into the picture, a living being. One wants to say: surely that makes a difference; surely meaning, in all its splendid animation, is some-

where at hand! The thought that is apt to occur now is that a person makes a difference, not as a potential source of sound and other commotion (many things are that), but as the locus of a *mind*. Thus, the demonstrative utterance "this way" introduces meaning into the situation because it introduces someone who *thinks* or *intends* the sign in a certain way. Indeed, it seems that *thought* is really the essential thing here, for it might have occurred—and meaning might come into the picture—even without the giving of any further signs.

The motive here is understandable enough: since further signs (texts or linguistic items) merely redouble the problem of the sign's impotence, it becomes tempting to think that "interpretation" must refer to some essentially *mental* act of thinking the sign one way or another. What we need, the thought goes, is not another inert bit of nature, but a mind; not essentially interpretations (*qua* signs) but an interpreter, alive and present.

7. Alas, this solution can make us happy only for a moment. Suppose it is asked, "What does his thinking or intending the sign *this* way rather than *that* way consist in?" After all, if we can doubt what the original sign requires, it should be possible to raise a question about what he intends or what accords with his intention. There seem to be only two general possibilities.

(A) We might say that his intending the sign *this* way consists in his *meaning* that, or meaning *that*. Clearly, this answer goes nowhere: it merely refuses the very notion— "meaning"—that "interpretation" was supposed to explain.[18] (B) We might try to identify something that went on "in his mind," considered as a region of goings-on that is left over once we abstract from the world and all the ("in themselves" meaningless) items to be found in it. However, this option looks no less hopeless. For one thing, if someone always follows the sign in the direction of the arrow (or points out the mistake when other people don't), then we shall say that he grasps its meaning no matter what actually goes on "in his mind." In fact, the search for a meaning-creating item in his mind only returns our original problem. Lots of things might have occurred to him, some of which (like the pang of hunger or impatience he felt) seem irrelevant. But if anything occurs to him that does seem relevant (perhaps he thought "to the right" or perhaps he saw a picture of the traveler turning right in his mind's eye), it is bound to disappoint us, for it is just one more discrete item that, like our original sign, can always be projected and applied in different ways. So, it too stands in need of an interpretation. This result shouldn't surprise us. For it amounts to what much twentieth-century philosophy has told us anyway: that we can't really make intelligible to ourselves how a thought occurring in someone's mind—for example, "turn right"—can be such as to be any more determinate, or less in need of interpretation, than a text representing that thought. We can't really understand what it would be for there to be an item in the mind that had the requisite normative properties of meaning but that was not, from the get-go, subject to the conditions or requirements of representability (or communicability) in signs.[19]

Actually, there is a third possibility for attempting to answer the question "what does his thinking or intending the sign consist in?" we might try to identify something that goes on "in his mind," considered not as a region apart from the world, but as something that *includes* a lot of happenings there—for example, what other people say and do. Fish's idea of an "interpretive community"— or of a subject whose mental life is what it is only "by virtue of his membership in a community of interpretation"—is a version of this idea. I shall postpone commenting on it because my endeavor is first to get into a position to describe its appeal more fully ("Why" 83).

8. Our hypothetical interpreter might throw up his hands at this point and say something like this: "Clearly, an interpretation is needed to get meaning into this picture, but the idea of 'interpretation' needed is just that of a very unique and remarkable spiritual power to make signs mean *this* rather than *that*—somewhat like the power to give life to dead matter. 'The Mind' is that unique kind of thing that has such remarkable powers. 'To interpret' is mentally to present oneself with a 'meaning.' And meanings sort things out in a way that is—we know (today) not how—immune to any further interpretation."

This response is not just a reuse of the term "meaning." When it is seriously entertained, it purports to explain the meaning of signs through the mind's grasp of entities called "meanings." Such a proposal—often dubbed "platonism" by its detractors—is sometimes thought to arise as a kind of self-standing conception at the beginning of philosophical inquiry into meaning; it is what the skeptic, in pointing to the indeterminacy of texts "in themselves" is supposed to be reacting against. But it should be clear at this point that "platonism" can just as well, or better, be given a different pedigree. It can be understood as a late (and desperate) product of a way of thinking that *begins* with a skeptical thought, a thought that then creates a felt need to explain the general possibility of meaning because it latently suggests, contrary to everyday experience, that meaning is in fact *impossible*.[20]

9. A metaphysically occult idea of meaning does indeed seem to be forced upon us here. This is so because we are eventually led to see that in order for "interpretation" to function as a general condition of the possibility of meaning, there has got to be some last or final interpretation—that is, an interpretation not in need of any further interpretation—which is what we call "*the* meaning." In other words, our starting point commits us, after whatever twists and turns, to looking for some item that a meaning-endowing interpretation can consist in but which, unlike ordinary linguistic signs, will function as a *regress-stopper*. It comes to seem that only a unique act of mind can do that.

Of course, there still remains another bold option: bite the skeptical bullet and accept "the endless movement from sign to sign."[21] But the choice, within the present setup, seems clear: either (1) indulge a platonic mythology, allowing that there just *are* meanings, remarkable normative entities channeled through a mind; or (2) accept rampant interpretivism, admitting that anything can be made to accord with any interpretation of a text (on some interpretation of that interpretation), which is to say, for some people today, the choice is clear: we should avoid mythology, and accept the ubiquity of interpretation.

So much for the skeptical recital. It presents ubiquitous interpretation as the realistic or demystifying alternative to a suspect metaphysics of meaning. But doesn't demystification here look unnervingly like decapitation? Hasn't this line of thought in fact destroyed the very possibility (of plain meanings) that it was supposed merely to account for? If anything can be made to accord with a text (on some interpretation), it looks like we simply can't talk about accord or conflict and therefore can't talk about meaning (see Wittgenstein, *Philosophical* 202). Are we really to accept that on a clearheaded view of things, nothing really means anything, and that, could we but see to the bottom of things, we should see that our most everyday concourse with meaning ("Please come next weekend") is unreal?

It is just at this point that Fish wishes to make use of the notion of an "interpretive community." That notion comes into play as an attempt to hang onto the idea that "to understand is to interpret" while avoiding the skeptical consequences that seem to come in the wake of this idea. (I indicated the general possibility of such a move earlier.)

According to Fish, the impression of skeptical consequences—the decapitating "denial of just about everything"—arises only because we have not really disabused ourselves of a longing for a metaphysical ideal, by comparison with which the available notions of meaning and truth seem disappointing ("Reply" 65). To purge immodest hope, however, can be at once to allay unfounded fear. We can purge the longing by recognizing that there are no "interpretation-free" facts about meaning. But we can allay our fear by noting that in place of such facts, there is always something coming, for all practical purposes, close enough: a story to be told about our membership in communities of mutual recognition, about how we achieve good standing and credit in such communities, about the sanctions that attach to deviance, and so on. Essentially, Fish's thought is that the source of norms relevant to meaning is the community itself: someone who does not behave (for example, follow the sign) as the community does is in violation of one of its norms and may justifiably be said to "misunderstand" the relevant text. And given the mutually sustained communal framework, any dues-paying member will find the meaning of "———>" and many other signs to be as plain as day: they will go right, naturally. So, in the end, the attack on "theory-hope" is not a destructive one—or it is destructive only of bits of philosophy ("texts that are clear in and of themselves") that we have no need for anyway ("Force" 513). Thus, we can come to love interpretation, not fear it, for it suffices to account for all the plainness and stability we could intelligibly ask for to see how meanings are—by a kind of groundless self-enactment of the community—socially constructed and maintained.

Spectators and Agents, Theory, and Practice

The foregoing dialectic elaborates two paradigmatic moments that appear in a typical Fish essay. The first moment invokes a notion of *possibility*: "it is always possible" for a text to mean something else, no matter what—or how richly specified—the context; every text (and context) is surrounded by a space of interpretive possibilities; it does not just by itself determine, and so on.[22] Anemic as the notion of possibility invoked here is (that a doubt is *possible* doesn't mean anyone *does* doubt), this may seem alarming. At the second moment, however, we learn that we needn't worry about the first moment, for after the interpreter is located within a community, we are supposed to have the materials we need to reconstruct such normative notions as are indispensable to our everyday talk of texts and their meanings. Indeed, it turns out that we not only needn't worry, but needn't even be interested, unless we are interested in theoretical questions, for, according to Fish, the reconstruction of "plain meaning" (as an effect of interpretation) would leave everything, practically speaking, as it was: "When you come to the end of the antiformalist road, what you will find waiting for you is formalism." ("Anti-formalism," as several Fish essays make clear, is another term for "rampant interpretivism.")[23]

Remarks like the preceding one—archetypal in their structure (they tell of a journey and a return, of something lost and regained)—deserve special comment. At such moments, Fish goes so far as to invite us to regard rampant interpretivism as just a transitional step—a self-consuming artifact, if you like—the effect of which is merely to remove some mistaken bits of philosophy, but without consequences for practice.[24] On the other hand, Fish doesn't think that his interpretivism is *completely* self-consuming, for he clearly thinks that it is to be endorsed, at the journey's end, as the *right* view in place of the wrong one. This is evident from the way the foregoing passage continues: " . . . what you will find waiting for you is formalism; that is, you will find the meanings that are perspicuous for you, *given your membership in what I have called an interpretive community*" (*Trouble* 295; emphasis added). To anticipate what I will have to say about Fish's view, it is worth noting an ambiguity here. Is "your interpretive community membership" *within* the intentional scope of "what you will find" at the end of the road, or is it merely the general precondition—itself unfound or unrecognized—of everything else you will find? The ambiguity isn't surprising, ultimately, because neither option should sit well with Fish. If communal interpretivism is part of what you will find, in what sense have you come back to "formalism"? If, on the other hand, communal interpretivism is only the (unthought) precondition of what you will find, why should anyone accept it as true? How could they? The significance of these questions will become more apparent in a moment. For now, it may be remarked simply that, at the last stop (or what he regards as the last), Fish is prepared to find not just practice unchanged, but practice regained through the right bit of theory.

This is not the place to examine every stop on this road. I limit myself to three observations. These observations will lead to the following conclusion. Fish's interpretivism would be more satisfying if it were utterly self-consuming: something to be recognized, at the last stop (if not before), as complete nonsense. In this role—as a piece of transitional nonsense—the interest of interpretivism obviously could not be, as Fish thinks, that it shows us the truth about texts and their meaning: nonsense is nonsense. Rather, its interest would be that it shows us something about *ourselves*—namely, (1) that we are sometimes prone to imagine that we are making sense when we aren't, and (2) that this illusion is connected to our wish to say something philosophical, our wish, that is, for there to be a philosophical perspective on things. The recognition of ourselves as harboring this wish—hence, as calling on words like "interpretation" outside the practical settings in which they have their significance—is the last stop. From such a cognition (of our wish to speak philosophically as one that would not be satisfied insofar as what we said made sense) there follows a loss of attraction to philosophical investigation—or not. In any case, my remarks here amount to friendly encouragement to Fish to take another step along the road and not chicken out. My reasons for so encouraging him will shortly become apparent.

Reason Number 1

To begin with, we need to see why the interpretive community story cannot provide a satisfactory account of meaning. Such a story is clearly aspiring to be a kind of down-to-earth pragmatism, as against metaphysically suspect conceptions of meaning. But it is really lacking in the perspicuity it would need to be that. Some of Fish's commentators have drawn attention to problems in the definition of "community" (What constitutes the relevant community? Can there be different but equally "right" answers for different communities? If so, can we really not intelligibly aspire to any more full-blooded objectivity than this?), but the problems I have in mind here are much more basic: they arise no matter how the community is spliced.[25]

Notice how things appear from the first-person point of view, that of the agent engaged in hands-on transactions with meaning. The question is what the text means, not what other people think it means. For a judge, the question is what the rule requires not what other people (or other judges) think it requires. Of course, it is possible for a judge to ask him or herself what other judges think, but this is only because *someone* is asking the hands-on question; someone is having thoughts about what the rule requires. The hands-on question is a critical question, as we may call it, not a sociological one.[26] Of course, all of us are, everyday, such hands-on agents, for, as indicated, there would be no sociological questions to ask about texts if there weren't, in the first place, agents whose relation to them is the engaged or critical one. (The sociology of meaning, if there is one, concerns the thoughts of such agents.) In this sense, the agent perspective on meaning is *primary*: it is possible to think of a world in which people only ask the critical questions, but not a world in which the only questions about texts are sociological ones.

Now this is not, just by itself, likely to be perceived as an objection by Fish. He is apt to say that the competent agent has internalized the community's way of seeing things and so has no need to consult anything but the "rule itself" as it appears within the relevant communal-interpretive framework. So the perspective of practical agency, Fish will say, is preserved in his story. But things are not that simple. We might ask: How does such a picture manage to be a picture of *meaning* (with its normativity intact) at all? For that a certain decision is required by a rule consists, according to this picture, in nothing more than the community agreeing that it is required. How does this differ from the picture of a community merely *pretending* to agree—or collectively sustaining the myth—that something is required by the rule?[27] How, this is to ask, can an agent so much as "agree" that something—anything at all—is genuinely *required* by the rule if he or she is not entitled to the view that the rule requires this no matter what others might think? The most he or she can say, it would seem, is something about what the community thinks. But no one in the community is in any better position. They, likewise, are not entitled to the view that the rule imposes a determinate requirement regardless of what anyone else might think. And since no one in the community is in a position to say anything stronger than something about what the community thinks, the perspective of agency vanishes here. (And of course, when this vanishes, there can also be no "communal way of seeing things," internalized or not.)[28]

Thinking about the primacy of the agent-perspective is instructive here. It means that what communal agents are being asked to agree to— the subject of their possible agreement—is, in the first place, what the rule requires, not what the community thinks it requires. The later is a possible question only because there are agents in the community who are not asking it, who have other things on their mind. But the problem, for Fish's story, is to see what entitles any of community's agents to represent (to themselves or to others) that the rule (for example, "no vehicles in the park") genuinely prohibits such-and-such events, once it is understood that whether one has gotten things right, must ultimately be a question of what the community agrees the rule prohibits.

All of this points to the same general conclusion. The *ersatz* notion of "correctness in judgment" provided by the interpretive community story can't really sustain the notion of their being *meaning* (that is, of there being agents subject to genuine normative requirements) once it is seen, that at the basic level, underneath talk of "what a rule requires," there is nothing but mere convergent behavior—or (one might again say) mere soundings-off. Fish's account of meaning, someone might feel, is really no less skeptical than the skeptic's account it is meant to combat. (As will become clear in a moment, it is also no less "theoretical" than the theoreticism it is meant to combat).

The objection advanced here is essentially that the interpretive community story does not make room for the attitudes toward meaning that agents must have if there is to so much as *be* an interpretive community (a community agreeing in its critical judgments) at all, for the story tells agents that in making such judgments—that is, that the rule requires such-and-such no matter what others might think—they are engaging a philosophical illusion. Given this structure, an understandable way of trying to defuse the objection would be to acoustically separate the judgments of practical agency from the deliverances of "theory." Thus, it might be said that *theory* (the right story about the possibility of plain meanings and correctness in judgment) is one thing, and *practice* (the engaged concourse with texts and their meanings) is quite another. According to this rejoinder, an agent can judge (and represent to all the world) that the "no vehicle in the park" rule genuinely prohibits such-and-such events because, in making this judgment, he or she is acting (and seeing the world) in his or her capacity as agent, not as a detached theorist of meaning. Such a person is playing the legal game, as Fish is apt to say, not the theory game. The motive here is obvious: those who judge that such-and-such is *required* by a rule—required as a plain fact—had better not be those who also see, by means of the right theory, to the deeper level of things, at which it becomes apparent that such notional "requirements" and "facts" are only *such* by courtesy of interpretation. The theoretical truth about meaning, in other words, had better not get around, for it hardly seems clear how the attitudes agents must have in their practical concourse with meanings could be psychologically stable ones once it does.

But is this separation plausible? What is supposed to stop the theoretical truth from getting around? One way of trying to stave off the possibility of reflective conflict would be simply cleaving everyone in two. Thus, it might be said, "Let the truth get around as it will. Still, at any moment, we are either having transactions with meaning *qua* practical agents or theorizing about it *qua* knowing-spectators; but these two parts of ourselves can never shake hands, for they may never be present at once." Of course, this looks desperate. Why can't they be present at once? Simply because agents would be psychologically unstable in their attitudes if they were? That is *my* point: it argues against a theoretical view that puts agents in the way of such conflict, not against the evident possibility of conflict on the grounds that practices and their agents are, after all, reflectively stable ones.

However these problems are to be developed, we might note that it is surprising to see Fish appealing to the split-agent picture as much as he does, for this is precisely a picture of a self-standing realm of "theory," laying bare the grounds of possibility of practice, yet somehow separated or detached from the judgments of practice. Isn't this ground-giving just what Fish everywhere says is "impossible," a hopeless attempt to look at oneself (*qua* agent) from sideways-on? (Evidently, Fish doesn't see this, so I will address this question—and not just ask it rhetorically—in a moment.)

Reason Number Two

The inadequacy of the interpretive community story about meaning would explain the matter I mentioned earlier: why Fish's work is liable to give some readers the impression that it intends a kind of skepticism. Fish's argument depends on following a skeptical (interpretivist) progression of thought up to a certain point, and then heading off its apparent unacceptable consequences by appeal to the notion of "community" as a source of ("always-already") interpretive stability.[29] The trouble is that although Fish's intention is a nonskeptical one, the solution remains too much in league with the skeptic, follows the skeptic too far down the road. Fish might ask himself whether such an account of "correct judgment" (as that view that the community realizes from among the interpretive possibilities) really squares with the Miltonic notion of correctness as judgment in accord with God's will.[30] It would seem that a notion of correctness as "community agreement" must remain a second-best notion, something falling short of some ideal as illusory (and not just unattainable).

Reason Number Three

How far down the road should one follow the skeptical progression of thought? A satisfactory response to it requires questioning, sooner or later, its *very first* step, the step at which the notion of a sign or text

"considered in itself" is introduced. If one accepts that step unquestioningly, then it will be natural to accept the thesis that to grasp a meaning
is to interpret; and if one accepts this thesis, it will be natural to feel
obliged to choose between "platonism" and some social-pragmatic story
about meaning. But there is another option: we might come to see that we
have no use for such notions as signs or texts "in themselves" unless we
are trying to give a *philosophical account* of the meaning of a sign or text.
And (taking a hint from the proverbial man suffering from carrying
around a heavy rock who found an astonishing solution: drop it) we could
simply stop trying to give such an account.

What is meant by this can be indicated by thinking about what
happens when we give everyday explanations of meaning—that is,
explanations in situations where questions about the "conditions of
possibility" of meaning are not in play. Generally, we rely on the
responses and uptake of others: we count on them, for example, to follow
in the direction of the pointed finger, not the opposite direction. Everyday
explanations are (thus) directed toward removing or averting such doubts
as, under the circumstances, actually arise—not every "possible" doubt,
whatever that might mean. In contrast, a philosophical account seeks to
explain how the meaning of a sign gets fixed from *among all the
possibilities*. (Remember, what justifies talk of ubiquitous interpretation,
for Fish, is not that there are always real doubts—some cases are plain
ones—but that doubts are "always possible.") The burden of a philosophical account, to put this another way, is not simply to rule out such
doubts as might, under the circumstances, arise, but to specify the
meaning of a sign *absolutely*.[31]

Now, the notion of a sign or text "in itself" is a natural starting point
for such an endeavor. Why? Because this notion is formed by abstracting
the sign from our practical concourse with it—that is, the natural
(circumstantial) responses and uptake on which everyday explanations
rely. By means of this abstraction, we in effect represent doubts that are
merely notionally possible (they might arise in some circumstances) as
somehow already present to an agent considering the sign. Such a
representation is clearly the mirror image of the platonic notion that
grasping a sign's "meaning" determines (in the present moment) its
application in all possible circumstances, excluding all possible doubt.
What the platonist and the interpretivist have in common, then, is the
endeavor to give an account of the fixity of meaning, as it were, in light
of all the possibilities. (Both express what someone might call "the
metaphysics of presence.")

What happens if, in contrast to both, we were to free ourselves of the felt need for such an explanatory endeavor? We should have no use for speaking of signs "in themselves," save perhaps in the practically useful way that, for example, lawyers sometimes do—namely, to distinguish between a text ("the rule itself") and someone's gloss on it. And if we had no use for such an abstraction, we should also have no use for the thought that there must always be an interpretation that fixes a sign's meaning. "What gives life to signs," we will be inclined to say (if we must say something about this), "is that they are part of the weave of *our lives*. It is we who are the life of signs." This is to be heard not as a further bit of rock-carrying theory, but simply as expressing that one no longer feels compelled to try to account for the normative aspect of signs by means of whatever materials remain in view after one abstracts from the sort of practical activities and attention that comprise our sign-filled lives.

Given this possibility (of rejecting the argument's first-step), it seems clear that we are not compelled to embrace the interpretive community story in order to head-off the argument's nihilistic consequences. We might instead come to recognize, in light of those consequences, that the thought "to understand is always to interpret" is—just as it intuitively seemed to be—an absurdity. The ubiquity of interpretation, communalized or not, is not intrinsically plausible. At best, it comes to look plausible as the result of a philosophical setup that makes it look as if platonism and nihilism—theory hope and theory fear—were the only other options. In such cases, the solution is always to figure out what we need to do to scrap the setup. Here, this would mean asking what has happened—what doubts have arisen—to make an account of the very possibility of meaning seem like something we need. (That there must or could be such an account—a substantially correct one—is of course not something that Fish, for all of his good cautionary advice about "the unavailability of cosmic doubts," ever questions.)[32]

Why doesn't Fish recognize that his interpretivism is cut from the same philosophical cloth as the platonism it would oppose? Recognizing this would require that he see more clearly what is wrong with the platonic or foundationalist idea of "absolutely fixed meaning." Fish tends to speak as if the trouble with this were just a suspect wish to find a "universal mechanism"—to give assurance to judgment from the outside. But a more fundamental question is whether we can so much as make out what is being said here—"fixed in light of *all* the possibilities"? If intelligibility (rather than substantial truth or falsity) is the trouble, no satisfaction is to be gained from *denying* that meaning could be so fixed by asserting that, on the contrary, all meaning is subject to interpretive conditions. To assert the later (that it is *always possible* for the text to mean something else) is to join ranks with what one means to be opposing: it is to suppose that one has managed to make sense of the idea of an absolute space of meaning-possibilities, the space of what a text *could* mean. (It is to entertain "cosmic doubts.")

An example of Fish's might help to make this clearer: "As yet two plus two equals four has not become . . . a flash point of disagreement, but it *could*. . . . Until two plus two equals four crosses someone's ambition, it is a fact agreed on by all the parties, but this doesn't mean that there are truths *above* ideology but that there are (at least by current convention) truths *below* ideology" (*Trouble* 271; emphasis on "could" added). The passage is virtuosic, as so much else in Fish, in purporting to exhibit how virtually anything, including the supposedly hard facts of mathematics, can be reconstructed as effects of interpretation. (No facts, to put this somewhat less benignly, are capable of getting in the way of Fish's interpretivism.) But to pursue further the intuition of "possibility" invoked here ("it *could* . . . "), we might ask, From what point of view does this possibility—that two plus two equals four could (intelligibly) cross someone's ambition—appear? From what point of view does it appear, for that matter, that a case that is perfectly plain under a rule *could* (tomorrow) come in for doubt? (See "Force" 512). Certainly, not *our* point of view as practical agents, at least if "could" means that we can make sense of these possibilities. (And if it doesn't mean that, what does it mean?) After all, some cases are so clear that to "doubt"—or to try to doubt—merely announces to others that you are not someone with whom it is going to be possible to speak; and if there is no speaking with you, there is no disagreeing, or feeling crossed by you, either. God's point of view then? A deeper diagnosis of what is wrong with foundationalism—its reliance on such a notional point of view—should have led Fish to see that his own interpretivism falls by the same axe. Interpretivism is the negative image of foundationalism. And a general moral to be grasped here is that one does not get rid of philosophical foundations by denying that there are any. That is merely a way of preserving the structure of the question (the demand for an explanation of how plain meaning is possible) that foundational views take themselves to be answering.

Practice, or the View from Straight-On

To conclude, it is worth recalling a point mentioned earlier—namely, that the everyday idea of interpretation is at home in cases of real doubt or uncertainty, cases that occur against a background of "plain cases" in which there is no call for interpretation. I have been arguing that to assert (in contrast to this) that an interpretation is always required because no text is immune to *possible* doubts is essentially to entertain, in league with one's philosophical opponent, the idea of a "philosophical perspective" on meaning, an account of how meaning is fixed from among "all the possibilities." When we give up this idea, we can return the word "interpretation" to its ordinary use, whereby interpretation is sometimes needed and sometimes not (it is no longer a general requirement). By the same token, we can return the expression "text itself" to its ordinary use, which marks a distinction between a text and an interpretation or gloss someone has put on it.

For all of his pragmatic aspiration, Fish misses this possibility—the possibility, you might say, of trusting in how things ordinarily appear. At the last stop, it seems that he wants there to be a philosophical perspective on meaning, an account for him to be "right" about; that idea—philosophy's traditional idea of itself—never ceases to attract him. His attraction to it, and his blindness to the intellectual possibilities it occludes, are ironic, of course, because the rejection of philosophical dogmas—including the dogma that there must always be room for good answers to philosophy's "how possible" question—-is one of his big themes.

The conflict I'm describing comes directly into view in remarks like this: "Theory's project—the attempt to get above practice and lay bare the grounds of its possibility—is an impossible one" ("Change" 156). How, we will want to know, is the general account Fish seeks to be described if not as an attempt to give grounds of the possibility of our concourse with meaning? Isn't that just what is in the offing when a question like "What makes it the case that *this* action is in accord with the utterance 'a diet Coke please'" meets with answers like "some community-informed interpretation," as opposed to the sort of answers that actually figure in our practical activity, answers that merely direct attention to features of the text in question or to the situation in which it was uttered? In contrast to what I have called the everyday use of interpretation, "interpretation" as a ubiquitous requirement begins to look like another name for—an occupant of the same explanatory place as—divinity: it is the terminus of all other explanations of meaning. So, this looks like "theory's project" more or less as Fish describes it: not a "universal mechanism," to be sure, but still an attempt to get above practice and exhibit its grounds of possibility—an attempt, in Fish's words, to look "sideways at oneself" ("Theory" 772; see also *Trouble* 305–56). Looking from *straight-on*—to continue the metaphor—it will appear that an interpretation is needed only when there is some actual doubt, not the mere notional *possibility* of doubt, to be cleared-up or averted.

Fish's mistaken sense of his own philosophical radicalism comes out again when he quotes a remark of Hilary Putnam's that is a modern variation on Plato's myth of the cave: "What if all the philosophers are wrong," Putnam asks, "and the way it seems to be is the way it is?" Fish approvingly glosses the question like this: "What if the answers philosophers come up with are answers only in the highly artificial circumstances of the philosophy seminar, where ordinary reasons for action are systematically distrusted and introduced only to be dismissed as naive?" (*Trouble* 294). But now it should be plain that, with respect to the refusal of philosophical tradition gestured toward in this question, Fish's interpretivism is on the wrong side, for that an interpretation is required in every case is *not* how things appear from the (naive) point of view of practical activity. (Imagine the server, with no special—circumstantial—prompting, replying, "I interpret that to mean you'd like a certain beverage now." Is the server mad? Or just doing a bit of literary theory?) In fact, it is *only* in the caves of the seminar room that the term "interpretation" shows up as part of an account of how it so much as possible for certain signs to be meaningful and hence to afford agents with reasons for action. Thank God, wise is He, for that.

From the straight-on perspective, the answer to a question (should it arise) like "What makes it a fact that he ordered a diet Coke?" must surely be *not* a communal interpretation, but rather (perhaps after reminding the questioner of the richly-woven world of restaurants, menus, orders, servers, meals, preferences, beverages, and so on): "look, you can see that's what happened yourself."[33] A final point to be dealt with involves being clear about the status of the material I have put in parentheses here.

The parenthetical material reminds us of the practical situation or setting. But the point is not to say that it is really, in the end, *practi*ce that determines a text's meaning or that mediates between a text and what accords with it. *That* would be another bit of theory; and we should then have to ask whether we really have a notion of "practice" as behavior that is describable without attributing "meanings" to anyone, and also whether behavior, so described, is really sufficient to give us the notion of "accord," and hence of meaning with its normativity intact. After every-thing I have said, it must be clear that I don't mean the parenthesis in this way, as finally the best theory of all—the "practice theory"! The paren-thesis is there rather to remind us that from the *practical* (engaged, straight-on) perspective, no *general* gap between an order and what accords with it appears. (It only looks like there is a general gap when we consider the order "in itself.") Since there is no general gap, there is no general need for the explanatory (gap-filling) work of "interpretation," "practice," or anything else.

Speaking as practical agents, what we shall say is simply this: sometimes there is a gap (and an interpretation is useful in bridging it), and other times there isn't (and then there is no call for interpretation). Of course, this is not a philosophical remark. It is merely something that practical agents can see and (often enough) agree on, in just the way that they (often enough) agree about such things as someone's having ordered a diet Coke. No explanation of the possibility of such agreement in judgments (or the possibility of "plain meaning") is on offer here, no attempt to go deeper than the fact that we do (often enough) agree. Is an explanation therefore *missing* here? A certain traditional philosopher is apt to be certain it is. Of course. But *Fish*? He ought to have said that it isn't compulsory to think so, for from the primary standpoint of practical engagement, an explanation is not merely not needed—it isn't even wanted. Despite his anti-theoreticism, Fish never really gets this intellec-tual possibility fully into view. Yet, from much of what he says, I think it is what he was after.

Notes

1. See also Fish, *Trouble* 243–48, 263–70.

2. More recent work by Fish extends these themes by proposing that we see "Liberalism" (as he writes it) as presenting a political analogy to the suspect forms of theory depicted earlier. See, for example, *Trouble*. This proposal is off the main line of my discussion.

3. The following remarks stem from a seminar I taught in the Spring of 1998 in Duke's Program in Literature; they retain here the style and sound of their pedagogical origin. My focus is only on the main nerve of Fish's argument. A broader treatment can be found in my contribution to John Gibson and Wolfgang Huemer's *Literature after Wittgenstein*. Related issues are also touched on in my "Wittgenstein on Deconstruction."

4. See Grossman. On the general connection between Fish's reading of *Paradise Lost* and his later interest in "interpretation," see the Preface to the second edition of his *Surprised by Sin*.

5. The idea of idolatry—the false representation of divinity—provides the point of intimacy, which Fish later explores, between Milton and the politics of Roberto Unger. See "Unger," especially 403 and 412.

6. Or perhaps the experience of clinical depression—though it seems more accurate to say that depression is more often the feeling that it is useless to act (Hamlet).

7. See "Dennis." Part of what makes sports both important and pleasurable is that the meaning (and other effects) of action are completely tractable within the game. Related to this is the fact that the point or goal of action is in general completely perspicuous: to win. Most everyday activities are not like this, and the law is a far cry away.

8. Reasoning about what will lead to what often comes into reasoning about what to do in a particular situation, but it is not distinctly practical in the present sense.

9. This was noticed by Kant. See *Critique* and "On." The point also arises in Wittgenstein's discussion of "accord with a rule" (*Philosophical* §§138–202).

10. I develop this idea in the context of debates in legal theory in my "Legal."

11. For purposes of simplicity, I am not questioning the thought that explanations that make judgment deductively available would obviate the need, in principle, for "practical discernment." But the better view is that *all* judgments—even deductive ones—rely on something like the kind of discernment that is out in the open in cases of practical conflict. As John McDowell has argued, this may be taken as one of the lessons of Wittgenstein's remarks on "accord with a rule." (There is a similar point in Cavell. As McDowell suggests, this lesson should allay the temptation to think that judgment in hard cases (where the need for discernment is conspicuous) must suffer in its credentials of objectivity by comparison with a deductive case, conceived as a paradigm of objective judgment, for the lesson is that even the deductive case does not live up to the notional ideal of a discernment-free path to judgment that structures the invidious comparison. See "Virtue."

12. "Non-natural meaning" would be more precise. See Grice. The idea, at any rate, is just to focus on the concept of meaning at stake when one says, for example, "That is not what the text means," as opposed to, say, "These tracks mean that a lion was here."

13. The implications of the idea that the interpretability of literary works is a function of the kind of interest we take in (what we call) "literature" are developed in my contribution to *Wittgenstein after Literature*. The idea is not completely foreign to Fish—see, for example, "Fish v. Fiss" 137 (contrasting literature and law)—but it never leads him to question the generality of the interpretivist thesis. To the contrary, such differences as may appear between literature and law are, for him—given that thesis—to be considered as effects of interpretive activity.

14. Fish writes, "The question is not whether there are in fact plain cases—

there surely are—but, rather, of what is their plainness a condition and a property" ("Force" 513). See also "Working" 101.

15. I say that Fish's formula is "provisional" (for us) because its sense is part of what needs to be investigated here. In the end, I think there should be no problem saying that some cases are "inherently plain"; that could strike us as just a bit of practical commonsense.

16. The dialectic sketched here retraces a few passages in my "Wittgenstein on Deconstruction." It is under investigation in Wittgenstein's discussion of the concepts of meaning and understanding.

17. This seems to be true even of "performing interpretations" (for example, Gould's interpretation of the *Goldberg Variations*), which don't at first look like explanations. Even here, however, the sense is that a performance helps to elucidate aspects of a work of art that would not otherwise be fully perspicuous.

18. The point here is not that we can't give analytic explanations of what "intending" or "meaning" something consists in; Grice and others do that. The point is that, given the dialectical setup (one suggesting that meaning is in fact impossible), the kind of explanation we need here must be one that does not make use of any normative notions closely related to meaning. Gricean and other analyses of "meaning" do not meet this requirement. This is the answer to a question that George Wilson asked me at a talk I gave at Johns Hopkins several years ago. I regret that I was only able to give a confusing answer at the time.

19. Of course, there is more to say on this point. It must suffice here to note that it is common ground between both Wittgenstein and Derrida, different as they are.

20. The point here is that this pedigree can be historically accurate even if the implications of the originating skeptical thought are not recognized until later on—even after the "platonic" moment. McDowell develops a similar idea in *Mind and World*, to which I'm indebted here.

21. This phrase is meant to echo Derrida in the context of a similar dialectic. See, for example, *Speech* 103, 149 and *Writing* 292.

22. See, for example, "Compliments" 51. For examples of the appeal to notional "possibility"—or its cousin, the "absence of necessity"—see *Doing* 296, 512 and *Trouble* 271.

23. *Trouble* 294–95. Also see "Introduction: Going," especially 4–6.

24. Martha Nussbaum notices this structure in Fish and finds an analogy in the notions of "*epoche*" (suspension of commitment") and "*ataraxia*" ("freedom from disturbance") from Pyrrhonian skepticism. See "Skepticism" 107. This somewhat obscures the philosophical register in which Fish is operating. What Fish seeks to gain freedom from is not, as Nussbaum says, "all normative judgment," but rather certain philosophical accounts of its possibility (726). A better analogy for Fish's gesture of self-consumption would be the use of a similar self-conscious literary strategy in, for example, the early Wittgenstein: "My propositions serve as elucidations in the following way: anyone who understands me eventually recognizes them as nonsensical. . . . (He must, so to

speak, throw away the ladder after he has climbed up it.)" *Tractatus* §6.54. On eludicatory nonsense, see Conant and Diamond.

25. Fish writes, "Of course, members of other communities will not see what you point to or will see something else, but that's life" (*Trouble* 295).

26. This could be refined to accommodate the fact that in many legal systems, judicially correct judgment involves following precedent, even when prior decisions are "wrong" on the merits. In such cases, the critical question isn't abandoned in favor of a question about what other judges think. Rather, a higher-order norm is applied—namely, the norm that precedent is binding—and the critical question is what precedent requires, not what other judges think it requires. Conventional rules—like "drive on the right"—are also not an exception to the present point. It is true that the reasons for following such a rule depend on whether other people follow them, but this is different from saying that what the rule means depends on what other people think it means.

27. See McDowell, "Wittgenstein," for a helpful exploration of these questions.

28. To put this another way, if talk about a "community framework" makes sense here, it records the fact that insofar as it is possible to speak at all, it must be possible to speak for others ("this is what *we* call a vehicle") without having to consult them or do a bit of sociolinguistic research first. But talk of "internalizing" the community's perspective doesn't itself put us in a position to see how such "speaking for" is possible once we are obliged to suppose that whether, for example, something really is a vehicle is just a matter of whether the community agrees it is one. To the contrary, it now looks positively irresponsible to speak for other community members without checking with them first. On the idea of "speaking-for" as inherent in speaking, and on the centrality of this idea to the procedures of "ordinary language philosophy," see Cavell, chapter 1, and "Must."

29. Fish often finds his critics to be mistakenly positing a moment of interpretive freedom that then needs to be constrained, whether by texts, rules, conventions, communities, and so on. See for example, "Working" and "Critical," especially 458–59. I insert the parenthesis—"always-already"—to make clear that nothing in my criticism incurs a commitment to this allegedly suspect conception of freedom/constraint. That is, I'm happy to follow Fish in saying that a community's interpretive framework is always-already internalized by its agents, or that subjects are always already "inscribed" within an interpretive framework. My question is how, on Fish's story, there could so much as *be* an interpretive framework to be inscribed in.

30. Fish cites Rorty, who in response to Alasdair MacIntyre having said "In your view, the worst thing someone can say about the Soviet Union is that it is un-American," shrugged and replied, "What could be worse?" Fish approvingly glosses Rorty's response as follows: "I would be hearing in [Rorty's] . . . line a thicker statement and a serious question. The statement would be a rehearsal of the interlocking values, investments, and social commitments . . . we implicitly

refer to when we say 'America.' The serious question would be, 'What could be worse than a state and an ideology opposed in every way to everything we cherish and believe in?'" ("Reply" 63). The question seems easily answered: worse than a state opposed to everything we believe in is a state that *conforms* to everything we believe in when our beliefs are evil. Clearly, there is something better than being guided by our most cherished beliefs, something most of us would want more: being guided by just and correct beliefs, or at least by not unjust or incorrect ones. Even Hitler (or Satan) was guided by his most cherished beliefs; there's nothing especially good about that just *as such*.

31. I owe a debt to Cora Diamond for this formulation. See 68–69.

32. Fish writes, "Schlag's mistake can be seen by considering the nature of the 'doubts' he considers 'requisite'. . . .They are cosmic doubts, not doubts about this or that, but doubts about the entire cognitive structure within which 'this' or 'that' emerge as objects of inquiry. That form of doubt is not available to situated beings . . ." ("Minimalism" 772). Fish ought to have seen that his own interpretivism falls by this axe. My argument here may be expressed, in the terms of this passage, by saying that (1) rampant interpretivism presupposes the intelligibility of doubt not about *this* or *that* text (there are plain cases), but about the possibility of textual meaning *as such*; and (2) such a form of doubt does not appear intelligible from the point of view of "situated beings"; it requires a notional God's-eye point of view. "What was required," Fish writes, "was an explanation that could account for both agreement and disagreement, and that explanation was found in the idea of an interpretive community" ("Change" 141). Fish is speaking here about introducing the notion of "interpretive community" to address certain issues in literary theory. But at the time this was written, this was also the central notion, for him, in an account of the possibility of the determinate meaning of any text. See, for example, "Compliments" 43.

33. I'm indebted to David Finkelstein for voicing a similarly flat-footed response in "Wittgenstein on Rules and Platonism."

Works Cited

Cavell, Stanley. *The Claim of Reason*. 2nd. ed. Oxford: Clarendon, 1979.

——. *Must We Mean What We Say*. 2nd ed. Cambridge: Cambridge UP, 2002.

Conant, James. "The Method of the Tractatus." *From Frege to Wittgenstein: Perspectives on Early Analytic Philosophy*. Ed. Erich Reck. Oxford: Oxford UP, 2002. 374–462.

Derrida, Jacques. *Speech and Phenomena*. Trans. David B. Allison. Evanston: Northwestern UP, 1973.

———. *Writing and Difference*. Trans. Alan Bass. Chicago: U of Chicago P, 1978.

Diamond, Cora. *The Realistic Spirit: Wittgenstein, Philosophy, and the Mind*. Cambridge: MIT P, 1991.

Finkelstein, David. "Wittgenstein on Rules and Platonism." *The New Wittgenstein*. Ed. Alice Crary Read and Rupert Read. London: Routledge, 2000. 53–73.

Fish, Stanley. *Doing What Comes Naturally: Change, Rhetoric, and the Practice of Theory in Literary and Legal Studies*. Durham: Duke UP, 1989.

———. *Is There a Text in this Class?: The Authority of Interpretive Communities*. Cambridge: Harvard UP, 1980.

———. "A Reply to My Critics." *The Responsive Community* 12.3 (2002): 63+.

———. *Self-Consuming Artifacts: The Experience of Seventeenth-Century Literature*. Berkeley: U of California P, 1974.

———. *Surprised by Sin: The Reader in Paradise Lost*. Cambridge: Harvard UP, 1998.

———. *The Trouble With Principle*. Cambridge: Harvard UP, 1999.

———. "Theory Minimalism." *San Diego Law Review* 37 (2000): 761–76.

Grice, Paul. "Meaning." *The Philosophical Review* 64 (1957): 377–88.

Grossman, Allen. *The Long Schoolroom: Lessons in the Bitter Logic of the Poetic Principle*. Ann Arbor: U of Michigan P, 1997.

Kant, Immanuel. *Critique of Pure Reason*. Trans. Norman Kemp Smith. New York: St. Martin's, 1929.

———. *Political Writings*. Trans. H.B. Nisbet. Ed. Han Reiss. Cambridge: Cambridge UP, 1970.

McDowell, John. *Mind and World*. Cambridge: Harvard UP, 1994.

———. *Mind, Value, and Reality*. Cambridge: Harvard UP, 1998.

———. "Wittgenstein on Following a Rule." *Synthese* 58 (1984): 325–63.

Nussbaum, Martha. "Skepticism about Practical Reason in Literature and the Law." *Harvard Law Review* 107.3 (1994): 714–44.

Stone, Martin. "On the Old Saw, 'Every reading of a text is an interpretation': Some Remarks" *The Literary Wittgenstein*. Ed. John Gibson and Wolfgang Huemer. Routledge, forthcoming.

————. "Focusing the Law: What Legal Interpretation is Not." *Law and Interpretation: Essays in Legal Philosophy*. Ed. Andrei Marmor. Oxford: Oxford UP, 1995.

————. "Legal Formalism: The Task of Judgment." *Oxford Handbook of Jurisprudence and Legal Philosophy*. Ed. Jules Coleman and Scott Shapiro. Oxford: Oxford UP, 2002.

————. "Wittgenstein on Deconstruction." *The New Wittgenstein*. Ed. Alice Crary and Rupert Read. London: Routledge, 2000. 83–117.

Wittgenstein, Ludwig. *Philosophical Investigations*. Trans. G.E.M. Anscombe. Oxford: Blackwell, 1958.

————. *Prototractatus: An Early Version of Tractatus Logico-Philosophicus*. Trans. D.F. Pears and B.F. McGuinness. Ed. B.F. McGuinness, T. Nyberg, and G.H. von Wright. Ithaca, NY: Cornell UP, 1971.

Fish and Dworkin on the Work
of Interpretation in a Democracy

Gary S. Wihl

Ronald Dworkin's "Law as Interpretation," published in 1983, advances his efforts to establish a philosophical framework for all levels of law by characterizing jurisprudence as a "mode of knowledge" that exists inside "interpretation as a general activity." Ideas and arguments presented in this essay reappear in his major treatise on the structure of law, *Law's Empire*, published three years later. The essay is also reprinted in his first major volume of writings on the law since the publication of *Taking Rights Seriously* in 1977, *A Matter of Principle*, published in 1985. Dworkin's entire position as a critic and theorist of jurisprudence rests on having a rather more robust, fully articulated concept of interpretation than most jurists and legal scholars would accept. The field of legal studies is governed by the notion that courts and judges interpret the law but do not write or make laws. Making law is the privilege of the people and their elected representatives; therefore, interpretation would normally be limited to following the expressed intent of the people wherever possible in applying statutes or the Constitution, or to earlier decisions taken by judges in matters of common law. A great deal of heated debate occurs at the borderline of what is brought forward in the name of the record of existing opinions and decisions by judges, or positive law, and what is invented, presumably intended, or "morphed" out of the law (to use Antonin Scalia's term of art) through the democratic process.

Dworkin is not an advocate of judicial prerogative—far from it. But he does assert the importance of a philosophical dimension in matters of

law, an inevitable contextualization of legal decisions within deep structures of belief about fairness, equality, tolerance, and freedom. Interpretation may not invent laws, but it is necessary to the realization of law as
a just institution that serves publicly held goods. Without a strong sense of
interpretation, laws may go astray and fail to serve the principles of justice
that people hold in common within a democratic state. Can one be
philosophical about justice and other democratic values and still stay within
the boundaries of the separation of powers, within the boundaries of court
actions that uphold rather than invent the meaning of laws? That is the
vexing question of interpretation for Dworkin.

The Dworkin-Fish Debate

Dworkin's reasonable assumption at the time of the writing of "Law as
Interpretation" is that disciplines that are based in interpretive activity,
such as literary criticism or aesthetics, probably have worked through
difficult issues about the limits and the philosophical horizons of interpretation. The work of these disciplines could be helpful to legal scholars
and law professionals who struggle with issues like intention, canonical
authority, semantics, and, most difficult of all, forms of agreement that
are poorly characterized as subjective or objective in nature. In the
opening of his essay, Dworkin states, "Lawyers would do well to study
literary and other forms of artistic interpretation. . . . Not all of the battles
within literary criticism are edifying or even comprehensible, but many
more theories of interpretation have been defended in literature than in
law, and these include theories which challenge the flat distinction
between description and evaluation that has enfeebled legal theory"
(252). But the overriding purpose of his essay remains philosophical.
Legal judgments have an interpretative component that may involve the
intended but unstated meaning of a statute, or a canonical shift in
legislation brought about by a Supreme Court decision on due process, or
the establishment of the right to privacy (nowhere explicitly spelled out
in the Constitution), or equal access to education. These judgments and
decisions interpret law because they determine how laws are applied over
time and because the courts expand and contract those applications of
law. Interpretation is the pathway to better law, a better civil society—
indeed, a democratic, constitutional society. In the conclusion of his
essay, he states, "It may be a sensible project, at least, to inquire whether
there are not particular philosophical bases shared by particular aesthetic

and particular political theories so that we can properly speak of a liberal or Marxist or perfectionist or totalitarian aesthetics. . . . I have no good idea that this project could be successful, and I end simply by acknowledging my sense that politics, art, and law are united, somehow, in philosophy" (270).

The problem solving of literary critics, particularly about intention and objectivity, enables certain obstacles to better legal interpretation to be cleared out of the way. To paraphrase William Blake, the excess of confusion about interpretation leads to the royal palace of better freedoms, protections, and forms of equality, where the law has produced the best conditions of a democratic society. In a very important sense, one has to read Dworkin's essay on law as interpretation as a *dialogical* exercise. He shows little interest in addressing literary critics on one side or another of any literary controversy—say, between New Critics and reader response critics, or structuralists and humanists—and when he resorts to literary examples, from Agatha Christie or John Fowles, the task of the author is little more than a trope for the protocols of common law, in which judges build their opinions by quoting the relevant opinions of judges before them. His famous example of the chain novelist, which he continues to employ in *Law's Empire*, and which became one focus of his exchange with Stanley Fish, is just such a trope that all legal readers of his essay would recognize immediately as a description of the process of common law rather than literary invention. Justice Antonin Scalia describes the process nicely in his own essay on law and interpretation:

> Oliver Wendell Holmes's influential book *The Common Law* . . . talks a little bit about Germanic and early English custom. But mostly it talks about individual court decisions, and about the judges, famous and obscure, who wrote them: Chief Justice Choke, Doderidge, J., Lord Holt, Redfield, C.J., Rolle, C.J., Hankford, J., Baron Parke, Lord Ellenborough. . . . Holmes's book is a paen to reason, and to the men who brought that faculty to bear in order to *create* Anglo-American law.
>
> This is the image of the law—the common law—to which an aspiring American lawyer is first exposed. . . . (4)

Judges in common law cases write opinions based on their identification and use of previous judges' decisions. Without this chain of authorship, common law would not exist. Dialogically, a narrow set of literary problems, centered upon issues like intention and objectivity, are relevant to the development of a legal concept of interpretation. Literature and law are analogous enterprises when it comes to very specific questions about interpretation, but Fowles and Christie have very little significance or philosophical weight when compared to *Regents of the University of California v. Bakke*. If law and literature ever should meet directly, it would be, as Dworkin says, in some unspecified realm of philosophy, at a core of shared beliefs and values about an entire social order.

Dworkin assumes that literary critics' heavy lifting of the concept of interpretation provides him with examples and terms to continue his arguments with the schools of positive law and intentionalism. He is primarily interested in addressing his legal peers in the language of literary criticism because he thinks it vanquishes his efforts to bring a higher level of philosophical insight to bear on matters of law. Crucially, he has very little stake in learning how debates over the status of literary discourse are reshaping the canons of literature. He repeatedly invokes the realm of aesthetics to bring forward the "best" interpretation, the one with the greatest "integrity" and "coherence," as if debates about interpretation in literary criticism have little or no impact on the formalism of literary studies or on its revisionist efforts to assess the impact of literature upon the most diverse, democratic readership since the inception of the printed book. While literary interpretation could demonstrate the naiveté of judges' assumptions about the application of a statute or common law case in a specific trial, it can have no effect, as far as Dworkin is concerned, on topics like intrinsic value or beauty or canonical authority, topics where the relationship between interpretation and values would be strained to a degree not suitable for Dworkin's philosophical purposes. Better interpretations of law enable the law to enhance the protection of individuals, to preserve autonomy of choice in fundamental matters of religion, or to put a check on majoritarian domination of the legislature.

Dworkin has remained committed to these values in all of his works since 1983, and they are perfectly fine liberal values that are among the core values held by most citizens in democratic societies. But he would dread the thought of importing into law the rather more turbulent doctrines of postmodernism, psychoanalysis, or Rorty's arguments about the philosophical contingency of liberalism—arguments that would radically separate the fundamental rights of life, liberty, and property from any shared assumption of human selfhood. Controversies in literary criticism are limited to those areas where literary interpretation may support the task of common law, civil law, and constitutional law within an overall philosophy of liberalism. "Philosophy" in Dworkin's writing is a shorthand term for the project of acquiring the values of personal dignity, tolerance, equal protection, and constitutional order. Interpretation is not an opportunity for the law to take on contests over identity, self-image, or unconscious, highly contradictory sets of beliefs that have emerged in many areas of literary analysis. Perhaps those sorts of controversies belong to the private realm, where the courts have no business. Perhaps they exist as a consequence of legally protected freedoms and personal beliefs. But as far as Dworkin is concerned legal interpretation operates within the "aesthetic" bounds of order, consistency, integrity—more like a Cleanth Brooks' well-wrought, organically unified Grecian urn than Walter Benjamin's image, from his essay on the task of the translator, of a broken, fragmented urn from the kabbala.

It is not surprising, therefore, that Dworkin's essay ran into a major roadblock from the domain where it was least expected: the writings of Stanley Fish. Fish is cited once in the essay on law as interpretation, on the grounds that his strengthening of interpretative practice in the field of literary criticism supports Dworkin's efforts to locate the larger political stakes in debates about legal interpretation. Dworkin's limited interest in the effects of Fish's work on the "philosophical" side of literary studies, or indeed on particular works of literature, blew up into a major controversy when Fish responded not in kind, with agreement and support for a fellow traveler, but rather with accusations that Dworkin's entire approach to interpretation is flawed by halfway measures and halfway insights. Take interpretation for what it is—an increasingly pragmatic exercise in agreement formation (not a pathway to philosophical reason)—or leave law to carry out its business in its prescribed settings without attempting to draw any philosophical inferences about civil society in general or about personal freedoms that come from some special insight into the overall nature of law. Dworkin suddenly discovered that the philosophical consequences of legal interpretation were being contested, or simply dismissed as irrelevant in the name of interpretation—precisely the opposite effect of his whole effort to collaborate with literary criticism, and from the one literary critic who would seem to have the greatest affinity with him in putting aside the narrow doctrines of intentionalism and positive law. What I am calling the dialogical quality of Dworkin's essay, its use of literary criticism as a means of addressing an audience of legal scholars, exposed Dworkin as out of touch with, perhaps even hostile to, changes in the field of literary criticism, many of them influenced by the pragmatism and antitheoretical writings of Fish. Literary criticism, Dworkin quickly discovered, had moved far beyond its earlier status as a branch of neoclassical aesthetics and had become a rather more polymorphously perverse enterprise, capable of turning Hamlet into a treatise on psychosis or putting Agatha Christie in the same league of writers as Dostoevski on the grounds of their comparable inquiries into the nature of evil. Imagine the result if this band of literary critics were let loose into the courts. While some "morphing" of the Constitution of the United States was indeed necessary to its fullest interpretation, if that interpretation were governed by polymorphous interpretation, the consequences would be worse than anything Dworkin could attribute to a Supreme Court nominee like Robert Bork or a Supreme Court justice like Antonin Scalia—two of Dworkin's greatest legal nemeses because of their antiliberal values and beliefs about what protections the Constitution offers.

Dworkin and Fish are two highly sophisticated, combative writers, each with a stake in the other's area of greatest expertise. They have debated each other most strenuously over those issues where in fact they share the greatest similarities, with results that have been adverse for the development of their respective positions on law and literature and for our own understanding of the crucial issues they have identified. The engagement with literary criticism in "Law as Interpretation" may be a dialogical exercise in comparison with his longer, systematic analysis of law, but there can be no doubt that the investment in a robust concept of interpretation is greater in Dworkin than in any other contemporary writer on American constitutional law, be it from Gadamer or Fish. (I purposely leave aside Habermas' *Between Facts and Norms*, since his work would introduce another set of problems connected with the relationship between Enlightenment legal history and philosophical rationalism. Habermas' philosophical position places him at an even greater distance from Dworkin than Fish.)

Since the exchange with Dworkin, Fish has continued to write extensively on the law in *Doing What Comes Naturally*, *There's No Such Thing as Free Speech*, *The Trouble with Principle*, and *Professional Correctness*. In polar opposition to Dworkin, Fish increasingly downplays any philosophical role for the law, arguably even a political role for the law. That is because the beliefs and values that come into play in the interpretation of a particular work of literature fall within the aims and goals of interpreting works of literature, Fish argues. Literary interpretations do not have any consequences for the larger public sphere, for if they did they would no longer be literary interpretations. The same goes for judges' rulings in legal cases. It is difficult if not impossible to attach any philosophical consequence to a court's decision, whether the issue is contracts or affirmative action. The drivers of that decision have to be specified to a very high level of detail and analysis in order to account for the outcome of a case and its possible aftereffects on other cases. To take the most recent example of this line of argument, Fish writes in *Professional Correctness*,

> Justification—the process by which a move in a game is declared valid—is always internal and is never a matter of looking for confirmation to something outside the law's immanent intelligibility. The client who complains that his experience of an event has not been accommodated by the law's rewriting of it will remain unhappy because "the crucial consideration is not what happened, but how one is to understand the justificatory structure that is latent in the legal arrangements. . . ." (22)

Fish proclaims the irrelevance of theoretical discourse to the practice of law, to its professional training, or to its operation in judgments, in contracts, or in the exercise of freedoms and protections. His remarkable grasp of the dynamics of interpretive activity, where he excels above all his friends and opponents, absorbs all philosophical argument into the working through of the case at hand. Rather than invoking higher philosophical purposes, Fish makes interpretive activity identical with close readings, the detailed maintenance of a coherent assertion in a dense field of opposed or conflicted possibilities. Interpretation as close reading owes some of its formulations to Fish's earlier opposition to New Criticism and formalism and some to his analysis of Milton's epical and theological poetic arguments. But the currency of close reading is not inherently literary or poetical at all. In a field of contested meanings and values, a field that surely encompasses law as much as literature, interpretation is the exacting, precise hold on the specific beliefs and values that are being contested by the other interpreter(s). No philosophical intervention will settle or obviate the battle of interpretation, whether the beliefs are about social justice or about the value of Shakespeare or about the inclusion of disadvantaged minorities in institutions of higher learning. Like Dworkin, Fish calls the contest of beliefs and values "interpretation" because the battle is not about self-evident facts per se or merely personal preferences. A social, indeed political outcome is at stake, but not in a way that can be settled by calling for the application of an unambiguous, higher-order principle.

Law and Literature in a Democracy

I have drawn Dworkin's and Fish's positions on law, interpretation, and philosophy as economically as possible. My purpose is to frame a set of issues that demonstrate the critical importance of their debate. There is nothing to gain from yet another rehearsal of the epistemological terms of their debate, where they have the lowest stake. The importance of their debate consists in the reminder it offers us about the relationship between a legally constituted regime—a constitutional democracy, in short—and the volatile, conflicted organization of values and beliefs that it manages to contain. Having taken on the problem of interpretation, Dworkin must account for the most conflicted areas of the law, where interpretative actions take their deepest root. He is required to redirect or at the very least limit the philosophical aspirations of law without giving up his goal of finding for the law a context of robust, strong convictions about the issues that matter most to a liberal, constitutional democracy.

Fish believes that his own best insights into interpretive activity lead to the conclusion that interpretations of literary works are largely inconsequential to actual matters of law or politics; they are different language games, played for different purposes. In strengthening the role of interests, beliefs, and convictions in matters of interpretation, Fish cannot offer any account of the democratizing process by which these beliefs have multiplied, coexisted, or displaced each other with a sufficient degree of stability. There is a palpable extravagance—or the opposite, what Dworkin calls "banality"—in his examples and arguments: there is no such thing as free speech? In what rhetorical context could such an assertion be taken seriously? Because Fish's best insights into the maintenance of beliefs exist at the most contested end of the spectrum, his work has the effect of turning all beliefs into their most extreme case in order to maintain the practical correctness of his approach to interpretive activity. But such degrees of contestation are actually quite rare in the political and aesthetic orders.

The stability in legally constructed conflicts of belief is probably greater than in literary conflicts, and, by the same token, the stakes are higher when that stability disintegrates. A battle between the President and Congress over the legality of the New Deal, or the application of equal protection to the states' jurisdiction over education, provokes greater mobilization of social forces than do revisions of the literary canon. Interpretations that provoke political change, particularly if they enhance democracy, require a fuller account than interpretations that do not. This is not a question of showing that Agatha Christie could be read by some, even many, as if she were Dostoevski, but rather that an interpretation of the Ninth Amendment will hold in the face of deeply conflicted religious interests and beliefs and thus allow women to exercise one of the most difficult choices anyone could ever make: the termination of a life. Democracy means the inevitable conflict of deeply held beliefs and convictions. Interpretation as the specification of where those beliefs conflict to the highest degree should not be rendered inconsequential too hastily by literary criticism. Literature may yet share in the circulation of those beliefs and the strengthening and weakening of them before and after they appear inside certain legal venues. It is premature to assert that the beliefs and values that may be contested and richly articulated in works of literature do not transfer over to conflicted beliefs that appear, in purposefully restricted form, inside courtrooms where decisions will rule actions by citizens. Walt Whitman may not be able to articulate the Fourteenth Amendment in the same manner as the courts, but that does not mean that *Democratic Vistas* cannot share in the promotion, testing, strengthening, or acceptance of values attached to the act of voting and the expansion of the franchise after the Civil War.

As a matter of fact, one unexpected consequence of Fish's own energetic pragmatizing of literature appears in the work of Steven Knapp, when Knapp finds that much of the belief and value that gravitate to works of literature connect with readers' lives in a democracy: as a pragmatist, Knapp believes we are more or less thrown into a world of competing values and beliefs and gradually acquire the dispositions that enable us to live in a "modern, Western, liberal, quasi-democratic form of life." Which is not to say that values are randomly significant, or randomly dropped or acquired, but rather that they are not self-evident or intrinsically valuable. Having the disposition to fight slavery or colonialism or legal injustice has something to do with the way you are put together as a specific person. Entering the arena of moral or political conflict, therefore, is part of tracing and developing the central values that define the individuals that we are: "The kind of person we happen to value—by no means the kind of person valued at every time in every human society—is the kind that wants to check itself out, know how it feels, be aware of its inconsistencies, whether or not fixing them is either possible or desirable. Whether or not its particular choices and actions are the right ones from some external perspective, we might just say that such a person fits in better with our . . . quasi-democratic form of life" (101). Literature plays a great role in determining these dispositions and degrees of fit within a democracy.

The conclusion I'm going to put forward about the Dworkin-Fish debate is that it is best seen as a timely, powerful version of what *legal and literary* discourse goes through in a constitutional democracy. Fish is right to dismiss philosophy as the hidden god of democracy. Democracy does not aspire to the condition of philosophy. But Dworkin is actually much closer, for all the limitations imposed on what law may describe, to the actual working through of conflict and contestation, where the law finds its place in a democracy. One needs to read Dworkin in order to absorb and use arguments about academic freedom, abortion, or the tyrannies of popular opinion. Fish's extravagant presentations of beliefs make the point about their relative weakness and strength when pitted against each other, and such presentations may also serve an important democratic purpose. "Philosophy" may not be a very good name for that purpose, particularly when Dworkin uses the term to characterize some higher state of reflection and repose, where art unites with law. But by the same token, Fish's vigorous mapping of specific conflicts of belief hovers between exaggeration and banality unless it can find its purpose within rather more broadly shared debates and public venues.

Once we move the Dworkin-Fish debate out of the sterile zone of epistemology and into considerations of law and literature in a democracy, their writings begin to complement each other in ways that I believe surpass most of the existing academic scholarship on the relationship between law and literature. I am going to put forward the claim that the relationship of Dworkin's and Fish's positions is like the relationship between Madison the representative to the constitutional convention and Madison the "Publius" of *The Federalist* papers, as described by Jack Rakove. After the lengthy debates that concluded in the drafting of the Constitution, the debate over its ratification took to the streets. Rakove says that "calm deliberation" could hardly be expected because the debate would inevitably bring forward numerous passions, interests, local points of view, and jealousies, a lot of the material Whitman once referred to as the "blab" of democracy. Rakove writes that the debates that took place through and around *The Federalist* "took the form not of a Socratic dialogue or an academic symposium but of a cacophonous argument in which appeals to principle and common sense and close analyses of specific clauses accompanied wild predictions of the good and evil effects that ratification would bring" (132). But for all that, the essays from *The Federalist* remain to this day important glosses on the Constitution, evidence of the framers' intentions, and superb examples of rhetoric.

I am not asserting that Stanley Fish is Publius and Ronald Dworkin Socrates. I am asserting that in a democracy, rhetoric and the law will intersect most crucially around core values and beliefs, precisely what the Dworkin-Fish debate on interpretation brings to the forefront of our attention. Their positions become complementary, and politically significant, once we learn from them how contested beliefs stabilize and circulate in a democratic public sphere, sometimes in the morphing process of the law in a democracy, sometimes in the particularities and structures of highly articulated beliefs that may be found in literary works by Whitman, George Eliot (a brilliant student of Machiavelli and popular opinion), Milton, Philip Roth, Robert Penn Warren, and so on.

Dworkin's and Fish's Positions as Complementary

To make good on this claim, I will conclude with three pieces of supporting evidence from their writings that demonstrate:

1. How their writings converge on the topic of substituting interpretative beliefs for epistemologies and then differ slightly on their accounts of what stabilizes conflicting beliefs.

2. How Dworkin and Fish foreshorten their best insights into the relationship of law to literature because of the confusing status of philosophy in their writings, an unspecified intrinsic value in Dworkin and a celebration of inconsequentiality in Fish.

3. How their writings are equally valid and relevant for those who wish to see the relationship of law and literature from the special perspective of democratic processes, where conflict and stabilization are essential features of beliefs. In fact the study of democracy is the true home for their writings.

As I said earlier, Dworkin's use of literature as an analogy to law is limited to certain aesthetic ideals: formal integrity, the effort to make the work appear in its "best" possible light, its coherence of meaning. Beliefs about literature are therefore carefully circumscribed within these aesthetic norms. The analogy works to a great disadvantage when it comes to those matters of law where beliefs will carry the highest stakes:

majoritarian dictates about personal morality, the conflict between federal and state rights, or the termination of life. In "Law as Interpretation," beliefs displace false assumptions about objectivity, the neutral ability to describe a legal situation, or intentional meaning. But even within the aesthetic order, beliefs may become "banal." Because Dworkin's essay never brings law squarely into the realm of politics, Fish offers important correctives to Dworkin's picture of how interpretation operates. The issue of banality is one that will return, however, and it bears careful scrutiny at the outset. Dworkin writes,

> Interpretive styles are grounded in different theories of what art is and what it is for and what makes art good. The point is so banal that it might as well be put the other way around: different theories of art are generated by different theories of interpretation. If someone thinks stylistics are important to interpretation, he will think a work of art better because it integrates pronunciation and trope; if someone is attracted to deconstruction, he will dismiss reference in its familiar sense. . . . No doubt the aesthetic hypothesis is in important ways banal. . . . Interpretation becomes a concept of which different theories are competing conceptions. (It follows that there is no radical difference but only a difference in the level of abstraction between offering a theory of interpretation and offering an interpretation of a particular work of art.). . . . Of course no important aesthetic claim can be "demonstrated" to be true or false, no argument can be produced for any interpretation which we can be sure will commend itself to everyone. (256)

The answer to the dilemma of multiple theories, concepts, and interpretations is to see that beliefs about works of art and literature (and laws) are parts of an "enterprise, a public institution," as Fish has been arguing all along. The connection between what you interpret and what you believe is worth interpreting is banal because it is common, uncontroversial, not particularly illuminating of anything, but it is also the ground over which laws and works of art enter a public realm and acquire much greater force and stability.

Finding the precise balance between the banal level of interpretation and public acceptance is the first issue in the Dworkin-Fish controversy. Their words are practically interchangeable when it comes to characterizing interpretation as an exercise of belief and evaluation. They differ sharply when it comes to invoking the banal quality of interpretation, or at least confusing it with the public quality of interpretation. If it is banal to say that one reader looks for stylistics in a poem, another for reference, and another for the author's intentions and socio-historical context, that is because the views of these readers make no difference to anyone except perhaps a small number of theoretically minded, professional readers of the same poem—hardly a "public" in the usual sense of the word. But if a citizen believes that the First Amendment prohibits school prayer, and a state court disagrees, there is no resolution in simply stating that different people interpret the First Amendment according to different beliefs about freedom. A Supreme Court must decide which belief about freedom of religion will prevail, and in which particular settings. And that is where the real work of interpretation, connecting the text of the law with publicly upheld views about freedom, takes hold.

Fish and Dworkin spill a lot of ink over epistemological questions such as objectivity in interpretation, or whether a text exists as a "brute fact," untouched by beliefs as to its value and importance. But the true crux of their debate rests in their respective efforts to turn the banal version of interpretation into the public version. Fish sums up the issue perfectly in his first response to Dworkin: Dworkin "distinguishes between simple cases in which the words of a statute bear a transparent relationship to the actions they authorize or exclude . . . and more difficult cases in which reasonable and knowledgeable men disagree as to whether some action or proposed action is lawful . . . even in a simple case the ease and immediacy with which one can apply the statute to the facts is the result of the same kind of interpretive work that is more obviously required in the difficult cases" (284). The banal, simple level of interpretation is, for Fish, always rich in "stipulated (and potentially controversial) definitions, terms, modes of inference, and so on." Fish is simply pressing Dworkin to get on with it, to make interpretation count, by putting aside the cautious use of banal instances of interpretation and probing to where conflict and stability actually occur.

When Dworkin comes closer to the conflicted end of the interpretative spectrum, the connection between interpretation and belief weakens, whereas of course for Fish we should be going in exactly the opposite direction. Dworkin dismisses controversies about semiotics and narratology in Agatha Christie as banal because such interpretations appear to coexist as free options for different readers. There appears to be nothing at stake in going one way or the other. In law, however, the constraints on interpretation are felt much more acutely because of the limits imposed on judges' ability to change the law. Interpretation must stand clearly apart from rewriting statutes or legislation, even though the law aspires to a very broad system of beliefs about fundamental rights and protections. Dworkin's solution is to fudge the difference between orders of beliefs and core and peripheral beliefs—the kind of fudging Fish relentlessly challenges as unstable and unworkable. Dworkin writes,

> People interpret texts and statutes and cases and pictures. The most striking fact about this practice is a certain shared conviction. Interpreters for the most part assume that interpreting a text is different from changing it into a new text, that one interpretation may be better than another even when it is controversial, that arguments exist for and against interpretations. . . . Together these second-order beliefs compose what we might call a "right-wrong" picture of interpretation. . . . The second-order beliefs I describe are part of the practices that constitute the institution of interpretation; they are, in fact, at the center of that practice. (289)

A second-order belief is a belief about the correctness of the belief that went into the textual analysis in the first instance. So, for example, courts may disagree sharply over states' authority in matters of school prayer, trade secret protection, abortion, and voter eligibility, but if some of these matters can be framed as constitutional, second-order beliefs will enter to govern the outcome of the first-order controversy. Second-order beliefs might include constitutional beliefs about equality, the protection of the individual, or the violation of limited monopolization granted under the Constitution. Practice, of course, gives Fish the edge in this discussion, since the two orders are much more deeply intertwined than Dworkin will allow; they continue to occupy the courts with controversial challenges and rulings. Nothing seems to be gained by deferring controversies at the first order to something with clearer value, or a clearer outcome, at the second level. Or else, second-order beliefs are allowed to exist under the special, undefined condition of "philosophy"—about which I will comment further very shortly.

So Dworkin on interpretation moves legal theory in the direction of a broader framework of values and beliefs, but he is unwilling to risk the limitations imposed on legal interpretation, holding to variously undefined ideas of order, belief, and aesthetic distance to avoid collapsing interpretation into chaos and invention. The overall result is banal, unless the precise interlocking of beliefs and how they stabilize or modify can be spelled out. Fish presses this point by questioning the hollowness of terms that are used to prop up belief without actually contesting any specific beliefs. Dworkin stabilizes the inherently controversial, conflicted nature of legal decisions by resorting to some inarticulate background of higher-order beliefs, sometimes called "aesthetics," sometimes "philosophy." Whatever they might be called, they bear little resemblance to controversies over matters of justice, fairness, or equality that permeate the public realm in a democracy. The question still remains: what gives the public order sufficient stability?

But Fish is not entirely free of problems either. He is so wrapped up in the specificity of controversy and debate that he often appears extravagant, equally out of touch with a genuine public. From his debate with Dworkin, he has gone on to write extensive commentary on the works of many legal scholars, but usually by repeating his attacks on formalism, intentionality, and the supposed neutrality or objectivity of the law. The upshot of his position, however, has been to characterize law, or literature, or institutional norms, in ever more discrete terms, to point out that they appear to have no important contact with each other. In an essay entitled "The Law Wishes to Have a Formal Existence," he writes, "The law . . . is not philosophy; it is law, although, like everything else it can become the object of philosophical analysis, in which case it becomes something different from what it is in its own terms" (*There's* 177). This is odd phrasing, on the one hand attacking philosophical readings of law in the way New Critics used to attack philosophical readings of poems, on the other hand hypothesizing something called "its own terms," in the way New Critics used to talk about the heresy of paraphrase. Only a poem can tell us what a poem means, and the same goes for law. Fish continues, "As soon as an argument has proven to be persuasive to the relevant parties—a court, a jury—we say of it that it is right, by which we mean that it is now the law . . . that it is *legally* right. Of course, we are still free to object to the decision on other ground, to find it "wrong" in moral terms or in terms of the long-range health of the republic. In that event, however, our recourse would not be to an alternative form of the legal process but to alternative arguments that would be successful—that is persuasive—within the same general form" (178). Fish's original intervention in the 1980s was the establishment of "interpretive community," an early version of what has since become professional practice, various language games, or institutional (largely academic) norms. Interpretive community was a decisive and major break with the formalism that dominated Western literary criticism since the 1940s, in Europe as much as in North America. But the idea has contracted as it has strengthened accounts of stability within the interpretive process. Gaining rightness or closure of interpretation, be it about Milton or the courts, limits the degree to which a particular interpretation can engage broader public discourse. Would Fish be prepared to argue, therefore, that the Constitution is an incoherent document because legislative discourse, in the name of the people, overlaps with a canon of decisions taken by Supreme Courts, or, even better, with the Congressional right to approve Supreme Court justices based on their likely support for issues of concern to the public? I might not be prepared to call this overlap "philosophy" anymore than Fish is, but it is unreasonable to argue that the rigor and precision by which courts apply rules of evidence or procedural rights or decide what constitutes cruel and unusual punishment is so constraining in practice as to exclude public values and beliefs from their deliberations.

Dworkin and Fish both fail to use interpretation as a bridge between textual analysis and publicly shared values and beliefs. That failure points us to the second issue that underscores their debate: the foreshortened status of philosophy. By "philosophy," I do not mean a governing set of concepts but simply the bigger, more robust beliefs and values that are woven into a republic, more specifically a democratic constitutional regime. After all, it is just such a political regime that has become the main theme of their writings in recent years, such as in Dworkin's *Reading the Constitution* or Fish's *The Trouble with Principle*. I still maintain that together they offer some of the best writing on how values and beliefs are authenticated, maintained, and balanced. But we need to continue to read them a bit further against the grain of their explicit arguments about interpretation or about philosophy and metaphysics (Dworkin) or about legal principle (Fish).

Life's Dominion is the most sustained consideration of a specific legal issue—namely, abortion and euthanasia—that Dworkin has written. It deliberately brings together all of Dworkin's major concerns as a theorist and analyst of constitutional law: profound conflict of belief, deeply philosophical values about the value of life that draw on Catholic as well as feminist literature on the subject, and arguments about the proper use of the Constitution in settling this deep controversy. The book is a remarkably nuanced, sophisticated study in constitutional politics, too complex to be dealt with adequately in this brief essay. I only wish to call attention to one feature of the argument that continues the issue Fish has identified: in this book, it is the special reliance on "intrinsic value" and the comparison, once again, of certain features of the abortion debate with problems in aesthetics.

In a nutshell, Dworkin is troubled by the fact that the Supreme Court has interpreted the Ninth Amendment in a way that protects a woman's right to choose and so has taken control of the debate about abortion. He is not against the right to choose, or against abortion—far from it. He is against the error of having the courts rule on a matter of profound belief. First, he is opposed to the courts' usurpation of law writing, a prerogative that is properly vested in the people. Whatever the outcome, the controversy over abortion needs to be sorted out through the legislative process rather than the courts, a powerful instance of the doctrine that courts interpret rather than make laws. Second, he is opposed to a reading of the Constitution that attributes unspecified rights and interests to "persons" by assigning an arbitrary definition to when personhood begins, thus offering partial constitutional protection to the unborn and muddying the waters of what rights and interests might mean in constitutional literature and the legal process. Here we have, if anywhere, a tight intersection of philosophical value, constitutional law, interpretive theory, and the public domain of legislation. True to his theorizing since "Law as Interpretation," Dworkin's intervention in this debate is to find the "best" reading of the Constitution that will add philosophical depth to the law (aligning it with some of the most difficult questions of life that may be asked) but that will also maintain a certain consistency of interpretation and will not "invent" new rights and meanings. Here's how he sums up his project:

> I hope to show that we cannot make sense of the constitutional controversy in the United States—the great legal and political argument about *Roe v. Wade*—if we construe that controversy as being centrally about the rights and interests of a fetus. It is widely assumed that the critical question in *Roe v. Wade* is the question of whether states have the constitutional power to treat a fetus as a person; but if that were true, then *Roe* would be obviously, almost uncontroversially, correct, and the great opposition to it, among not only anti-abortion activists but some renowned constitutional scholars as well, would be wholly inexplicable. What was really at stake in that important case was whether state legislatures have the constitutional power to decide which intrinsic values all citizens must respect, and how, and whether legislatures may prohibit abortion on that ground. (25–26)

Dworkin offers a unique way out of this constitutional error: he makes "intrinsic value" refer to that special area where art and life and law meet—that is, the realm of philosophy—but which the law itself can only protect and circumscribe in the name of protecting individuals who actually uphold those intrinsic values free of public interference. He argues, "Most of us believe that human life has intrinsic value, but also . . . this explains why we disagree so profoundly about abortion. How can that be? How can a shared assumption explain the terrible divisions about abortion that are tearing us apart? The answer, I believe, is that we interpret the idea that human life is intrinsically valuable in different ways" (70). That level of deep belief, though conflicted, can be protected by the law, in the same way that the law protects freedom of religion. So long as we can be assured that some deeply held conviction is at stake in a moment of choice, that the decision to terminate a life is not frivolous, the law can appropriately protect that constitutional freedom. That sort of freedom belongs properly within the category of protected rights. We reach that assurance about what the Constitution may protect by looking to life as an intrinsic value. The case of protecting something intrinsic differs radically from the present situation of state legislatures' taking control of that definition because the Constitution has been erroneously applied to ascribe certain "rights" to the unborn.

This is not an essay on constitutional law, or on the abortion controversy. But Dworkin's argument about abortion helps us situate him rather more clearly in the debate with Fish. Dworkin's resorting to intrinsic value, even his direct comparison of life's intrinsic value to the intrinsic value of certain works of art, works brilliantly in this book, not because we know or can uphold intrinsic value, but because it makes a strong case for correcting an anomaly in constitutional law. It shifts constitutional discourse from undefined rights upheld on a state-by-state basis to a recognizable constitutional right within the canons of legal interpretation.

It may be argued that intrinsic value is another instance of Dworkin's disengaging of second-order beliefs from first-order beliefs, another instance of his abandoning the field of contestation, where beliefs are tested, for a field of neutrality where individuals may decide deeply personal issues for themselves. Perhaps. I cannot say. I *can* say that Dworkin offers a constitutional reading that reconciles conflict in the public sphere with consistency of constitutional interpretation and thereby lowers the authority of the Court over the lives of people. In this instance, it is less important that a certain belief about life is not fully articulated, because the main belief that is at stake is the kind of protection and jurisdiction that the Constitution may offer in a society made of deeply held, contradictory beliefs. From that insight, it may be possible to work back to the specifics of interpretation and find the right thread that enables contradictory beliefs to coexist inside a framework of core values. Dennis Patterson's book, *Law and Truth*, makes the point that Dworkin is essentially a constitutional thinker. Applying Dworkin and Fish's debate to all matters of law is bound to fail. In Dworkin's case at least, a robust theory of interpretation, one that is linked to strong beliefs, avoids the pitfalls of banal insight and vague philosophy by focusing on constitutional problems that arise in democracy. The abortion debate is a perfect case in point.

In *The Trouble with Principle*, Fish writes directly on constitutional issues, particularly the First Amendment. His position has also developed considerably since his encounter with Dworkin. Constitutional problems are closely linked to problems about liberalism in general, to the dominant political discourse of tolerance, neutrality, and the settling of disputes by abstract principle. Given the strengthening of belief as a premise of interpretation—all the way from the early work on interpretive communities and formalism to his most politically engaged writing on racism, sexism, and hate speech—it is not surprising that Fish is more vigorous than ever in locating the exact moments and terms of conflict in the public sphere. There is no reaching for abstract protections inside conflicted positions, for that would be an untenable solution, according to Fish. By the same token, the Constitution itself is totally subsumed inside specific conflict, and one has to wonder what relevance it actually has to Fish's analysis of the First Amendment. Unlike Dworkin, he does not contest any Supreme Court decision, although he does frequently quote opinions by justices such as Scalia or Holmes. My point is simply that he is not addressing his arguments to constitutional scholars and experts in the same way as Dworkin is when writing on *Roe v. Wade*. In invoking the Constitution, Fish is really talking about how debate happens very much in the public sphere, not behind the doors of a courtroom with all of its careful procedures. Discussion of the First Amendment matters because tolerance and freedom of speech are being put under severe strain *inside the public sphere*—by hate groups who advocate racism, by acts of discrimination that practice racism in the name of false equality, by the inability of liberal tolerance to manage and resist these social terrors. In a very real sense, Fish is combating a publicly held fantasy about the law and how it may regulate our lives (which it actually does to a very limited extent). He does not oppose injustices with more constitutional abstraction, but rather goes in exactly the opposite direction: directly combating racism and sexism through advocacy, rhetoric, coalition building, and public speaking.

But then the question is, why is his rhetoric and public speech more forceful and persuasive than that of his opponents? Fish explains,

> This is what almost always happens when the courts hand down a principled First Amendment decision: the issues that truly concern the parties disappear in the solvent of a so-called "higher" argument—an argument pitched at a level that refuses to recognize the legitimacy of what actual persons either fear or desire—with the result that substantive matters are displaced by the attenuated and attenuating logic of abstraction. When principle enters the picture and takes it over, no one is able to talk about what is really on his mind. (*Trouble* 90).

Of course, we recall that, in an earlier quotation from *There's No Such Thing as Free Speech*, Fish suggested that people leave their true feelings and desires outside the courtroom because the professional conditions and practices of law could not accommodate those feelings and still be called law. The quotation about the First Amendment simply shows that Fish doesn't like it when the direction is reversed and the language of the courts turns into public speech or particular stances within a contested public sphere. His position is actually quite consistent, and the main point is that the focus of Fish's writing has shifted to where he excels above all other public intellectuals: in specific contestations of belief in the public sphere, which is not the same thing as debates over interpretation that must take place inside courtrooms.

Dworkin has not convinced anyone that it is possible to philosophize inside a courtroom, though his interest in philosophy gives him special purchase when it comes to making arguments about the morphing of the Constitution, a process that is driven imperfectly by the turbulence of a democratic public sphere. In fact, his recent writing on interpretation, in response to Justice Scalia's lectures on legal interpretation at Princeton, explicitly states that the problem of interpretation in legal studies is not the old chestnut of objectivity and intentionalism but rather the relationship of law to the democratic process. Increasingly, Dworkin has become concerned with the pressures of majoritarian politics on fundamental freedoms and rights. Fish is the only literary critic I can think of who is doing today what F.R. Leavis, I.A. Richards, Raymond Williams, Irving Howe, and Alfred Kazin did before literary studies turned completely professional—namely, stand up as a public intellectual. He can do this not because of special insights into the nature of the law or the nature of literature, but because his antiformalism brings back into view the weaving and unweaving of beliefs that occur inside a democratic public sphere. He facilitates that checking out of the kind of democratic persons we are as described by Knapp.

Stanley Fish and Ronald Dworkin do not need to be opposed to each other, anymore than do Madison and Publius. All of the interesting questions start with their degrees of overlap, where the complex layers of belief that make up the restricted speech of the law draw energy from the testing and stabilizing of different beliefs inside a democratic public sphere. These are questions that have been posed by literary authors and political theorists—by George Kateb on freedom of association and the poetry of Whitman, by Richard Rorty and Judith Shklar on cruelty and George Orwell, by George Eliot and Quentin Skinner on Machiavelli's Florence, and by Robert Penn Warren and J.A. Pocock on the American obsession with virtue and commerce. Stanley Fish and Ronald Dworkin could not exist without the work of each other. Together they offer a remarkable picture of the most pressing problems of assessing the role of literature inside constitutional democracies.

Works Cited

Dworkin, Ronald. *A Matter of Principle*. Cambridge: Harvard UP, 1985.

———. *Freedom's Law. The Moral Reading of the American Constitution*. Cambridge: Harvard UP, 1996.

———. *Law's Empire*. Cambridge: Harvard UP, 1986.

———. "Law as Interpretation." *The Politics of Interpretation*. Ed. W.J.T. Mitchell. Chicago: U of Chicago P, 1983. 249–70.

———. *Life's Dominion: An Argument about Abortion, Euthanasia, and Individual Freedom*. New York: Knopf, 1993.

———. "My Reply to Stanley Fish (and Walter Benn Michaels): Please Don't Talk about Objectivity Any More." *The Politics of Interpretation*. Ed. W.J.T. Mitchell. Chicago: U of Chicago P, 1983. 287–314.

Fish, Stanley. *Doing What Comes Naturally: Change, Rhetoric, and the Practice of Theory in Literary and Legal Studies*. Durham: Duke UP, 1989.

———. *Professional Correctness: Literary Studies and Political Change*. Cambridge: Harvard UP, 1999.

————. *There's No Such Thing as Free Speech, and It's a Good Thing, Too.* New York: Oxford UP, 1994.

————. *The Trouble with Principle.* Cambridge: Harvard UP, 1999.

————. "Working on the Chain Gang: Interpretation in the Law and in Literary Criticism." *The Politics of Interpretation.* Ed. W.J.T. Mitchell. Chicago: U of Chicago P, 1983. 271–86.

Knapp, Steven. *Literary Interest: The Limits of Anti-Formalism.* Cambridge: Harvard UP, 1993.

Patterson, Dennis. *Law and Truth.* New York: Oxford UP, 1996.

Rakove, Jack N. *Original Meanings. Politics and Ideas in the Making of the Constitution.* New York: Knopf, 1996.

Scalia, Antonin. *A Matter of Interpretation. Federal Courts and the Law: An Essay.* Princeton: Princeton UP, 1997.

PART TWO

PHILOSOPHICAL INTERVENTIONS

Deconstructed to Death? Fish on Freedom

Michael Robertson

One of the things I like about Stanley Fish's work is the provocative way he makes his points. A typical Fish move is to take something cherished by orthodox thinking, and then declare that it does not exist. So we find him declaring that liberalism does not exist, and theory does not exist, and principles do not exist, and there's no such thing as free speech.[1] He could be the poster boy for both *trahison des clercs* and *épater les bourgeois*. In addition to the aesthetic pleasure to be derived from such bravura, I appreciate the way it generates work for academics like me to do. Many Fish readers rise to his provocations and summarily dismiss his position as obviously untenable without really engaging with his arguments. Consequently, there is a job to be done in collecting and presenting Fish's arguments in a way that is less likely to provoke outrage and rejection. What makes this job valuable is that Fish is right. Sitting behind the provocative statements are powerful and insightful arguments that move beyond orthodox thinking on important topics. What I propose to do in this chapter is explain and expand Fish's critique of the orthodox thinking about freedom.

Freedom, especially freedom of the individual, had been a key concept in Western philosophy and politics even before the rise of liberalism.[2] It is an important legal concept too, as can be seen in the protection granted to freedom of speech and freedom of religion in the various liberal bills, declarations, and charters of rights that seek to protect the individual from oppression. As well, there are institutional settings where freedom of a more particular kind is a fundamental value.

99

This can be seen in universities, where academic freedom for professors is held to be crucial.

What this valued freedom means is a little more contentious. Some have understood it negatively, as meaning that no one can interfere with an action you have decided to take. Those supporting negative freedom typically argue that the state should leave individuals alone. Others have understood it positively, as meaning that you have a range of different actions available to you. Those supporting positive freedom typically argue that the state needs to act so that individuals have more and better choices open to them. But notwithstanding this familiar dispute, these two understandings of what freedom means have a lot in common. They both stress the importance of unconstrained individual choice, and they both see freedom and constraint as being fundamentally opposed. Whether the source of the freedom-threatening constraints is the interfering actions of other people, or the structural constraints of poverty, racism, or lack of education, the goal is to eliminate those constraints and so maximize freedom.

Fish's provocative move in the face of this orthodox thinking is to reject the position that freedom and constraint are fundamentally opposed and that one moves toward freedom by eliminating constraints. Instead, his arguments deconstruct any hard dichotomy between freedom and constraint and reveal how freedom always presupposes constraint. Consequently, the standard discourse about freedom is revealed as describing an impossible project. Or, as Fish might put it, freedom doesn't exist and so there's no such thing as free speech, *if* what you mean by "freedom" and "free speech" requires the absence of constraints.

It might seem that Fish is saying nothing new. After all, careful philosophers have already pointed out that if I have a right to free speech, for example, then it follows that some others have a duty not to interfere with my speech, and so they suffer constraints on their freedom of action. Hence, freedom for me will sometimes logically imply constraint for you.[3] But as we shall see, this is not Fish's argument for the inseparability of freedom and constraint. He presents novel arguments that go beyond the standard discourse on the subject, and this is why it is worth unpacking and examining them more closely. It is precisely because these arguments do step outside the standard discourse, however, that it can be hard for readers to take them in. I will therefore seek to present Fish's position in a way that prepares the ground for his unconventional treatment of freedom. That is, I will start by setting out what I take to be the philosophical commitments upon which Fish's work rests, and then indicate briefly how many of his characteristic positions flow logically from these commitments. I will then turn to consider in more detail Fish's treatment of the freedom versus constraint dichotomy as a particular example of this logical progression, and I will conclude by looking at the concrete example of academic freedom, to which Fish devotes particular attention.

Fish's Conception of the Self [4]

It is my contention that Fish's work is best understood as the project of tracing out the logical implications, in different contexts, of a certain conception of the self. It would require a separate essay to evaluate the soundness or coherence of this account of the self, and such a work would not devote much space to Fish, because others have devoted more effort to elaborating and justifying it.[5] All I seek to do here is describe this conception of the self and indicate how some of Fish's important claims flow from it. This allows me to focus on what is unique about Fish, because although others have endorsed the same conception of self, they have not seen the same implications of such a commitment.

Fish emphatically rejects the Kantian understanding of the self that has been so influential in Western philosophy. For Kant the key to understanding the nature of the self was to abstract away from any local and contingent features of people to find the common and enduring human nature underneath them. Different human individuals and groups will choose different values and ways of life at different times, but subsisting behind this welter of difference lies our common nature as autonomous, rational choosing agents. This is the true essence of the self and is therefore what must be respected and protected. How particular autonomous agents exercise their free will at any particular time—that is, what they choose to do or value—is a secondary, less important matter. In this concept of the self, as Fish puts it, you are defined as "the bearer of rights—the right to believe, the right to speak, the right to choose—and those capacities, rather than what you happen to believe, or happen to say, or happen to choose, are what is important and what must be protected" ("Sauce" 41).[6]

According to Fish, Kant—and after him, John Rawls—is moving in exactly the wrong direction.[7] The key to understanding the self is to focus on the enabling and constraining role of the local context. Rejecting the concrete and particular in favor of an abstract, contextless "self" is a fundamental error for two reasons. First, it fails to see that the fundamental beliefs and values that differentiate people are not contingent and accidental features of the true self ("opinions" or "mere preferences") but instead constitute that self. Second, it misdescribes these local commitments as being—at least ideally—"choices" of an autonomous agent. For Fish they are preconditions of being an agent in the first place, and so they cannot be subsequent choices of such an agent (see "Sauce" 41–42).

In Fish's competing conception of the self, all human thinking, perception, and action are only made possible by being embedded within local communities and absorbing the beliefs, values, categories of thought, and practices of those communities. Being locally embedded thus simultaneously constitutes, structures, and enables us: "Selves are constituted by the ways of thinking and seeing that inhere in social organizations. . . . " (*Is There* 336). Being locally embedded provides the cognitive and perceptual tools humans use, but these tools will always bear the marks of their origin in some particular community and its fundamental beliefs, values, and practices. Fish writes that an interpretive community was "not so much a group of individuals who shared a point of view, but a point of view or way of organizing experience that shared individuals in the sense that its assumed distinctions, categories of understanding, and stipulations of relevance and irrelevance were the content of the consciousness of community members who were therefore no longer individuals, but, insofar as they were embedded in the community's enterprise, community property" ("Change" 141).

Implications of Fish's Conception of the Self

In Fish's account, being embedded in local communities is a precondition for being a human self, and it is therefore impossible for humans ever to transcend the grip of the local in any strong way. From this starting point, Fish proceeds to draw the conclusions that have gained him notoriety. One logical consequence he draws is that many intellectual projects turn out to be impossible, because transcending the grip of the local in a strong way is just what they want to do. Conservatives want to be true to a substantive conception of the good that is not merely relative or dependent upon some local context. Liberals want to find neutral principles that regulate from the outside disputes between those with competing local conceptions of the good. Multiculturalists want to enable people to reflect critically upon their substantive local beliefs and commitments, realize their ideological or contingent nature, and, as a consequence, hold them more lightly or tentatively, with greater tolerance for the commitments of others. All of these intellectual projects would be instances of what Fish means by "theory" when he says that theory is impossible (see Robertson, "What").

Another implication Fish draws from the conception of the embedded self is that many of the important organizing categories of thought in our culture need to be reconceived. The organizing categories in question take the form of opposed pairs, or dichotomies, such as the following:

Reason vs. Faith
Knowledge vs. Belief
Freedom vs. Constraint
Open vs. Closed
Neutral vs. Biased
Objective vs. Subjective
Principle vs. Rhetoric
Procedure vs. Substance

In our liberal, secular, post-Enlightenment societies, the items on the left side are generally felt to occupy a superior or more desirable position than those on the right. As a guide for conduct, it is felt to be a good thing to seek to move toward the values in the left column and to eschew or even completely eliminate the ones on the right. But Fish, in his characteristically provocative way, has consistently swum against this current, and his writings have instead championed the disparaged items on the right. He vigorously defends the role of rhetoric, and he asserts that local moral, social, or political substantive commitments hide beneath any purportedly neutral procedure or principle. He develops an epistemology that stresses that facts and reasons only exist for us because some deep local beliefs are in place, rather than facts and reason being independent neutral tools that stand apart from and evaluate subjective beliefs. He denies that it is ever possible to be open, neutral, or tolerant in the strong sense desired by orthodox liberal thought.

We can see now that Fish takes these surprising positions because they follow logically from his conception of the embedded self. If one's consciousness and perception are enabled and structured through being embedded in local communities, and if it is impossible ever to transcend this state, then the items on the left side of the standard dichotomies become deeply problematic. They all seem to presuppose the ability to rise above local embeddedness to an Olympian position outside it. For selves, who are necessarily embedded, the state of being enmeshed in local (and therefore "closed," "biased," "constraining," "subjective") systems of belief and practices is inescapable.

But does this mean that Fish is claiming that the items on the left side of the dichotomies do not exist? Has he deconstructed them to death? Not at all. As Fish himself comments in "Profession Despise Thyself," "One deconstructs an opposition not by reversing the hierarchy of its poles but by denying to either pole the independence that makes the opposition possible in the first place" (211). The standard dichotomies create a hard opposition between the items on the left and those on the right and seek to avoid or eliminate the items on the right. But for Fish, the items on the right are the inevitable byproduct of our nature as embedded selves. He does not conclude from this that the items on the left do not exist—rather, that their existence is only possible because of the existence of the items on the right. So instead of the polar oppositions of the standard dichotomies, we find interdependence, with the items on the right being the hidden preconditions for the items on the left.

This explains some of the misunderstanding of Fish's work. Many of his readers are deeply committed to thinking within these dichotomies as conventionally understood. Within such an understanding, if Fish is speaking in favor of one of the items on the right side, then he must be seeking to disparage or even deny the existence of the opposed value on the left side. They consequently attribute to Fish a desire to deny the existence of facts or objectivity or freedom. But what Fish is challenging is the cogency of the whole dichotomy, not just one of its poles.[8] He is seeking to give a description of what we do that does not rely on the standard understanding of these organizing dichotomies.

Fish has different ways of trying to dissolve the understanding of these dichotomies as opposed pairs. In the following passage from *Is There a Text in this Class?* we see him trying to describe how textual meaning arises while resisting having his account slotted into the conventional objective versus subjective dichotomy:

> [I]f the self is conceived of not as an independent entity but as a social construct whose operations are delimited by the systems of intelligibility that inform it, then the meanings it confers on texts are not its own but have their source in the interpretive community (or communities) of which it is a function. Moreover, these meanings will be neither subjective nor objective, *at least in the*

*terms assumed by those who argue within the traditional frame-
work*: they will not be objective because they will always have
been the product of a point of view rather than having been simply
"read off"; and they will not be subjective because that point of
view will always be social or institutional. Or by the same reasoning one could say that they are *both* subjective and objective: they
are subjective because they inhere in a particular point of view and
are therefore not universal; and they are objective because the
point of view that delivers them is public and conventional rather
than individual or unique. (335–36; first emphasis added)

In other places, he has sought to release us from the grip of the standard
understanding of the reason versus faith and knowledge versus belief
dichotomies by showing how reason, facts, and knowledge are not
opposed to local deep beliefs or faiths but instead rely upon them being
in place.[9] (I shall return to this point in more detail at the end of this
chapter.) As we shall now see, he uses the same technique when seeking
to dissolve the freedom versus constraint dichotomy. His goal is to show
that constraint is not the simple opposite of freedom, but rather that
freedom always requires constraint to exist.

The Freedom Versus Constraint Dichotomy

With the hope that the ground has now been prepared, I shall proceed to
a more detailed description of Fish's deconstruction of the freedom
versus constraint dichotomy. Earlier I claimed that Fish presents some
novel arguments regarding the relationship of freedom and constraint.
Here they are:

> Argument 1: In order for me to be free, I must also be constrained.
>
> Argument 2: In order for me to be committed to freedom, I must
> also be committed to the constraint of others, even where their
> actions do not interfere with my actions.

Both of these arguments seek to make Fish's deconstructive point that
freedom presupposes constraint, rather than freedom and constraint
being inherently opposed. Both of these arguments are different from the
more familiar argument that in order for me to be free, other people must
be constrained from interfering with my actions. (As mentioned earlier,

if I am free to do X because I have what Hohfeld calls a legal claim-right to do X, other people will be under a duty not to interfere with my doing X, and so they are constrained.) But as they stand, both of these arguments seem paradoxical and contradictory. We shall have to consider each in more depth to unpack Fish's reasoning and dispel this impression.

Argument 1: In order for me to be free, I must also be constrained.
This claim follows from Fish's conception of the embedded self. According to this conception, as we have seen, it is a precondition of being a self that you are embedded within particular local communities. But another way to describe this is to say that it is a precondition of being a self that you are constrained. You are constrained by the particular beliefs, values, and practices that come with that local embeddedness. In the standard understanding of the freedom versus constraint dichotomy, to be constrained is a bad thing; but in Fish's account, it is a good thing in that this constraint is what enables you to think, perceive, and act in the first place. More particularly, it is this constraint that enables you to act freely. Fish writes,

> I do not mean that we are never free to act, but that our freedom is a function of—in the sense of being dependent on—some other structure of constraint without which action of any kind would be impossible. This may seem counterintuitive to those who are accustomed to identify freedom with the *absence* of constraints, but, in fact, such a state, if it could be achieved, would produce not free actions, but *no* actions. An action is only conceivable against a background of alternative paths, a background that is already a constraint in that by marking out some actions as possible it renders unavailable others that might emerge as possibilities against a different background. To imagine a world with no background in place, with no prearticulation of the directions one might take, is to imagine a world where there would be literally nowhere to go, where, since every path is the same path, the notion of doing this rather than that—of acting freely—would be empty. ("Critical" 459)

The background constraint provided by being embedded in a local community is a necessary precondition for being free—that is, for being a self that sees a range of possible actions and has a reason to choose one over another. Elsewhere, Fish applies this general understanding of freedom and constraint to the more particular case of freedom of speech:

> Absent some already-in-place and (for the time being) unquestioned ideological vision, the act of speaking would make no sense, because it would not be resonating against any background understanding of the possible courses of physical or verbal actions and their possible consequences. Nor is that background accessible to the speaker it constrains; it is not an object of his or her critical self-consciousness; rather, it constitutes the field in which consciousness occurs, and therefore the productions of consciousness, and specifically speech, will always be political (that is, angled) in ways the speaker cannot know. ("There's" 115–16)[10]

But it might seem that Fish's analysis has delivered us a paradox that undermines the very existence of freedom. He says that we can't have freedom without also being constrained and that this constraint is a precondition for freedom. Does this mean that freedom and constraint cannot be separated and that our everyday judgments distinguishing between them thus need to be abandoned because they rest upon a philosophical mistake? Fish's answer would be no, because of his view of the relationship between philosophical analysis and everyday life.

This brings us to Fish's position on theory, which is complex and novel enough to require a paper all its own.[11] The conventional view of theory is that it allows us to abstract away from our current local beliefs, values, and practices in order to find deeper, more enduring principles behind or above them. We can then use the fruits of our theoretical labor to order our local beliefs and practices in a more coherent and principled fashion. According to this understanding of the role of theory, if our reflection upon the nature and preconditions of freedom lead us to see freedom and constraint as interdependent, then this has to have consequences for our everyday use of the term.

For Fish, of course, the strong theory project so described is impossible because it requires us to transcend completely the locally embedded state that is a precondition of our being thinking, perceiving, choosing selves at all. However, he acknowledges that there can still be forms of abstract intellectual work that have more realistic goals. One of these is philosophy, but philosophy still abstracts far enough away from any substantive content that it has no consequences for everyday life. What goes on in philosophy seminars occurs in a local disciplinary context that gives the questions meaning, but that context is very different from the contexts in which such words as *liberty, equality,* and *justice* are used in everyday life. Philosophical reflections on the nature and preconditions of freedom in general (such as he provides in this first argument) have no consequences at all for distinguishing between free and constrained actions in everyday life, Fish claims. The two practices are different and do not have an impact on each other. The only consequences of philosophical reflections on the nature of freedom are the answers one would give to some traditional questions dealt with in philosophy seminars.

Now, this sounds very counterintuitive. How can Fish have it both ways? How can he assert that freedom does not exist without constraint at one level of analysis, dealt with by philosophers, but that freedom and constraint can be distinguished in uncontroversial, familiar ways at another level of analysis, the level of everyday life? Surely, the two levels must interact in some way. Surely, some skeptical consequences must ensue. Let me try to support Fish's rejection of this objection by offering my own experience as a puzzled first-year university student in a philosophy class. The teacher thumped his fist on the table, demonstrating to us that it was solid and stable. But then he reminded us that this very table was made up of atoms and that these atoms consisted of a nucleus, around which electrons were moving at great speed. Not only were the electrons moving, but they were also, relatively speaking, a long way away from the small nucleus. So was the table really solid and stable? Or was it composed largely of empty space and rapidly moving particles? Which was the real table?

In that class long ago, I experienced the same intellectual vertigo I imagine some readers of Fish experience when he says both that constraint is a precondition for freedom as a philosophical matter, and that freedom can be distinguished from constraint in everyday life. How can both statements be true? Well, they can both be true in the same way that the atomic physicist's statements about the table and the ordinary person's statements about the table can both be true. Whatever one has to say about the table at the atomic level has no consequences at all for everyday use of and descriptions of that table. Its solidity and stability have not been undermined or rendered suspect in everyday life by what physicists might have to say about it. Indeed, the atomic spaces and particle movements are the preconditions of the solidity and stability we deal with in everyday life. Similarly, Fish's philosophical remarks about the preconditions of freedom do not affect or undermine the use of that term by any particular interpretive community.

Here is another simple example to support Fish's claim that the enabling background constraint that comes with embeddedness has no consequences for our ability to distinguish between free and constrained actions in everyday life. Consider this very chapter you are reading. My action in writing it would be categorized as a free action. I was not forced to write it, nor, once I had chosen to do so, was I constrained by anyone as to the topic or the arguments. My employer did not seek to approve its contents or to prevent me from using university property, such as my office and word processor, to compose it. Fish would have no complaints about this everyday use of the term "free action." His point is that this admittedly free action of mine is only possible because I am subject to certain background enabling constraints, which it is the goal of his analysis to expose.

The nature of these constraints is various, and unpacking them would be a mammoth task.[12] Some would be the constraints associated with academic freedom, which I shall deal with in more detail shortly. But there is an even more basic form of background constraint at work enabling my free action in this case. Consider my use of a word processor to write the chapter. When I first started to learn how to use word processing software, I had to proceed through the instruction manual slowly and painfully. Little seemed intuitive, and many instructions seemed to presuppose knowledge that I did not have. I kept finding the instructions and commands ambiguous. Instead of the text clearly telling me what to do, many of its directions raised a host of other questions about what exactly I was being told to do, because I could see alternative meanings. Eventually, I absorbed enough to use many functions of the computer program quickly and easily. But this process of training and learning, while it enabled me to do more and different things than I could before, and so enhanced my freedom of action, was simultaneously a process of constraint. I could only be brought to the point of seeing my computer program's commands and options as intuitive and obvious by having alternative understandings—such as those producing the ambiguity that vexed me initially—rendered *un*-seeable. My training involved shaping and structuring my perceptions and reactions, but any shaping of perceptions and reactions involves constraining them, too. It involves blocking possible perceptions and reactions that would interfere with the performance of the desired activity.

So, from this simple example we can see how background constraint can coexist with an ability to distinguish between free and constrained acts. Learning to use a word processor involves training and constraint in the way I have just described, but that has no consequences for our ability to distinguish between being free to write what you want on your computer, and being constrained from doing so by the actions of the state or your employer. Pushing this example a little further reveals some of the other background constraints in place. To be free to write plays on my computer, for example, I must not simply be left alone, or even be provided with a government grant. I must have first learned a language, learned to read and write that language, learned that plays are a possible and valued "language-game," and learned the conventions of writing plays (that is, how writing plays is different from writing contracts or telephone books). But any such learning was a process that shaped and constrained me even as it enabled me, just as learning to use a word processor did.

For Fish there are two levels of analysis that have to be kept separate and that do not affect each other. There is the philosophical point that all humans are always embedded and so are always constrained, and there is the particular use of the terms *free* and *constrained* developed and used by those humans embedded within a particular community. This means that while different societies might disagree about which provided greater freedom to its members, at the philosophical level of analysis all humans are equally constrained because they are equally embedded:

> It follows, then, that it makes no sense to imagine conditions of *no* constraint, and it follows, too, that there can be no continuum which differentiates institutions or structures as being more or less constrained, more or less free, because freedom, in whatever shape it appears, is another name for constraint. Rather than a continuum, what we have is an array, an array of structures of constraint, no one of which is more constraining than another, and each of which is differently productive of actions that are, in the only sense the word can have, free. Depending on which of those structures one inhabits or by which one is inhabited, things will be very different, including one's sense of what is free and what is constrained, but those differences can never be characterized in the terms that are crucial to the critical project. What the critical theorists call liberation or emancipation is nothing more (or less) than the passing from one structure of constraint to another, a passing that will always be attended by the "discovery of new possibilities," but of possibilities that will be no less (or more) constrained than those that have been left behind. ("Critical" 459–60)

It is crucial not to conflate the two levels of analysis, for if one neglects to keep them apart, one could make the mistake of reading this passage as denying that it is possible to assert, for example, that the USA is a freer society than the old USSR was. This is not Fish's point. Rather than seeking to deny the ability to make discriminations between freedom and constraint, he is trying to explain how this is possible for embedded selves. The equality of constraint Fish is noting at the level of philosophical analysis is akin to the equal constraint we all feel from the weight of the earth's atmosphere above us. It forms part of the unnoticed enabling background within which we act and within which we make valid distinctions between free and constrained acts. Because we are locally embedded, we will never fail to have at hand the tools to make such distinctions. The necessary criteria come with being socialized into and constituted by the relevant community.

Our nature as embedded selves also means that one's access to these tools is not rendered uncertain or suspect by the philosophical point that they are local products only. Fish rejects both the fears of some that our nature as embedded selves means that things like truth, reason, and objectivity cease to exist, and the hopes of others that once we realize that our current conceptions of truth, reason, and objectivity are contingent and local, we can be less gripped by them. The fears rest upon a desire for an unachievable foundation outside any human experience, while the hopes depend upon a conception of the self that is no longer constituted by its local commitments but that can float free of them.

Argument 2: In order for me to be committed to freedom, I must also be committed to the constraint of others, even where their actions do not interfere with my actions.

Fish's first argument for the inseparability of freedom and constraint is focused solely upon the background constraints that come with embeddedness. His claim is that the constant presence of these constraints means that as a philosophical matter freedom cannot be correctly conceived of as the absence of constraints. But the constraint in question turns out to reside in the background, rather than the foreground, of our lives and has no consequences for the way those embedded within particular interpretive communities use the concepts "free" and "constrained" in everyday life. So might it be the case that at the level of everyday life, freedom can properly be understood as the absence of constraints? This brings us to Fish's second argument, which denies this possibility. He argues that even when you look at the way "freedom" and "constraint" are employed at the local level, the hard opposition between them that is found in the standard dichotomy cannot be maintained. Even here, constraint turns out to be inseparable from freedom, though for a different reason than was exposed by the first argument.

The keystone of Fish's second argument is the claim that freedom can only be valued because it produces valued consequences. If freedom is valued only because it produces such consequences, then it follows logically, Fish argues, that actions that undermine those consequences have no claim to be protected as free actions. Not only are they not entitled to protection, such actions must actively be constrained by those who are committed to freedom and the consequences it is valued for producing. Such constraint is an expression of the commitment to freedom, not a falling away from it.

The passages where Fish makes this point most forcefully occur in his analysis of freedom of speech. In liberal societies, free speech is valued because it is believed to produce desired consequences such as more truth, better democratic politics, and more individual self-development. But this means that any freedom of speech principle carries with it a commitment to constrain speech that destroys these things. Alternatively put, a commitment to free speech necessarily carries within it a commitment to censorship:

> This is not an empirical but a logical inevitability; for if you have what has been called a consequentialist view of the First Amendment—a view that values free speech because of the good effects it will bring about—then you must necessarily be on the lookout for forms of action, including speech action, that threaten to subvert those effects.... And, to continue the logic, at the point you discern such a threat and move against it, you will not be compromising the First Amendment; you will be honoring it by performing the act of censorship that was implicit in it from the beginning. ("Dance" 115)[13]

Two objections arise at this point. First, why should we accept Fish's claim that only a consequentialist argument can explain why freedom is valued? Some people certainly do not rely on consequentialist arguments to justify the importance of individual freedom. Instead, they talk of such freedom as a basic human right to which people are entitled because of their nature as autonomous beings. And if freedom need not be valued on consequentialist grounds alone, then this undermines Fish's argument that a commitment to freedom of speech logically implies the constraint of speech antithetical to the valued consequences.

Fish has two responses to this objection. The first is that attempts to hold non-consequentialist positions on free speech tend to self-destruct because they are "always sliding over into consequentialism."[14] That is, eventually the putative non-consequentialist starts bringing valued consequences into his or her reasons for having freedom of speech. His second response is a *reductio ad absurdum* of the non-consequentialist position. If the consequences of speech are not the reason why free speech is valued, then the actual content of the speech must be irrelevant. But if the content of the speech is irrelevant, then the freedom of speech principle just amounts to the right to make noise. And why should a right to make noise be given the status of a fundamental right?

This surprising argument needs to be unpacked. The position that the consequences and content of speech are irrelevant to the free speech principle is, Fish claims, inherent in the Kantian conception of the person. As we have seen, in Kant's account the self is defined in terms of an abstract capacity, the capacity to exercise autonomous free choice, rather than the concrete choices actually made by exercising that capacity. These concrete choices are contingent and revisable characteristics of persons; they are not what is essential and enduring. In this view of the self, what is important about free speech is not the actual content of what is said, or the consequences of saying it, but the fact that an autonomous human had the will to say it and was able to do so without constraint. Fish writes,

> In the legal culture, as crystallized in First Amendment jurisprudence, what counts is the moment in which a lone speaker rises and, in defiance of the forces that press in on him, gives utterance to the inner voice of conscience. In [this] scenario . . . the person is reduced, or exalted, to the status of pure mind, a bodiless agent whose paradigmatic act is either of forming an expression or expressing it. Everything else is accidental, in the strict philosophical sense; everything else is dross. . . . [T]he point, and the only point, is to preserve the autonomy of individual moral choice. In the contexts informed by high liberal thought, it is not the consequences of an action—its real-world community effects—that matter but the extent to which the action is free, that is, the product of an uncoerced will. ("Of an Age" 50)

But if what is important about free speech is the fact that an autonomous human had the will to say something and was able to do so without constraint, not the actual content of what is said or the consequences of saying it, then the right of free speech is indistinguishable from the right to make noise:

> Freedom of expression would only be a primary value if it didn't matter what was said, didn't matter in the sense that no one gave a damn but just liked to hear talk. . . . In ordinary contexts, talk is produced with the goal of trying to move the world in one direction rather than another. . . . You assert, in short, because you give a damn, not about assertion—as if it were a value in and of itself—but about what your assertion is about. It may seem paradoxical, but free expression could only be a primary value if what you are valuing is the right to make noise; but if you are engaged in some purposive activity in the course of which speech happens to be produced, sooner or later you will come to a point when you decide that some forms of speech do not further but endanger that purpose. ("There's" 106–07)[15]

And why should a right to make noise be valued in and of itself? Fish has a ready answer to this question: "The choice is clear; either acknowledge that, like other items in the Constitution, the First Amendment has a purpose and that in the light of that purpose some acts of toleration make sense and some don't; or acknowledge that the free-speech clause has no purpose beyond itself, and face the conclusion that there is no compelling—that is, serious—reason for adhering to it" ("Jerry" 123).[16] The position that free speech is not valued because of its consequences thus destroys the importance of free speech, in Fish's analysis.

　　The second objection to Fish's position that can be raised here is that it is empirically disproved. He has claimed that a commitment to free speech simultaneously carries with it a commitment to censor—to constrain speech that seriously harms the consequences that speech is valued for producing. But in liberal societies that profess to adhere to the free speech principle, we do not see wholesale censorship. Rather, we see speech that most people would see as objectionable and opposed to wider social values being tolerated and protected.

　　Fish has two responses to this objection too, both based on his *first law of toleration-dynamics*: "Toleration is exercised in an inverse proportion to there being anything at stake" ("Almost" 217). One response is that he is not claiming that *any* speech opposed to important social values will be censored, only such speech that is perceived to be likely to cause real harm to those values. Since liberal societies, unlike others, judge that most unorthodox speech is unlikely to have widespread and serious negative consequences, these societies display more tolerance. Some objectionable voices might have to be permitted to wail in the wilderness, and some sensibilities might be hurt because of this, but no serious harm will result from leaving them alone. His other response is that at some point, when serious harm *is* perceived to be looming, toleration will run out even in liberal societies, and censorship will kick in. But typically this constraint of speech is concealed by being categorized as something else. In this way, the impression can be maintained that freedom of speech is diametrically opposed to constraint, rather than admitting Fish's point that freedom of speech logically requires constraint of speech.

Fish finds many examples of such concealment of constraint by recategorization in the First Amendment law. Again, his detailed treatment of this body of law requires a paper of its own, but for our purposes the following passage gives the flavor of his position:

> Hard-line First Amendment advocates will vigorously protest this account of their sacred text, but the protest is belied by their own activities, for they typically play the regulation game behind their own backs. They insist up front that they read the text without exceptions ("shall make no law") but then smuggle in the exceptions by declaring them not really to be speech or to be speech "brigaded with action." . . . A so-called principled analysis is . . . ad hoc behind its back; it is continually engaged in saving its own appearances by inventing (and then reinventing as needed) distinctions that hide from itself what is really going on. ("Jerry" 124, 127)[17]

Fish is referring to the distinction drawn in First Amendment law between speech, which cannot be regulated, and action, which can be regulated without constitutional impropriety. When something that looks like speech is to be regulated, the potential difficulty is avoided by recategorizing it as action rather than speech. But Fish claims that the speech/action distinction cannot do the work the First Amendment purist wants it to do. It cannot serve to separate two distinct categories, because speech can nearly always be redescribed as action and thereby moved from one side of the line to the other. His argument for this position is based on his rebuttal of the first objection posed earlier. There he argued that a concept of free speech that was not inherently connected with consequences was empty and uninteresting. It dealt only with the right to make noise. Since any speech that is not mere noise can be connected with possible consequences, any such speech can be redescribed as action seeking to bring those consequences about.

Academic Freedom

We have now surveyed Fish's unconventional claims about the nature of freedom. Rather than freedom being opposed to constraint, he says, freedom can only exist for those who are constrained themselves; and, moreover, freedom can only be valued by those who are prepared to constrain others. In *The Trouble with Principle*, the main examples Fish uses to explore these points are the freedoms of speech and religion, and academic freedom within the university. Since I have considered freedom of speech and freedom of religion elsewhere, I will concentrate more on academic freedom here.

Although they may squabble about many things, academics are typically united in their conviction that academic freedom is crucial both for the health of the universities and for the long-term good of society (see Menand). It is seen as protecting the ability of the academic to push back the boundaries of knowledge by questioning accepted wisdom. It is seen as leaving the academic a wide zone of freedom in which to teach and research without constraints being imposed on him or her by an employer, or by those in society who might object to any radical challenges to the status quo. Fish's approach to academic freedom, however, is consistent with his general analysis of freedom. Even as academics go about their work of teaching and researching under the shelter of the academic freedom umbrella, he says, they are both constrained and prepared to constrain others.[18]

His first argument for these claims follows from his point that any form of local embeddedness will constrain and enable at the same time. Just as learning to use a word processor is simultaneously the expansion of options and the imposition of constraints, so the routine teaching of university students will both enable and constrain them. Teaching students to venerate a canonical author like Shakespeare simultaneously opens and closes their minds. Acquiring beliefs about the high value of canonical materials opens their minds to the beauty and power of the canon, but simultaneously constrains their ability to see comparable beauty and power in material excluded from the canon. And, of course, the university teacher, as an embedded member of the interpretive community of Shakespeare scholars, is constrained in just the same way. The teacher's academic freedom to teach Shakespeare involves imposing the same constraints on the minds of the students as the ones that currently structure his or her own thinking. Hence, Fish says, there is a real sense in which the invocation of a canonical author like Shakespeare functions not to encourage thought but to stop it. Canonical materials, when they are exerting their full force, draw a line in the sand, but with an air suggesting that the sand is a monument of steel. When a piece of the canon is invoked in this way, it is assumed that there is nothing more to say. In fact, there is always more that could be said; it is just that the structure of canonical authority is such that one is discouraged from saying it, or even from thinking it. . . . If Shakespeare is on your side of the argument, the argument is over. ("Of an Age" 47)

Fish also applies his second, more local, argument about the inextricability of freedom and constraint to the academic context. He notes that within the university, free speech is valued because it is perceived to have consequences that advance the particular goals that universities are established to promote. In liberal societies, these goals would include using reason (the scientific method, critical analysis, and so on) to reach the truth, and teaching the young to be good democratic citizens by encouraging them to engage in open-minded debate with those who hold opposing viewpoints. But, in Fish's analysis, it would follow that universities need not be tolerant of speech that was perceived as seriously harming such goals.

As a very simple example of such constraint of speech at work within academia, consider what the result would be if, instead of lecturing to my students, I spent the entire hour insulting each of them on the basis of their haircuts, clothing, accent, gender, perceived sexual orientation, and so on. What would be the response if, after the inevitable complaints, I tried to defend myself to the dean on the grounds that I was simply exercising my academic freedom to think and teach in unconventional ways? Obviously, the dean would say that the university's commitment to academic freedom isn't meant to cover speech like mine, which is not devoted to seeking truth or encouraging student learning and participation. In fact, my speech is likely to harm all of these goals by making students feel inferior and less likely to attend classes and participate. My insulting speech would certainly be constrained, but this would not be categorized as restricting freedom of speech or academic freedom; rather, it would be described as insisting that I get on with what I was paid to do. I would be told to stop acting like a fool and start behaving as an academic professional should. But that instruction relies on an in-place understanding of what the proper role of a university academic is, and that in turn relies on an understanding of what the institutional goals of a university are. These understandings form part of the background context that embedded members of the academic community share and that Fish has argued constrains them.[19] If a member of the academic community acts in violation of these understandings, that person will be disciplined or constrained by the other members. However, such constraint will not be categorized as a violation of academic freedom; rather, it will be seen as ensuring that academic freedom is used responsibly, with integrity, and with a full appreciation of the duties that go with such a privilege. This demonstrates Fish's point that speech that undercuts the goals of the particular free speech regime will quite appropriately be restricted, and that such restriction is not a violation of the free speech principle but a way of being true to it.

This simple example leads us to the more complex problem of how to deal with hate speech on campus. Should hate speech directed at some ethnic or religious groups on campus by teachers, fellow students, or on-campus organizations be restricted or banned by campus hate speech codes? Some hold that the liberal principle of freedom of speech requires blanket toleration of such views. But in Fish's analysis, freedom of speech can never require blanket toleration of any viewpoint, regardless of its content. Such a lack of concern with content or consequences would reduce the free speech right to the right to make noise. Speech that undercuts the goals for which free speech is valued is properly constrained, and so there is a pragmatic judgment that cannot be avoided in the case of on-campus hate speech: Is allowing such speech to continue unrestrained in a particular context likely to cause more serious harm to the institutional goals of the university than attempting to ban or constrain it? (see "Putting" 285 and "There's" 111). This is a difficult judgment to make, and Fish himself seems to have changed his mind over time on which way to jump.[20] But if the result of this pragmatic judgment about local consequences is to restrict hate speech on campus, Fish is unequivocal that this does not represent a failure to respect freedom of speech; rather, such constraint is a way of being true to a commitment to free speech in the university.

Another example of constraint within academia is the treatment of conservative Christians, according to Fish (see my "Limits"). Among the institutional goals of the university in liberal societies are rational inquiry and critical evaluation of opposing viewpoints. Open-minded debate requires that the participants hold themselves ready to change their minds if reason favors their opponents. Since these commitments are fundamental to the liberal university, it would be expected, according to Fish's analysis, that those gripped by competing religious commitments that reject the primacy of human reason and the obligation to change one's mind as the result of open-minded debate would face constraint. They might be tolerated if they had little chance of actually changing anything, but the more efficacious such anti-liberal viewpoints became, the greater the likelihood of their restriction within the university. Fish's analysis also anticipates that such restriction would not be categorized as violating freedom of speech or academic freedom. Rather, it would be described as preventing irrational fanaticism or zealotry from destroying freedom of speech and academic freedom:

> What this means is that academic freedom, rather than being . . . "open to all points of view", is open to all points of view only so long as they offer themselves with the reserve and diffidence appropriate to Enlightenment decorums, only so long as they offer themselves for correction. In short, academic freedom places severe limits on what can go on in its playground, and is in fact a form of closure. Academic freedom is not a defence against orthodoxy; it is an orthodoxy and a faith. . . . What academic freedom excludes is any position that refuses that obligation, any position which rests, for example, on pronouncements like "I am the way" or "Thou shalt have no other gods before me." (Sauce" 40)[21]

For some conservative Christians, human reason is rendered fallible by original sin and is therefore distrusted and "rejected as a way of knowing in favor of scripture and revelation" ("Wolf" 189). Other conservative Christians object to the assumption that there is only one reason, one logic, that is a neutral tool that can be applied to all substantive positions to see how they stand up. Fish also rejects "reason" as a candidate for the neutral procedures or principles that liberalism constantly seeks, for he sees it too as a partisan historical product.[22] Secular liberals often dismiss conservative Christians for abandoning reason in favor of faith, but Fish argues that each group has different conceptions of reason that stem in each case from the different fundamental beliefs, or faiths, that come with being differently embedded. Rather than subjective beliefs standing in opposition to objective reason and facts, as in another familiar dichotomy, Fish's deconstruction shows that it is deep fundamental beliefs, operating like articles of faith, that determine what we will accept as reason, or evidence, or fact. Just as he has argued that the constraint that comes with embeddedness is necessary for us to have freedom, now he argues that the beliefs that come with embeddedness are necessary for us to have facts and reason:

That is to say, evidence is never independent in the sense of being immediately apprehensible; evidence comes into view (or doesn't) in the light of some first premise or "essential axiom" that cannot itself be put to the test because the protocols of testing are established by its presumed authority. A "creationist parent whose child is being taught . . . evolution" protests not in the name of religion and against the witness of fact; he protests in the name of fact as it seems indisputable to him given the "central" truth that "God is real". Given such a "starting point and the methodology" that follows from it, "creationism is as rational an explanation as any other" and from the other direction, you might say that given the assumption of a material world that caused itself . . . evolution is as faith-dependent an explanation as any other. This is not to debunk rationality in favor of faith but to say that rationality and faith go together in an indissoluble package; you can't have one without the other. ("Why We Can't" 255)[23]

What happens to conservative Christians within a secular liberal university? They will be left in peace if they accommodate their religious beliefs to the liberal "assumptions of fallibilism (all points of view are partial and corrigible) and pluralism (the more points of view in play the better)" ("Playing" 240). But if they reject fallibilism and pluralism as distorting and truncating their more fundamental religious beliefs and insist on the one truth and religious ways of knowing, the liberal university will respond to such a threat to its own fundamental beliefs. This response can range from censure, restriction, or expulsion, depending upon the seriousness of the threat:

To be sure, a champion of academic freedom would say that such positions are not excluded at all; rather, they are invited into the seminar, where they can be discussed, interrogated, reasoned with, analyzed. But of course, this is not what the proponents of doctrinaire agendas want. They want to win; they want to occupy, and be sovereign over, the discursive space, and expel others from it. And this academic freedom will not permit (it wants to win too, and does by exiling from its confines any discourse which violates its rules). In short, academic freedom invites forceful agendas in only on its own terms, and refuses to grant legitimacy to the terms within which such agendas define themselves. . . . [R]eligion can be part of university life so long as it renounces its claim to have a privileged purchase on the truth, which of course is the claim that defines a religion as a religion as opposed to a mere opinion. ("Sauce" 40)

If conservative Christians move out of the secular universities and set up their own, these religious institutions will not be fully respected as proper universities by the secular academics. Fish describes how the American Association of University Professors "denies to religiously based institutions the name of 'university' because 'they do not, at least as regards one particular subject, accept the principles of freedom and inquiry'" ("Sauce" 37). What they will not allow to be questioned is their own foundational beliefs about God. But Fish's position is that secular universities are exactly the same as religious universities in not allowing dangerous questioning of their fundamental beliefs (see "There's" 107–08). The only difference between them here is the beliefs that occupy the fundamental position. Religious universities will not allow the questioning of God's existence; secular universities will not allow the questioning of secular reason's superiority over religious reason or revelation. As he says,

> The debate is never between the inclusive university and a university marked by exclusions; the debate is always between competing structures of exclusion. And the debate is over, at least for a time, when one structure of exclusion has managed to make its interests perfectly congruent with what is understood by the term "academic freedom." ("Sauce" 44)

Conclusion

Fish's project with respect to freedom is descriptive; it is neither destructive nor prescriptive. He is not arguing that freedom does not exist, nor is he urging us to modify or abandon our current use of the concept. Instead, he is seeking to provide a more adequate account of our current use of the concept that takes account of our nature as embedded selves.

Fish's position is that any adequate general description of the concept of freedom has to be more complex than simply positing freedom as the absence of constraint, and it is this more complex description of our existing practice that he provides. He is not seeking to change that existing practice, only to change the answers one would give to some philosophical questions about the nature and preconditions of freedom. Fish's philosophical analysis deconstructs the freedom versus constraint dichotomy by demonstrating the necessary interdependence of the two terms. But like all philosophical theorizing, he would say, it is conducted at a high level of abstraction and so has no consequences for everyday life.[24]

Notes

1. See "Liberalism," "There's," and *The Trouble*. For a detailed analysis of Fish's position on theory, see Robertson, "What."

2. The liberal stress on the freedom of the individual from the power of the state and an established church had its origin in the Protestant reformation in the sixteenth century and was developed particularly by the Puritans in the seventeenth century. See Tawney and Weber.

3. In an analysis of the different concepts clustering under the general heading of "right," Wesley Hohfeld notes that one meaning of right implied that others were under a duty and so constrained (38). Earlier, Jeremy Bentham made this same point in his "Anarchical Fallacies," written in 1796: "No right without a correspondent obligation. . . . How is property given? By restraining liberty. . . . How is your house made yours? By debarring every one else from the liberty of entering it without your leave" (57).

4. This section is taken from Robertson, "What."

5. The conception of the self that is central for Fish can also be found in the work of Charles Taylor, Alasdair MacIntyre, and Michael Sandel. It has been adopted by some communitarians, social constructionists, and even conservative thinkers.

6. See also "Sauce" 39 and 36, where Kant is identified as the source of the view Fish is criticizing. Fish can also be found criticizing this Kantian "theory of personhood" in "Of an Age" (50); "Boutique" (57–59); "Vicki" (157–58); and "Wolf" (197–98). He does not always clearly identify Kant as the source of the position he opposes in these passages, but other theorists who directly critique Kant along lines similar to Fish have made the connection explicit. See Sandel (11–17) and Radin (34–40 and chapter 5).

7. In "Prologue: Taking Sides," Fish writes, "By referring to these [matters hidden by the veil of ignorance in the original position] as restrictions on *information*, Rawls makes it clear that in his view the characteristics they remove from inspection are not essential to the person, who is what he is with or without these identifying marks of merely social relations: he is an agent with a capacity to imagine a condition of justice and a vision of the good; and it is this capacity, rather than any realization it happens to have, that defines him" (11).

8. Fish writes, "In general [critics] ignore my challenge to the binaries on which their arguments depend, and take to chiding me for failing to respect distinctions whose lack of cogency has been a large part of my point" ("There's" 117).

9. For more detailed discussions of Fish's epistemology, see Robertson, "Picking" (403–28); "Limits" (260–65); and "What" (365–67).

10. See also "There's" (108 and 117) and "Fraught" (93).

11. See Robertson "What." This paragraph and the next give a truncated summary of part of that paper.

12. In "Consequences," Fish writes, "In order to make even the simplest of assertions or perform the most elementary action, I must already be proceeding in the context of innumerable beliefs which cannot be the object of my attention because they are the content of my attention: beliefs on the order of the identity of persons, the existence of animate and inanimate entities, the stability of objects, in addition to the countless beliefs that underwrite the possibility and intelligibility of events in my local culture—beliefs that give me, without reflection, a world populated by streets, sidewalks and telephone poles, restaurants, figures of authority and figures of fun, worthy and unworthy tasks, achievable and unachievable goals, and so on. The descriptions of what assumptions must already be in place for me to enter an elevator, or stand in line in a supermarket, or ask for the check in a restaurant would fill volumes, volumes that would themselves be intelligible only within a set of assumptions they in turn did not contain" (326–27).

13. See also "Rhetoric" (85–86); "Introduction" (13–14); and "There's" (103–04).

14. For an elaboration of this argument (with Ronald Dworkin as the target), see "Introduction" (14–15).

15. See also "Rhetoric" (78) and "Fraught" (93).

16. For a slightly different version of this argument, see "Rhetoric" (86–87).

17. His work on the First Amendment is dealt with in more detail in Robertson, "Principle."

18. Free speech within academia is discussed in "Sauce" (34); "Of an Age" (46); "Rhetoric" (75); "There's" (107ff); "Jerry's" (127–28); and, most recently, "Holocaust."

19. He writes, "In the classroom, the established purpose—instruction as mandated by college and departmental requirements—would place obligations on both teachers and students that would restrict both the subjects to be discussed and the manner of their discussion" ("Jerry's 128).

20. He is in favor of hate speech codes in "There's" (115), but he is against them in "Boutique" (71–72).

21. For Fish applying a similar analysis to hate speech, see "Boutique" (67–72). In "Fraught with Death," Fish writes, "The rhetoric of general persuasion is the rhetoric of openness, but . . . the logic of general persuasion is strongly exclusionary. What it excludes (declaring them beyond the pale) are those who refuse to submit their core principles to the scrutiny and play of the marketplace; such persons are labeled 'irrational' or 'fanatical' and in the name of inclusiveness they are read out of the community" (109–10).

22. See "Wolf" (187ff). For instances of Fish giving the same analysis of

reason in his earlier writing, see "Anti-Professionalism" (222–25); "Force" (518–19); "Introduction" (17–18); and "Liberalism" (135–37).

23. In "Beliefs About Belief," he writes, "Belief is prior to rationality; rationality can only unfold in the context of convictions and commitments it neither chooses nor approves.... It is because belief is at some level inaccessible to consciousness that it is so crucial to—indeed constitutive of—consciousness. Moreover, if it is within belief that deliberation occurs and evidence becomes perspicuous and reasons persuasive, then what you believe will, as James suggests, be determinative of what you see, of what you notice, and, down the road, of what you do" (284).

24. I would like to thank Andrew Geddis, Richard Mahoney, and Stanley Fish for reading and commenting on an earlier draft of this paper.

Works Cited

Bentham, Jeremy. "Anarchical Fallacies." *Nonsense upon Stilts: Bentham, Burke, and Marx on the Rights of Man.* Ed. Jeremy Waldron. New York: Methuen, 1987.

Fish, Stanley. "Almost Pragmatism: The Jurisprudence of Richard Posner, Richard Rorty, and Ronald Dworkin," *There's No* 200–30.

———. "Anti-Professionalism" *Doing* 215–46.

———. "Beliefs About Belief," *Trouble* 279–84.

———. "Boutique Multiculturalism," *Trouble* 56–72.

———. "Change," *Doing* 141–60.

———. "Consequences," *Doing* 315–41.

———. "Critical Self-Consciousness, Or Can We Know What We're Doing? *Doing* 436–67.

———. *Doing What Comes Naturally. Change, Rhetoric and the Practice of Theory in Literary and Legal Studies.* Durham: Duke UP, 1989.

———. "Force," *Doing* 503–54.

———. "Fraught With Death," *Trouble* 93–114.

———. "The Dance of Theory," *Trouble* 115–50.

MICHAEL ROBERTSON 125

————. "Holocaust Denial and Academic Freedom." *Valparaiso Law Review* 35.3 (2001): 499–524.

————. "Introduction: 'That's Not Fair,'" *There's No* 3–28.

————. *Is There a Text in this Class? The Authority of Interpretive Communities.* Cambridge, MA: Harvard UP, 1980.

————. "Jerry Falwell's Mother, or, What's the Harm?" *There's No* 120–33.

————. "Liberalism Doesn't Exist," *There's No* 134–38.

————. "Of an Age and Not for All Time," *Trouble* 46–55.

————. "Playing Not to Win," *Trouble* 211–43.

————. "Putting Theory in Its Place," *Trouble* 285–92.

————. "Profession Despise Thyself: Fear and Self-Loathing in Literary Studies," *Doing* 197–214.

————. "Prologue: Taking Sides," *Trouble* 1–15.

————. "The Rhetoric of Regret," *Trouble* 75–92.

————. "Sauce for the Goose," *Trouble* 34–45.

————. *There's No Such Thing as Free Speech, and It's a Good Thing, Too.* New York: Oxford UP, 1994.

————. "There's No Such Thing as Free Speech, and It's a Good Thing, Too," *There's No* 102–19.

————. *The Trouble with Principle.* Cambridge: Harvard UP, 1999.

————. "Vicki Frost Objects," *Trouble* 153–61.

————. "Why We Can't All Just Get Along," *Trouble* 243–62.

————. "A Wolf in Reason's Clothing," *Trouble* 187–210.

Hohfeld, Wesley. *Fundamental Legal Conceptions as Applied in Judicial Reasoning.* 1927. New Haven: Yale UP, 1964.

Menand, Louis, ed. *The Future of Academic Freedom*. Chicago: U of Chicago P, 1996.

Radin, Margaret. *Contested Commodities*. Cambridge: Harvard UP, 1996.

Robertson, Michael. "The Limits of Liberal Rights: Stanley Fish on Freedom of Religion," *Otago Law Review* 10 (2002): 251–69.

———. "Picking Positivism Apart: Stanley Fish on Epistemology and Law" *Southern California Interdisciplinary Law Journal* 8 (1999): 401–65.

———. "Principle, Pragmatism and Paralysis: Fish on the First Amendment," unpublished manuscript.

———. "What Am I Doing? Stanley Fish on the Possibility of Legal Theory." *Legal Theory* 8 (2002): 359–85.

Sandel, Michael. *Democracy's Discontent: America in Search of a Public Philosophy*. Cambridge: Harvard UP, 1996.

Tawney, R.H. *Religion and the Rise of Capitalism: A Historical Study*. London: J. Murray, 1948.

Weber, Max. *The Protestant Ethic and the Spirit of Capitalism*. London: Allen, 1930.

The Trouble with (Arguing against) Principle: Stanley Fish's Incomplete Machiavellianism

Reed Way Dasenbrock

In *The Trouble with Principle*, Stanley Fish tries to precision bomb liberal political and legal theory, arguing at length against a notion central to liberalism: that we can agree on neutral procedural principles that we can then use to govern political, social, and legal disputes. Damage assessment after the raid suggests that the bombs hit their target—at least to the extent that I am not prepared to argue here for the procedural universals that were the official target of Fish's attack. But precision bombing is another in a long line of military oxymorons: in blowing one thing up, we tend to destroy other things as well. My focus here is the collateral damage caused by Fish's attack on liberal principles, and my argument is that Fish destroys a good deal of what he ostensibly is trying to defend as well as what he wants to destroy. The environment left after Fish's attack is not one in which anyone will want to live, and this suggests some serious flaws in the design of the raid.

Procedural and Substantive Universals

Fish's argument is finally a simple one, as he acknowledges, though he elaborates on it at length: the trouble with principle is that to act according to a principle requires setting aside one's particular situation in favor of a general rule, law, or principle; and, according to Fish, this is what we

127

never can or will do. We never can do it because it is our concrete and specific situation that gives rise to our actions and beings; we never will because to accept "neutral principles" is in fact to accept someone else's equally concrete and specific values masquerading as a set of formal or neutral principles. The claim Fish opposes is that "abstractions like fairness, impartiality, mutual respect, and reasonableness can be defined in ways not hostage to any partisan agenda" (2). Although these are presented as procedural principles that should govern the substantive fray—the more specific disputes about what the fair, impartial, and reasonable thing to do is—Fish's point is that the distinction between substantive and procedural is itself substantive since there is in fact nothing like universal assent to these procedural principles. They are in fact not above the fray but very much of it, actively defining the arena of contestation in a way that favors certain positions and disqualifies or severely weakens others. To cite an obvious example, impartiality is not and cannot be impartial in the contest between those who value impartiality and those who explicitly value partiality.

Fish shows this best in an extended discussion about the conflict between liberal principles and religious belief. We are all familiar with versions of this conflict, played out in every school system in the United States: what happens when the demands of a parent for a particular kind of content in the schools (either expressed positively as the demand for school prayer or negatively as the desire not to have one's child exposed, say, to sex education or material about other religions) encounters the liberal position that the school system should not explicitly endorse the views of a particular religious group? The parents in such cases as these cannot accept the liberal position as setting out the procedural landscape because if they do, the contest is already over—over in that the liberal principles dictate that they lose because their values are illiberal ones. This is part of a larger point: "If liberal neutrality cannot make good on its claim to be above the fray (and it certainly cannot), then it is of necessity embroiled in the fray, coming down on one side rather than another." Furthermore, "The assertion of interest is always what's going on even when, and especially when, interest wraps itself in high-sounding abstractions" (43, 45). No one is above the fray, and the claim of liberal principle to be above the fray is in fact its most ingenious and successful attempt to intervene in it.

If nothing is above the fray, what actually makes up the fray? How do we make decisions if we have no recourse to abstractions or general principles? Fish has two different answers. One is fairly predictable to anyone familiar with the milieu in which Fish has developed his critique of universalism. He cites Charles Taylor's call for "inspired adhoccery" and explains, "What it means is that the solutions to particular problems will be found by regarding each situation-of-crisis as an opportunity for improvisation and not as an occasion for the application of rules and principles" (63).[1] This is a theme encountered repeatedly in *The Trouble with Principle*:

> Our convictions have no support in anything external to their structure and history. (125)

> There is nothing which undergirds our beliefs, nothing to which our beliefs might be referred for either confirmation or correction; and, moreover, if that is the case, there is nothing interesting to say about belief in general because belief is a particular, not a general (i.e., principled), matter. (279)

> If you say that someone or something is wrong, you will often be asked to provide a basis for your judgment that is independent of the social, political, and biographical circumstances in which it was formed. The thesis of this book has been that no such basis is available and that the ordinary resources that come along with your situation, education, and personal history are both all that you have and all you need. (293)

In passages such as these, we should know where we are, since all of this is a fairly predictable expression of "antifoundationalism" or contingency theory that is in keeping with Fish's earlier work in literary theory. As I have argued at length against these views in other settings, I won't retrace that ground here; in any case, these passages aren't the interesting moments in *The Trouble with Principle*.[2] Far more interesting are the passages where he advances a different explanation of how we make decisions, an explanation harder to reconcile with this theoretical perspective. Fish's other answer about how we make decisions, somewhat surprisingly, is morality. If we can't rely on a set of neutral principles, we rely instead on "strong moral intuitions as to how the world should go combined with a resolve to be faithful to them." Or, again: "Where, however, does this leave us? First of all, it leaves us without a ground of justification more basic or higher than the grounds given us by our moral convictions and determinations of fact" (9, 146).

Tactically, one can see why Fish moves in this direction. So long as the two terms contesting the field are liberal principles and postmodern contingency theory, Fish is not rhetorically well positioned in the public policy debate he is entering and wishes to affect, for if one of the cardinal rules of literary theory is "never be outflanked on the left"—never allow the opposition to present itself as more political, more socially engaged, more radical than your position—the cardinal rule in the public policy arena is that to be on the left is to be outflanked. If all Fish has on his side is postmodern theory, he may win hands down in a humanities faculty meeting, but he won't fare well in any extramural setting. However, if Fish can invoke the language of morality against liberalism, he will be in a much better tactical position, as he can present himself as representing ordinary intuitions and feelings against an abstract and thin account of human action.

Nonetheless, the pursuit of tactical advantage without a coherent strategic concept or plan can lead to disaster, and I think that is the case here, for the language of morally informed decision making invoked here and elsewhere in *The Trouble with Principle* contradicts the language of contingency and adhoccery invoked throughout the book. Fish makes a heroic effort in the passage just quoted to erase the difference between them. When he says that we have "no ground of justification more basic or higher than the grounds given us by our moral convictions," he tries to merge the language of antifoundationalism and the language of morality, suggesting that moral convictions are simply part of the furniture with which we make ad hoc judgments, part of our "social, political, and biographical circumstances." On one level, this is certainly so: undoubtedly, we have the moral convictions we have in large measure because of where we are situated. Yet, this is a fact that anyone seriously committed to the discourse of morality must struggle against, not complacently accept, because the language of morality seeks to escape the contingent and context-specific precisely because systems of morality present themselves as universally applicable. The language of morality is no more an ad hoc language than the language of liberal principles, and one measure of this is that the far more common term for what Fish refers to as "moral convictions" or "moral intuitions" is "moral principles." While no moral system presents itself as nonsubstantive on the model of the liberal neutral principles Fish argues are false universals, neither do any present themselves as without a ground of higher justification or as ad hoc. Moral principles present themselves not as procedural universals but as substantive universals. In other words, morality is not another ad hoc practice for those who take it seriously; it is grounded in ethical universals that are seen to transcend the situations in which they are applied. Of course, it is easy to engage in a critique of ethical universals along the lines of Fish's critique of procedural universals, presenting any ethical principles with aspirations to universality as pseudo-universals reflecting the situation of a particular people in a particular place and time. This is a familiar move in the postmodern theory that Fish depends on for his critique of liberalism, and in fact the critique of universalism on which Fish draws is first developed in terms of ethics, in a tradition that goes back as far as Nietzsche.[3] Fish's relation to this critique of ethical universals is complex: he certainly doesn't explicitly invoke it; on the contrary, he invokes the language of morality as part of his situationalist critique of universalist principles. But his granting of that moral language only a contingent, local, or situational force reflects the Nietzschean critique and "evacuates morality" in much the same way as the liberalism Fish ostensibly opposes for this very reason.

The bob and weave this commits Fish to can best be seen in an astonishing passage in which he claims that the victory of the civil rights movement in the 1960s was not a victory of a set of principles but rather was "the accomplishment of politics rather than theory," a matter of "one vocabulary [falling] into [dis]favor and disuse while another stepped into the place it had formerly occupied" (204, 205). That there were contingent and political factors in the success of the civil rights movement no one would deny, but to argue that this is all there was is to make a much stronger claim. One has to say that it certainly didn't feel that way to any of the participants, since they regarded it as a victory for the principles of morality and justice. The language used at the time wasn't contingent or situation specific in the postmodern fashion. It used the strong universalism characteristic of the discourse of moralism: discrimination is wrong; we are equal in the sight of God. There is nothing ad hoc or contingent about the vocabulary used in that struggle. Here, as elsewhere, there is a crucial third term distinct from contingency theory and liberalism, and Fish's inability to allow for its existence is a troubling lacuna.

Now, I'm not telling Fish anything he doesn't already know when I remind him that the world is not divided into liberal procedural universalists and antifoundationalist contingency theorists, for otherwise he would not try to use the stance of substantive universalism against the procedural universalism of liberalism. But it's not clear to me that he *can* use it in this way, since morality is a matter of principle for those who call on it, and those principles have the non-ad hoc character Fish deplores about the principles of liberalism. This means that those committed to the language of morality will find common cause with liberalism against Fish in terms of the universal-contingency debate even if they might find common cause with Fish in terms of his critique of procedural universalism. Fish's fire is not aimed at the substantive universalism of morality but nonetheless his antifoundationalist vantage point is no more capable of taking this substantive universalism seriously on its own terms than is procedural liberalism.

Thus, when Fish says that there is no "ground of justification more basic or higher than the grounds given us by our moral convictions," he is trying to bridge a gap between postmodern contingency theory and traditional systems of morality—a gap that cannot be bridged. These systems contain within them the conviction that there is such a higher ground or more basic justification; such moral convictions are sustained by a belief that they are not contingent, not ad hoc, not situation specific. Although it is possible to develop systems of ethical thinking (or, perhaps more precisely, ways of thinking about ethics) without this universalist element (the "ethical turn" in postmodern theory is essentially such an effort), these systems are not the ordinary moral convictions that Fish is pointing toward in his depiction of liberalism's struggle with antiliberal beliefs.[4] These beliefs are principled beliefs, in sharp contrast to the antifoundationalist adhoccery Fish wishes to align them with. From this vantage point, his antiliberalism shares with the liberal views he attacks a commitment to proceduralism, an absence of commitment to substantive principles.

We therefore don't have, as Fish would have it, a sharp distinction between liberalism and all the rest. The situation instead seems much more like a game of rock, paper, and scissors. In essence, Fish treats the rock of moral principles as if it were the paper of contingency theory, implicitly denying that moral intuitions or convictions are principles. This is, of course, how he explicitly treats the principles of liberalism that are his object of critique, treating the scissors of procedural principles as an illegitimate attempt to universalize a particular set of values, fake or pseudo-universals whose proponents are attempting to put one over on us. In this respect, I see no logical difference between moral and liberal principles, no distinction that justifies Fish's different approaches to them; the justification is rhetorical or tactical. Fish has a purpose in *The Trouble with Principle*: he considers the influence of liberal procedural universalism on public policy debate in American society to be baleful because it teaches us to replace our specific reaction to specific situations with a set of abstractions that, according to Fish, clouds and inhibits those specific reactions; he therefore wants us to embrace the world as he sees it, a world where contingent situations are all we have, a world where we cannot take refuge in comforting abstractions. This world clearly looks more inviting to us if Fish can portray it as a world just like the world we inhabit except that the illusory procedural universalism of liberalism has been excised or at least has lost its talismanic force. But if we are persuaded by Fish's arguments against the nonsituation-specific principles of liberalism, we cannot stop in the comfortable halfway house of Fish's rhetorical presentation.

Fish's arguments in *The Trouble with Principle* are more explicitly Foucauldian than Fish has ever been, in that he presents the discourse regime of liberalism as attempting to convince us of the universal or noncontingent nature of its contingent premises as part of a will to power or will to order. He then presents his own discourse as counterhegemonic:

> Liberal neutrality does political work so well because it has managed to assume the mantle of being above political work; and if you don't like the political work it is doing, you must labor to take the mantle away, strip off the veneer of principle so that policies that wear the mask of principle will be forced to identify themselves for what they are and for what they are not. (44)

One might note, parenthetically, that this comes closer to what Fish criticizes as "theory hope" than any other moment in Fish's writings, since the claim here seems to be that contingency theory can lead to critical self-consciousness, a freedom from illusion that is enabling and liberating. But my point is a different one: to employ the solvent of antifoundationalism in this way is to hit a much larger target than Fish is aiming at. The language used here against liberalism is part and parcel of the critique of Christianity as a language of pseudo-universal principles used as a mask for a will to power, a critique that descends to us from Nietzsche through Foucault and many others. The root assumption is the same in both critiques: that because there are no universals, anyone invoking a language of universals does so in bad faith, with the intent of using that language to control others subject to the illusion. The language here of unmasking and stripping off the veneer reveals Fish's indebtedness to this tradition.

Now, Fish doesn't press this case against the claims of the ethical, nor am I assuming that he wishes to. But the case he presses against the principles of liberalism, because it is an argument against principles *tout court*, necessarily activates this parallel critique of ethical principles. He doesn't pursue this critique above all because it would make the water he is seeking to attract us into much less inviting. If in order to embrace the brave new world of adhoccery all we have to lose is our commitment to the impartial procedures of liberal democracy, that's one thing. If we also have to leave on the beach our commitment to any grounding of our moral convictions, then most of us are far less inclined to jump in. If the "assertion of interests is always what's going on," if any apparent universal claim masks a will to power and to organize our situation, why indeed should we assent to the apparently universal claim that there is no grounding in principle "deeper than or higher than" the situation in which we find ourselves? What interests are asserted here? Is it in our interest to abandon the language of principle and to accept that "inspired adhoccery" is all we have? Fish cannot argue that we should accept his description of the world because it is true, because it corresponds to the way things really are, since that would imply what cannot be the case: that he alone has escaped the landscape of interested descriptions he describes. To be consistent, the argument has to be that we should assent to his description because it works for us as well as for him.

Fish's Incomplete Machiavellianism

I have argued at length elsewhere that this is not a description that actually does work, either for the profession of literary studies or for society as a whole. It is not, in my view, in our interest that we accept Fish's argument against principles, and I do not find that Fish has any good, noncontradictory reasons to accept it. But as I have explored these other angles elsewhere,[5] I'd like to explore a different issue: where Fish might have found a model for the very peculiar embrace of the language of ordinary morality that he engages in in *The Trouble with Principle*. Fish has defined an intellectual trajectory behind his antifoundationalism that draws on a fairly predictable canon of postmodernist thought, but there is nothing in that tradition that remotely resembles Fish's treatment of morality. The dominant strain in that tradition is essentially a Nietzschean critique of ethics invoked by Foucault and others in French poststructuralist thought, and there are important commonalities between this tradition and the logical positivist critique of ethical language that is another important source for Fish. A secondary emphasis in this tradition is a somewhat after-the-fact attempt to recuperate some space for the ethical that nonetheless transcends and does not endorse the "ordinary moral intuitions" invoked by Fish. I don't see in Nietzsche or Heidegger or

Derrida or Levinas or Lyotard anything like Fish's simultaneous apparent endorsement of ordinary moral perceptions and theoretical rejection of the grounds these perceptions need to claim.

There *is* a model for this position, however: Niccolò Machiavelli. Machiavelli and Machiavellianism have, of course, come down to us as shorthand terms for a critical attitude toward any system of morality, and in Fish's own period of study, the English Renaissance, "Machiavel" virtually stood in for the Prince of Darkness himself. Contemporary scholarship has complicated the received image of Machiavelli enormously and usefully, reestablishing the centrality of *I Discorsi* as well as *Il Principe* in his oeuvre and establishing his indebtedness to a civic humanist republican tradition.[6] But the Machiavelli that I would suggest is important for Fish is closer to the old Machiavelli, and the key text is clearly *The Prince*.[7] That Machiavelli, however, has a much more complex attitude to traditional systems of morality than the traditional simplifications would have it. For Machiavelli, systems of morality are made by men, not by divine intervention: they are, as contingency theorists would say, "socially constructed" to achieve certain ends. The prince must see this fact clearly and not follow the dictates of ordinary morality in those cases where he needs to do evil in order to do great things:

> For there is such a gap between how one lives and how one should live that he who neglects what is being done for what should be done will learn his destruction rather than his preservation: for a man who wishes to profess goodness at all times must fall to ruin among so many who are not good. Whereby it is necessary for a prince who wishes to maintain his position to learn how not to be good, and to use it or not according to necessity. (127)

It is the last phrase that strikes the most modern note here and marks the gap between Machiavelli's actual position and crude "Machiavellianism." Machiavelli does not endorse the common morality as a given for all time and for all places but for a contingent culturally specific occasion. But that very contingency grants it a local force, which means that the astute prince ignores it at his peril—or, more properly, only where he absolutely needs to.

Here, we move into Machiavelli's classic distinction between seeming to be good and being good, which is to say the difference between inhabiting a system of morality and tactically deploying it: "It is not necessary, then, for a prince to have all of the qualities mentioned above, but it is certainly necessary that he appear to have them. In fact, I would go so far as to say this that having them and observing them at all times, they are harmful; and appearing to have them, they are useful" (147). It would be fatal for the prince to live within a system of morality, for moral codes to inhibit his action, because that might inhibit him from actions that he must take. But it is also a fatal error not to *seem* to inhabit such a system in every other situation besides those in which it is imperative to do evil: "A prince, therefore, should take great care never to say a single thing that is not infused with the five qualities mentioned above; he should appear, when seen and heard, to be all compassion, all faithfulness, all integrity, all kindness, all religion" (149). Of course, the key word here is *appear*, for it is "often necessary, in order to maintain the state, to act against your word, against charity, against kindness, against religion." That is, the prince "must not separate himself from the good, if he is able, but he must know how to take up evil, should it become necessary" (147, 149).

This necessary duplicitousness (when viewed from the perspective of traditional morality) or flexibility (as viewed by Machiavelli) finds its best statement in the classic passage on the lion and the fox, and I think this passage sums up both Fish's particular "Machiavellianism" and what is incomplete about it. Machiavelli begins this discussion with a passage known to all lawyers:

> You should know, then, that there are two ways of fighting: one with the law, the other with force: the first way is peculiar to man, the other to beasts; but since the first in many instances is not enough, it becomes necessary to resort to the second. Therefore, a prince must know how to make good use of the beast and the man. (145)

But as the passage continues, both man and beast, both guile and force, become figured as animals:

> Since a prince must know how to make good use of the beast, he should choose then the fox and the lion; for the lion has no protection from traps, and the fox is defenseless against the wolves. It is necessary, therefore, to be a fox in order to know the traps, and a lion to frighten the wolves. . . . But one must know how to disguise this [fox-like] nature well, and how to be a fine liar and hypocrite. (145)

Quoting Machiavelli is infectious, but I think the main lines of his approach should be clear. Ordinary morality is something that the prince must be able to inhabit when he can but abandon when he needs to, but he must seem to abandon it as seldom as possible. To put this in more modern terms, he must always have a meta-awareness of the provisionality and incompleteness of any system of morality, but he must never display that awareness because that would be disruptive of the public persona as a good person that he needs to maintain. The fox stays hidden inside the lion because the lion is admired in a way the fox is not.

I bring Machiavelli into the picture here both because his influence goes a long way to explain Fish's apparent inconsistencies on morality but also because Machiavelli suggests what is problematic and ultimately self-defeating about Fish's approach. The influence is above all that Fish is close to Machiavelli in the way that he invokes a conventional system of morality yet sees himself as above it and aware of its limitations at the same time. But Machiavelli tips his hand in a way that he suggests his prince should not. In other words, Machiavelli's advice to his prince and his own behavior are sharply distinct, since Machiavelli displays his meta-awareness of the situated nature of morality in a way he would advise his prince against. The prince must have this awareness but must not display it. Machiavelli can display his cynicism about morality because he is not a prince, but the prince can afford no such moments of candor, at least publicly.

Fish may have begun his career hoping to be Machiavelli—that is, a theorist who sees how things really work, sees the *verità effettuale della cosa*—but as his career has progressed, his aspirations have shifted toward the arena of action—that is, trying to get things done, trying in a sense to be a prince. This is true of his personal career, with the move first to become director of Duke University Press and then to become dean at the University of Illinois in Chicago, and it is true of his intellectual trajectory as well, as his work has engaged public policy questions such as affirmative action and as he has sought to be a player in the public policy arena. I find this move on Fish's part to be the most attractive part of his recent work, but the attempt to move from theorist to agent, from Machiavelli to prince, is beset with certain problems that the example of Machiavelli helps to pinpoint.

Machiavelli himself was famously unsuccessful in his own attempts to influence events. His dedication of *Il Principe* to Lorenzo de Medici seems to have led his republican friends to distrust him without winning him a position with the Medici, and he ended his life a political outcast, never having had the role on the Florentine stage that he would have liked: that of statesman. This could be taken as a sign that his own advice wasn't particularly good advice except for the fact that he didn't follow it. Accusations of impiety and atheism dogged Machiavelli throughout his adult life, and the point to make about this is not to wonder whether they were correct (for surely they were) but rather that this marks the difference between Machiavelli's advice and his own example. The prince is necessarily a hypocrite, aware that he is playing a role by pretending to accede to the morality around him and equally aware of everything that contingency theory might tell him about the unprincipled nature of these principles. Machiavelli recommends such hypocrisy but cannot practice it, given his role as a theoretician. But it is this very honesty, this willingness to display his meta-awareness for the benefit of his readers, that precisely displays this to his readers and prevents him from having the influence he might have wished.

Fish has, I think, strayed down the same path, with much the same results. By that, I mean that he has followed Machiavelli's example rather than his advice. It is key for a successful prince to be a fox, but the successful prince hides his fox-like nature—or, perhaps more precisely, the successful fox hides his fox-like nature. Hypocrisy is morality's name for this role playing. It is entirely to Fish's credit that he is not a hypocrite and that he is completely incapable of gaming us without then confessing that he is gaming us. But this shows how far he is from successfully inhabiting the policy world he would like to inhabit. To be specific, contemporary America even more than *cinquecento* Florence is an *ambiente* in which one must seem to be good and one must seem to inhabit the world of ordinary moral strictures. (Bill Clinton, of course, discovered this, with consequences we are all living through.) Clearly, Fish is not running for office, with all of the particular pressures forced on someone playing that role. But the theoretical meta-awareness about morality that he displays in his work reflects a similar fox-like nature failing to disguise itself as a lion. I don't think that any of those whom Fish hopes to convince that he is on their side because he invokes their moral intuitions will accept that he is on their side precisely because of the self-consciousness he displays about the situatedness of those intuitions. He is anxious to seem good, not to be good (in their terms), but he is also anxious to display to his more sophisticated, theoretical audience that this is a seeming, that he as well as we know and understand the antifoundationalist critique of morality's claim to be grounded. Unfortunately, the larger audience can catch and understand these asides as well, which means that they understand Fish's performance as a performance and are not taken in by it.

I don't know whether these remarks are to be taken as praise or dispraise, to use the Renaissance dyad. One would not have wanted Machiavelli to have followed his own advice, for then we would not have had that advice. One has to admire the *sprezzatura* of Fish's performance in arguing against free speech, against principles, against so many of the concepts we take for granted. But to admire is not the same as to agree with or to find persuasive. Fish wants but is unable to have his cake and eat it too. He wants to dazzle and to persuade, but the way he seeks to dazzle— Machiavelli's way—stands in the way of his successfully persuading us. Even if principles have only an ad hoc, contingent, or local validity, the language of principles nonetheless remains the language of political argument and persuasive discourse in our local situation. Fish's eschewal of this language renders him largely ineffectual in the public policy arena precisely because his principled commitment to the ad hoc and local runs up against our local (and perhaps ad hoc) commitment to principle. As Fish should be among the first to insist, the local inevitably trumps the general, which means that the available means of persuasion in the arena Fish has moved toward remains the language of principle. Thus, even if Fish is right in his critique of principle, his critique also suggests why that critique is unpersuasive in a context in which the language of principle remains dominant. Fish's Machiavellianism is therefore fascinatingly incomplete in a way that suggests the trouble with arguing against principle.

Notes

1. It should be noted that Taylor's invocation of "inspired adhoccery" is for Taylor himself more an ad hoc response and not the rather non-ad hoc principle that Fish constructs of it. Taylor's own work goes in a very different direction from the use Fish makes of it; see, in particular, *Sources of the Self* for a discussion of the place of the ethical much more nuanced than anything found in *The Trouble with Principle*.

2. See especially *Truth and Consequences*.

3. The line of influence from Nietzsche to French poststructuralism is fairly clear and has been widely discussed. At least as important for Fish in my view is the logical positivist critique of ethical discourse as unverifiable nonsense; the most accessible statement of this perspective is found in Ayer. It should also be said that the way I put this case reflects a Christian and Kantian view of ethical principles. Of course, there are other ways to characterize ethical principles, but I have used this language here above all because the people Fish wishes to appeal to in his invocation of morality would use this language. His appeal to them must

meet their concerns if it is to succeed, and, of course, my argument is that he does not, which is why it does not.

4. See *Who Comes after the Subject?* Also see Critchley and Critchley and Dews.

5. See Dasenbrock.

6. Key works here include those by Baron, Pocock, Skinner, and Viroli. Fish is aware of this body of work, if only from his co-residence at Johns Hopkins with Pocock.

7. One essay in which Fish cites Machiavelli is "Nice Work if You Can Get Them to Do It," and the entire essay is relevant to my argument here.

Works Cited

Ayer, Alfred Jules. *Language, Truth and Logic.* 1946. New York: Dover, 1952.

Baron, Hans. *The Crisis of the Early Italian Renaissance: Civic Humanism and Republican Liberty in an Age of Classicism and Tyranny.* 2nd ed. Princeton: Princeton UP, 1966.

Cadava, Eduardo, Peter Connor, and Jean-Luc Nancy, eds. *Who Comes after the Subject?* New York: Routledge, 1991.

Critchley, Simon. *The Ethics of Deconstruction: Derrida and Levinas.* Cambridge: Blackwell, 1992.

Critchley, Simon, and Peter Dews, eds. *Deconstructive Subjectivities.* Albany: State U of New York P, 1996.

Dasenbrock, Reed Way. *Truth and Consequences: Intentions, Conventions and the New Thematics.* University Park: Pennsylvania State UP, 2001.

Fish, Stanley. "Nice Work if You Can Get Them to Do It." *ADE Bulletin* 126 (Fall 2000):15–17.

———. *The Trouble with Principle.* Cambridge: Harvard UP, 1999.

Machiavelli, Niccolò. *The Prince.* Trans. and Ed. Mark Musa. New York: St. Martin's, 1964.

Pocock, J.G.A. *The Machiavellian Moment: Florentine Political Thought and the Atlantic Republican Tradition.* Princeton: Princeton UP, 1975.

Skinner, Quentin. *The Foundations of Modern Political Thought.* 2 vols.

Cambridge, Eng.: Cambridge UP, 1978.

Taylor, Charles. *Sources of the Self: The Making of the Modern Identity*. Cambridge: Harvard UP, 1989.

Viroli, Maurizio. *Machiavelli*. Oxford: Oxford UP, 1998.

Rhetoric, Emotion,
and the Justification of Belief

Gary A. Olson and Lynn Worsham

If anything can be said to unite Stanley Fish's interventions in so many disparate areas of inquiry, it is his belief in the centrality of rhetoric. Whether he is discussing how disciplines conduct their work, how political positions triumph, or how practice always derives from specific situations despite the grandiose theories employed to justify them, he consistently turns to the specific local, contingent context—to the rhetorical situation at play—to explain how something works. When he contends that a theory will not substantively affect the practice it seeks to elucidate, inform, or improve, he is saying that people fashion their practices within the specific constraints of the rhetorical situations they find themselves in. When he asserts that composition instructors have no choice *but* to teach situations and that they will not be able to reform writing pedagogy by appealing to theory, he is observing that they are always already located within rhetorical situations and that the very act of directing students to write to a particular audience for a particular purpose is precisely to engage themselves and their students in rhetoric. When he declares that a general principle such as fairness can be deployed as a weapon in political, legal, and ethical struggles to further the interests and objectives of one set of individuals over and against the interests and objectives of others, he is simply describing how agents operate rhetorically to achieve their ends. When he argues that despite all attempts to undergird multiculturalism with grand principles of tolerance and democracy, multiculturalism is a fact of life and the most productive response is to deal with any "problems" in their specific contexts (and that that's all we can ever really do anyway), he is insisting that all we can ever do is operate rhetorically within the specific situations that present themselves to us. As he says, rhetoric is the "necessary center," and "substantial realities are products of rhetorical, persuasive, political efforts" (qtd. in Olson 95). In fact, his insistence on the centrality of rhetoric is what led him to embrace Roger Kimball's description of him as "the contemporary sophist"—an epithet that Kimball intended to be derogatory but that Fish adopts with pride.

Conviction and the Structure of Belief

For nearly a half a century, scholars from practically every intellectual discipline have asserted a strong connection between rhetoric and epistemology. From Clifford Geertz to Thomas Kuhn, from Richard Rorty to the feminist standpoint theorists, scholar after scholar, despite their disagreements with each other on a multitude of issues, has affirmed the centrality of rhetoric in the making of knowledge. No one has been as consistent and undaunted in this endeavor as Stanley Fish. One factor that sets Fish apart from so many other writers, however, is his belief that our convictions are what have the strongest hold on us and that we then seek to justify those convictions rhetorically, not the other way around. As he comments in "Consequences," beliefs are a "prerequisite for being conscious"; they are "not what you think *about* but what you think *with*, and it is within the space provided by their articulations that mental activity—including the activity of theorizing—goes on. . . . [B]eliefs have *you*, in the sense that there can be no distance between them and the acts they enable" (326). People don't arrive at a position or belief because they have been persuaded by the logic or "reasonableness" of someone's argument; they arrive at a position or belief because it fits into the structure of beliefs already in play. They then seek the available means of persuasion to justify that belief, both to themselves and to others. Rhetoric, then, is not simply a rational, cognitive, mechanical operation as so many other scholars posit. This strong connection between rhetoric and belief is what distinguishes Fish's work.

Although Fish makes this point in a multitude of places throughout his *oeuvre,* one particularly cogent statement is "Faith Before Reason," a short essay exploring the relationship between religious faith and rational inquiry. This essay is a response to Father Richard Neuhaus, editor of *First Things: A Monthly Journal of Religion and Public Life*. Neuhaus had written a reply to Fish's "Why We Can't All Just Get Along," which had appeared earlier in that journal.[1] Fish argues that faith and reason are not in opposition; they are, in fact, mutually interdependent. Put succinctly, the difference between a believer and a nonbeliever (or any two individuals who hold differing beliefs) is not that one reasons and the other doesn't, or that one is rational and the other isn't; rather, each reasons from a central premise that the other denies. While a believer and a nonbeliever may well employ the same rules of evidence and the same kind of rational deliberation, they eventually will disagree about whether something does or does not constitute evidence, and such a disagreement cannot be settled by an appeal to the rules of reason because those rules "unfold in relation to a proposition they do not generate." In the context of a debate between a believer and a nonbeliever, the proposition "God exists or does not exist" is an article of faith, and despite the meticulousness of their adherence to strict rules of logical reasoning, both parties will necessarily end up in "completely different places" precisely because "it is from different (substantive) places that they began" (263). Each begins not from a logical argument but from a heartfelt conviction, and all logical reasoning, justification, and argumentation flows from that conviction.

Because a believer and a nonbeliever each begins from a different premise, a premise the other disavows, each will fashion any evidence that emerges into a shape that is dictated by the structure of his or her belief system. The belief system in play determines how all evidence will be read (interpreted) and how an individual will then be able to turn around and justify a belief and corresponding evidence rhetorically. In other words, we each begin from a position, a conviction, and that conviction and the structure of beliefs to which it is attached will cause us to interpret evidence in such a way as to buttress that conviction and belief system and to repulse challenges to them. We cannot rise above or step outside of our belief system in order to assess evidence or arguments. The central beliefs of a belief system—Christianity, for example— cannot be falsified or even challenged by "evidence" that a believer does not acknowledge (because of that very structure of beliefs) qualifies as evidence: "For one party, falsification follows from the absence of any rational account of how the purported phenomena (walking on water, feeding five thousand with five loaves and two fishes, rising from the dead) could have occurred; for the other the absence of a rational explanation is just the point, one that, far from challenging the faith, confirms it" (268). One's structure of beliefs is likely to be much deeper and much more compelling than any rationalizing that transpires detached from that structure.

An atheist, for example, might point to the Holocaust as clear evidence that God does not exist. If God is merciful and watches over all the world's creatures, then God never would have allowed such unimaginable atrocities to occur. Since these unimaginable atrocities did occur, then surely God cannot exist. The atheist's structure of beliefs causes him or her to receive the information about the Holocaust as confirmation of his or her belief system, and then this information becomes rhetorical support for an argument demonstrating the nonexistence of God. Confronted with information about the Holocaust, a believer might simply contend that such atrocities say more about humanity than about God and may thus dismiss such "evidence" as irrelevant to a discussion about the existence of God—as not evidence at all. Or the believer may well wrestle with the apparent contradiction between unimaginable atrocities and a merciful God, and if that believer could not simply dismiss the information as irrelevant or could not incorporate the information into his or her belief system, that individual would be in a "crisis of faith." But, says Fish, whatever that believer "did with the doubt, it will have been a doubt *for him* by virtue of what he believed and not because a challenge to his belief has come from someplace outside it" (268). Evidence (information, arguments) external to an individual's belief system is not powerful enough in and of itself to shake a person's faith or convictions; only doubt already lodged within the person's belief system would be sufficiently compelling to have such an effect.

In response to such arguments, Neuhaus contends that if an archeological expedition were to establish beyond a reasonable doubt that the remains of a certain body was that of Jesus Christ, then the truth claims of Christianity would be in grave doubt. But Fish replies that this depends on how one construes "reasonable doubt":

> If he means the kind of doubt an empirically minded nonbeliever might have, then the doubt is a foregone conclusion since it is implicit in the way he (already) thinks. "A virgin birth? A God incarnate? Give me a break!" But if Neuhaus means a reasonable doubt a Christian might have, then it would have to be a doubt raised by tensions internal to Christian belief, and not by tensions *between* Christian belief and some other belief system. (268)

The believer and the nonbeliever each adjusts incoming evidence to his or her belief system, shaping the information to support that structure of beliefs and dismissing as irrelevant anything that contradicts it. It would take much more than carbon dating to shake or topple a faith that is not founded on such kinds of evidence in the first place because carbon dating qualifies as evidence only in the context of assumptions that the believer does not share and, in fact, considers to be unequivocally wrong. Someone who believes a view to be correct simply cannot see what is seen by those who deny its very founding premises, and vice versa.

One might argue (as Neuhaus does) that people often encounter propositions that they can fully understand but that they nonetheless believe to be untrue. There is a substantial difference, however, between comprehending the literal meaning of a proposition and experiencing the truth of that utterance in a deeply heartfelt way. It is one matter to understand the semantics and syntax of an utterance; it is entirely another matter to inhabit the position that the utterance announces. These are two different senses of what it means to "understand." You might announce that you understand a statement and that it is untrue, but "understand" in this sense means that from your perspective the assertion has the form of a truth statement but no valid content: you understand it to be nothing, and consequently you understand it only in the most superficial sense—that is, you in effect do not understand it at all. Thus, in response to Neuhaus' declaration that a Christian can "understand" what an atheist is saying, Fish replies, "Sure he can: he will understand the atheist as saying error, that which is not" (270). The Christian may well comprehend the syntax and semantics of the atheist's declaration that God is a fiction, but because the believer begins from a first premise that is totally antithetical to the atheist's first premise, the Christian is unable to inhabit the position that the utterance announces—the atheist's statement, then, is truly incomprehensible to the believer, except in the most superficial way.

Believing Is Seeing

For Fish, then, people arrive at a position or belief because it fits into the structure of beliefs already in play, not because they have been swayed by the "reasonableness" of someone's argument; they then pursue the available means of support to justify that belief rhetorically, both to themselves and to others. People "understand" or are "persuaded" by a position or belief because it fits into a preexisting belief structure. This description of the relationship between faith and reason, rhetoric and epistemology is in sharp contrast to the prevailing liberal-humanist perspective that emerges from the tradition of Enlightenment rationality—a tradition that regards the mind as a kind of "calculating and assessing machine that is open to all thoughts and closed to none." In this rationalist conception, belief and knowledge are discrete and independent, and the mind is never closed, always open; in fact, committing to a value or idea in a fixed way is a sure sign of "cognitive and moral infirmity"—what is often labeled "closed mindedness" or "blind belief" ("Why" 247). Fish contends, however, that the mind must begin with a first premise, a fixed commitment to a value or idea, and this premise both enables thought about the subject at hand and is unavailable to thought precisely because it is thought's enabling condition: "One's consciousness must be grounded in an originary act of faith [about anything, not just religious issues]—a stipulation of basic value—from which determinations of right and wrong, relevant and irrelevant, real and unreal, will then follow" (247). For the liberal rationalist, the mind operates independent of any particular belief, coolly and rationally assessing contending beliefs to determine which make sense; for Fish, beliefs are the "content of a rationality that cannot scrutinize them because it rests on them," in the sense that rationality arises from beliefs and not the other way around (247). Consequently, Fish would exchange the liberal motto "Seeing is believing" for the seemingly counterintuitive "Believing is seeing," signifying that it is our beliefs that enable us to see in certain ways and not others. Furthermore, because what we see constitutes the boundary or limits of our knowledge, what we believe is coextensive with what we know (believing is knowing). And further, since we typically base our actions on what we know, then believing is acting; and since it is our actions that constitute who we are, in many ways we are what we believe. Put epigrammatically, "What you believe is what you see is what you know is what you do is what you are"—or, we are what we believe (247).

In a very real way, then, liberal open mindedness is impossible, in that we are never truly open to beliefs that flow from premises hostile to the premises and beliefs we begin with. We call a belief or position (and the person who utters it) "reasonable" when it corresponds to our own beliefs and positions. Because what we consider to be reasonable is based on a submerged core belief that itself determines what reasonableness is, we cannot subject that submerged core belief to a test of reasonableness; that would be tantamount to rising out of our own ideological perspective in order to examine that perspective from outside of itself—which, of course, is impossible. It is the ideological perspective that constitutes us and our notion of reasonableness in the first place. There is nothing outside of our structure of beliefs, then, that we can appeal to in order to validate or adjust our beliefs, no external or neutral arbiter against which to evaluate those beliefs. In fact, this is the thesis of Fish's "Beliefs about Belief." In that essay, he argues that because there is nothing undergirding our beliefs, "nothing to which our beliefs might be referred for either confirmation or correction," there is "nothing interesting to say about belief in general" (279). That is, belief is a particular, not a general; it arises out of a particular person's belief system under certain conditions and in specific contexts. There is no general way to characterize it or its operations since it is radically contingent.

Belief and Consciousness

Fish has consistently stated that an individual's belief about belief has no relationship to any particular belief the person might hold, unless the question being considered happens to be the nature of belief: "The thesis, baldly put, is that anything one believes about a particular matter is logically independent of the account one might give (and how many of us after all could give such an account) of how beliefs emerge or of what underlies them or of what confirms them or calls them into question" (280). A meta-level (theoretical) discussion of how beliefs are formed is disconnected from and of no consequence to a person's specific beliefs. One person may believe that his or her beliefs are firmly grounded in some solid foundation—God, truth, reason—and another may believe that beliefs are never supported by general principles detached from specific contexts and that if only everybody would arrive at this realization people would stop using their beliefs as the justification for social conflict, including war; however, both views somehow presume that a belief about belief can in some way have some general significance or repercussion. Neither of these two individuals' differing conceptions of the workings of belief will affect their respective beliefs; these individuals will not abandon their beliefs or alter them or exchange them or believe in them less or more firmly: "That is because there is no *relationship* between us and our beliefs; rather, there is an identity. The operations of my consciousness and the shape of my beliefs are not two entities somehow 'relating' to one another but one entity called by different names" (280). Beliefs are constitutive of consciousness and thus cannot exist independent of consciousness. This is yet another way to say that we are what we believe.

To say that beliefs are constitutive of consciousness is not to say that beliefs are groundless or have no support; rather, beliefs are supported by other beliefs in an intricate structure of beliefs, "a lattice or a web whose component parts are mutually constitutive." A person who is asked to justify a particular belief or position will immediately appeal to "the interlocking structure of understandings within which the particular belief in question seems obvious" (280, 281). Asked to support a belief about evolution, an individual would draw on theories of scientific evidence, a vocabulary of "genes" and "mutations," and a theory about the origins of life. Every fact and assumption proffered to bolster the position may in turn require support, in which case the individual would "point to those components of the picture not presently under the pressure of a demand for justification." While this process may well be circular, it is circular in the same way that the operation of a dictionary is circular: "one meaning explains another which explains another, which, somewhere down the line, is explained by the meaning with which you began" (281). We justify a belief, then, by turning to the structure of beliefs from which the belief derives its intelligibility and within which it is coherent, and we then seek to express that intelligibility and coherence rhetorically, establishing a case for the belief.

One might object to this description of a structure of beliefs and the rhetorical justification of belief by claiming that it does not account for how beliefs change. That is, if the structure of beliefs is composed of a latticework of mutually supportive beliefs and if the justification of belief is internal to that structure, what force or incentive could impel change? Fish replies that belief itself is the cause of a change in belief, and this will only seem paradoxical if beliefs are assumed to be discrete and independent entities; beliefs, however, are "components of a structure and exist in relationships of dependence and scope to one another, and among the beliefs internal to any structure will be a belief as to what might be a reason for its own revision" (281). Every individual will have his or her own threshold as to what might cause a belief to change, and there is no way to predict in advance what that threshold might be. As an example, Fish cites the case of a white supremacist who abandoned his former colleagues, renounced his previously heartfelt racist ideology, and worked to publicize the dangers of the white supremacist movement. This neo-

Nazi, whose daughter had a cleft palate, repudiated his previous worldview after his group's leader publicly denounced the physically disabled. This narrative of instant conversion illustrates that it is not possible to generalize a model of change from specific instances of change; each instance is so unique and context dependent that no useful general account of change could be extrapolated from one instance. What's more, there was no way to predict in advance that the neo-Nazi whose daughter had a cleft palate would renounce his faith; he might have responded by professing renewed allegiance to his group on the grounds that "the cause" was greater than any single individual, including his daughter. Explanations of a change in belief will always be constructed ex post facto, and no retrospective account of a change in belief will be useful in predicting what that person is likely to do in the future. Fish writes,

> Any authority, no matter how longstanding its hold on your imagination, can be dislodged in an instant, although that instant cannot be willed, cannot be planned for, and need not ever occur. But if it does, it will not be because an independent reality has presented itself in such a way that a structure of belief must simply bow to it but because embedded in that structure will be something—an allegiance, a fear, a hope—that is strongly affirmed in a crisis of decision or choice. The moment of its affirmation will be the moment at which the web of belief might undergo a basic alteration—you could leave the cult you have lived for or abandon the argument that has made your career—but the mechanics of that alteration will be entirely internal. ("Beliefs" 283)

The insularity of a structure of beliefs does not preclude the ability to change a belief; it is the very mechanism that enables the ability to change a belief.

In many ways, we have little control over our beliefs. No one shops for a belief and then consciously chooses one from an array of competing beliefs; rather, the act of believing is involuntary, more a matter of reflex than cogitation. Acquiring a belief is more akin to catching a cold than to selecting a new shirt.[2] Nor can we simply refrain from believing our beliefs through an act of will. Belief operates at a much deeper, subterranean level. This is why Fish says that we don't "have" beliefs; beliefs "have" us. To say that we don't have beliefs but that beliefs have us is not to suggest that beliefs or the actions that proceed from them are "irrational"; rather, it is to affirm that rationality—which includes the rhetorical processes of collecting evidence, providing examples and support, refuting opposing arguments, correcting errors, and so on—takes place "in the light of our beliefs." That is, belief precedes rationality. Or, put another way, rationality operates within a "context of convictions and commitments it neither chooses nor approves" (284).

If beliefs are constitutive of consciousness, if we are what we believe, then we have no access to how those beliefs operate; they are not accessible to the conscious mind, since access would assume that we could rise above them. The fact that we cannot rise above them is precisely why we can't, through an act of will, choose or reject or analyze them. Most importantly, it is only within our belief system that "deliberation occurs and evidence becomes perspicuous and reasons persuasive" (284). That is, rhetoric transpires within—in fact is enabled by and in turn helps justify—a belief system. Far from the simple mechanical process of marshaling the available means of support, rhetoric arises from and is part of the complex workings of an intricate web of beliefs altogether unavailable to consciousness. Rhetoric, then, is truly fundamental to how humans operate in the world. This is why Fish and others like him are moving rhetoric from "the disreputable periphery to the necessary center," for if the "highest truth" for any given person is what that person believes it to be,[7] then the skill that justifies belief and "therefore establishes what, in a particular time and a particular place, is true, is the skill essential to the building and maintaining of a civilized society. In the absence of a revealed truth, rhetoric is that skill" ("Rhetoric" 480).

Belief and Emotion

However central rhetoric may be in Fish's view of epistemology, there is one facet of the theory and practice of rhetoric about which he has little to say: the role that emotion plays in constituting belief and knowledge and in producing conviction and persuasion. Fish never explicitly addresses the role of emotion in epistemology or rhetoric, yet emotion is *there* in his concept of rhetoric and knowledge—implicit, unacknowledged, and unstated. When Fish claims that all reasoning, justification, and argumentation flow from a "heartfelt" conviction, he suggests, without explicitly articulating, a relationship between affect and belief. When he claims that we don't "have" beliefs but that beliefs "have" us, he brings into the discussion an unacknowledged notion of emotion that gives belief its power to possess the believer. Indeed, emotion is the missing term in Fish's critical lexicon, the term he needs in order to explain what makes a conviction "heartfelt" and a belief system compelling, perspicuous, and tenacious.

Fish is right to say that people don't just arrive at a position or belief because they have been persuaded by the logic or reasonableness of an argument; he is right to argue that people arrive at a position or belief because it fits in a preexisting structure of belief; and he is right when he claims that they then may seek to justify that belief rhetorically, to themselves or others, by utilizing other beliefs in the selfsame belief system. However, what he does not acknowledge is the role that emotion plays in the formation of belief and in the process of persuasion and justification. Consciousness begins, as Fish argues, with a heartfelt conviction; he does not tell us what makes a conviction heartfelt, what additional element is in play to secure the "stipulation of basic value" that grounds consciousness. Perhaps emotion has a stronger hold on us than does belief and gives the mind its first premise. Perhaps what inaugurates the mind is, as numerous psychologists and psychoanalytic theorists have argued, an early and fundamental affective mapping of the individual psyche that arguably begins even before birth. This affective mapping provides a rudimentary emotional orientation—or, in Fish's terms, "a stipulation of basic value"—that then makes possible a distinction between "inside" and "outside," "good" and "bad," "clean and unclean," "proper" and "improper," "real" and "unreal." This mapping provides the basis for the subsequent creation of an intricate and sophisticated structure of beliefs.

In other words, consciousness is composed not only of a structure of beliefs; it is composed of, and by, what Silvan Tomkins calls an "ideoaffective organization" (see Magai and Haviland-Jones 5-12). According to Tomkins, each individual is such by virtue of a particular ideoaffective system, or a structure of interrelated emotions and beliefs. An ideoaffective system itself arises from recurrent and salient affective "scenes" that take place over the course of an individual's lifespan, although a given emotional disposition is formed early in life through an affective mapping of the psyche that occurs before an individual acquires language (5; Worsham). This emotional disposition tends to shape all subsequent experience. In this view, emotion is central: emotion shapes and frames the content of thought as well as the process of thinking; it filters information and organizes experience; it is the active agent of consciousness and identity. A given ideoaffective system, composed of belief and emotion, will predispose an individual to see the world in certain emotionally colored ways and to assimilate new information into the existing system. It predisposes the individual to a particular course of action, reaction, or response. Likewise, it disqualifies from the outset (or renders "irrational") other possibilities of perception, interpretation, and action. Not only does rationality arise from beliefs, as Fish argues, but it arises, more accurately, from the particular structure of emotion and belief that makes a conviction heartfelt. Rationality and the practice of justification thus include more than the rhetorical processes of collecting evidence, providing examples, refuting opposing arguments, and correcting errors. Rationality operates within a context of convictions, commitments, and their emotional valences and arises from this context.

This view of the interrelation of emotion and belief explains what Fish fails to explain: the reason why acquiring a belief is more akin to catching a cold than to selecting a new shirt, why we have little control over what we believe. The reason we cannot simply refrain from believing our beliefs through an act of will, the reason the act of believing is involuntary, is that belief has more to do with emotion than it does with reason or will. The deeper, subterranean level at which belief operates—the sense that we don't "have" beliefs and that instead beliefs "have" us—is the more originary level of affect. In other words, the way in which beliefs have possession of us is through the workings of emotion. Stated in still other words, beliefs always have affective valences (just as emotions always have their "reasons"), and they are linked in complex, variable, and largely unpredictable ways to other beliefs and their affective valences in an intricate ideoaffective structure that arguably distinguishes one individual from another. Thus, the "content" of one's belief about the world or about the trustworthiness of other people is in large part affective and not merely cognitive, and it is linked to the "content" of other beliefs in an intricate "lattice" or "web," to use Fish's terms, whose component parts (emotion and belief) are mutually constitutive of what we typically mean by "individual identity."

Emotion, then, is not the opposite of reason. Nor is it simply the engine that provides the raw energy for a structure of belief; emotion is a constitutive part of the system. We are not only what we believe; we are also what we feel. Fish comes very close to suggesting something along these lines when he discusses the mechanics through which a change occurs in a person's belief system or what we have called an ideoaffective system. Fish explains that when change does occur it is because "embedded in that structure will be something—an *allegiance*, a *fear*, a *hope*—that is strongly affirmed in a crisis of decision or choice. The moment of its affirmation will be the moment at which the web of belief might undergo a basic alteration . . . but the mechanics of that alteration will be entirely internal" (283; emphasis added). In Fish's view, then, when change does occur, there is something internal to the system (a belief, an emotion) that forms the condition of possibility for change to occur.

Let's return for a moment to the case of the white supremicist who abandoned his heartfelt racist ideology and publicly repudiated the neo-Nazi movement of which he was a member after the group's leader denounced the physically disabled. We might speculate, absent further information, that this man's affection for his disabled daughter actually trumped his belief in white supremacy. We might speculate ex post facto (speculation after the fact is all we can do here) that his affection for his daughter had a prior (i.e., deeper and more particular) claim on him than did his belief in the more abstract, impersonal tenets of racist ideology. We might speculate that his identity (his ideoaffective organization) was more thoroughly regulated by his investment in his role as father and protector of his child than by his investment in his role as symbolic father and self-appointed protector of his race. We can imagine him saying, by way of justification of his actions, "I love my daughter and believe in her right to live much more than I love or believe in the cause of white supremacy," just as we can imagine him saying the opposite. Granted, his change of heart and mind need not occur. That is, an understanding that emotion plays a key role in an ideoaffective system, or that it plays a key role in a change in that system, does not enhance our power to predict future action. Instead, we might conclude that emotion gives belief a sense of heartfelt conviction; that emotion and belief precede and give rise to what, in that system, counts as "reason"; and that rationality not only takes place "in the light of our beliefs," as Fish has argued, but also in the color, so to speak, of our emotional dispositions.

Emotion, as we have suggested, provides the basis for the formation of a given belief system; thus, what Fish calls a "structure of belief" is more accurately termed an ideoaffective structure. This structure enables us to see in certain ways and not others; it determines what counts as evidence and what we will ultimately deem "reasonable." Argumentation, justification, and deliberation flow from this structure, from the unpredictable way in which affect gives conviction and belief a heartbeat. We cannot step outside of or rise above our own ideoaffective system in order to assess evidence or judge arguments independently of that system. The insularity of an ideoaffective system does not preclude a change in belief or affective ties, although beliefs are much more susceptible of change than are their underlying affective valences. This view moves emotion, along with belief, from "the disreputable periphery to the necessary center" of epistemology and rhetoric, and moves us well beyond the prevailing liberal-humanist perspective that emerges from the tradition of Enlightenment rationality.

Notes

1. Although the essay reprinted in *The Trouble with Principle* is titled "Faith Before Reason," the original was titled "A Reply to Richard Neuhaus." Neuhaus' essay was entitled "Why We Can Get Along."

2. In this discussion, Fish cites philosopher John Heil, who wrote that "acquiring a belief is equivalent to catching a cold" (283).

3 . In the preceding phrase, Fish is paraphrasing Protagoras.

Works Cited

Fish, Stanley. "Consequences." *Doing What Comes Naturally: Change, Rhetoric, and the Practice of Theory in Literary and Legal Studies*. Durham: Duke UP, 1989. 315–41.

————. "Beliefs about Belief." *The Trouble with Principle*. Cambridge: Harvard UP, 1999. 279–84.

————. "Faith Before Reason." *The Trouble with Principle*. Cambridge: Harvard UP, 1999. 263–75.

Magai, Carol, and Jeannette Haviland-Jones. *The Hidden Genius of Emotion: Lifespan Transformations of Personality*. Cambridge, Eng.: Cambridge UP, 2002.

Olson, Gary A. *Justifying Belief: Stanley Fish and the Work of Rhetoric*. Albany: State U of New York P, 2002.

Worsham, Lynn. "Going Postal: Pedagogic Violence and the Schooling of Emotion." *JAC* 18 (1998): 213–45.

Contingent Universals
and Rhetorical Pragmatism

Steven Mailloux

What you believe is what you see is what you know is
what you do is what you are.

—Stanley Fish

Can the complex reality of particular situations be cap-
tured by the abstract vocabulary of so-called universals?
No, in thunder.

—Stanley Fish

When Jerry Falwell blamed the events of September 11 on the pagans, the abortionists, the feminists, the ACLU, the gays and lesbians, and the People for the American Way, we witnessed one religious fundamentalism reacting to another. When the American Council of Trustees and Alumni condemned liberal professors for their cautionary comments regarding counterterrorism, we saw an intolerant patriotism responding to critiques of such patriotism. When a few cultural commentators linked academic postmodern relativism to the tolerance of dangerous fundamentalist ideologies, we heard radically different accounts of the current political scene offered by public intellectuals. My point in citing these various disagreements is not simply to continue the blame game but rather to suggest how better to understand it. I start by focusing on the relation between religious beliefs and postmodern theory and then briefly address problems with communication among contemporary intellectuals and lay publics. Finally, I turn to the issue of universals in the rhetoric of appeals for tolerance and understanding.

My way of proceeding will be through something I call "rhetorical hermeneutics," a cultural tracing of the rhetorical paths of thought in the public sphere.[1] This cultural tracing looks especially at the relation of rhetoric and interpretation, of using language and making sense in various cultural sites. Here, I do some rhetorical hermeneutics with the comments following close upon the tragedy of September 11. Of course, reactions to the attacks included not only the immediate public interpretations of the events and the rhetorical efforts to affect future action but also other cognitive, emotional, and (I have no other word for it) spiritual responses to the deaths, to the terror, to the shock, to the lingering chaos of thought. It is some of these other responses—related to what Kenneth Burke called "attitudes" and what Raymond Williams called "structures of feeling"— that I want to take into account in sorting through the cultural rhetoric of the post-September 11 environment.

Postmodernism and Universals

Let me begin by defining a couple of terms. These definitions are a bit skewed, since I will be trying to link them from the first to certain issues of rhetoric and interpretation. Today, the term *fundamentalism* often refers to a religiously held set of mutually-supportive beliefs and practices, including radical criticism of secular modernity, Manichean narratives of communal identity, selective interpretations of scriptural texts, rhetorical intolerance of ideological disagreement, charismatic leadership and zealous discipleship, and profoundly intense commitment to action for the cause. Various scholars of "religious fundamentalism" have complained about the slipperiness of the term, but most often they agree that it remains the most useful way to refer to the family resemblances among certain antimodernist movements within a wide range of traditional religions, including Christianity, Judaism, and Islam.[2]

Postmodernism is an even more difficult term to define than *fundamentalism*. Because I am tracing the rhetorical function of words in cultural conversations after September 11, I will point here to some uses of the term *postmodernism* by its critics and by academic theorists often labeled postmodernist by the national press. Shortly after the terrorist attacks, columnist Edward Rothstein wrote in the pages of the *New York*

Times that he hoped those events would lead to a rejection of postmodernism and its own "rejection of ideals and universals": "In general postmodernists challenge assertions that truth and ethical judgment have any objective validity." Rothstein claims that postmodernism is "partly an attempt to question the fundamental philosophical and political premises of the West," and it argues "that many of the concepts we take for granted—including truth, morality, and objectivity—are culturally 'constructed.'" As mere cultural constructions, they cannot provide us with the "transcendent ethical perspective" needed to judge events like those of September 11. Indeed, says Rothstein, when postmodern logic is taken "to its most extreme conclusions," and especially when it is combined with postcolonial theory, "the rejections of universal values and ideals leave little room for unqualified condemnations of a terrorist attack, particularly one against the West." Rothstein calls for an end to this "Western relativism of pomo."

In response to charges that "postmodern relativism" leaves us unable to condemn terrorist attacks, some so-called academic postmodernists objected that it just isn't so. Writing in the same *New York Times*, Stanley Fish explains, "Postmodernism maintains only that there can be no independent standard for determining which of many rival interpretations of an event is the true one. The only thing postmodern thought argues against is the hope of justifying our response to the attacks in universal terms that would be persuasive to everyone, including our enemies." We can still condemn terrorist attacks, just not in absolutist terms. Fish goes on to argue that "Invoking the abstract notions of justice and truth to support our cause wouldn't be effective anyway because our adversaries lay claim to the same language. . . . Instead, we can and should invoke the particular lived values that unite us and inform the institutions we cherish and wish to defend." Fish shifts the focus from the transcendental criteria of evaluation to the contingent rhetoric of effective response. Rothstein believes that the latter requires the former, Fish that the latter remains possible despite the loss of the former.

I pretty much agree with Fish on the theoretical and practical points he makes; that is, I am persuaded by his rhetorical pragmatist account of postmodernism and the rhetorical strategies he advocates. But I do think that he strangely misses something crucial: the full rhetorical force of the ideas hovering around the term *postmodernism* for some modernist academics and for many nonacademic commentators. It is, of course, helpful for Fish to point out the precise use of the term *postmodernism* among some academic thinkers, especially the limits on belief and practice built into postmodern theory thus understood. In this thinking, recognition, toleration, and acceptance are always contingently limited; the question is necessarily where do the limits end? And that is an empirical, historical question depending on the other beliefs and practices in place. I agree with Fish that no single metabelief (belief about beliefs), no antimodernist, modernist, or postmodernist theory can trump all the other beliefs in the communal set, loosening them up so radically that just anything goes, including the toleration of fundamentalist ideologies inspiring acts of international terrorism. But I think Fish fails to appreciate two things: first, that there are emotional or attitudinal effects resulting from the acceptance of even this conservative postmodernism for anyone who converts to it; and second, whatever the logical (non)connection between postmodernism (as he defines it) and other beliefs and practices, there may be rhetorical effects of advocating this or that philosophical theory in the public sphere—for example, more or less toleration of competing ideas. Of course, these two points are related. Let me illustrate.

Say you are a believer in Roman Catholicism. Perhaps one of the reasons you accept the Roman Catholic faith is that you not only believe in its doctrines but also that you believe that your doctrinal beliefs are absolutely true. If you then lose your philosophical belief in absolutism, it is at least possible that your other beliefs could be weakened, even if you further believed with Fish that beliefs about beliefs have no logical, necessary consequences.[3] For some people, a belief can be weakened not *logically* but *rhetorically* by the effects of new experiences, including being scandalized by someone you admire who holds a belief you also hold or by being persuaded that the philosophical status you once gave to your belief (that it was true absolutely) is no longer tenable.

It is all well and good for Fish to say that there is no logical connection between, say, absolutism and other beliefs, or postmodernism and other beliefs, but the transformation of a philosophical belief in absolute truth into a belief in postmodernism might have other rhetorical effects on related nonphilosophical beliefs. Though it is doubtful that deeply held beliefs about ethics or politics would be significantly affected by changes in beliefs about the metaphysical status of those beliefs, it is unpredictable what the attitudinal or emotional changes might turn out to be in the short or long run. Fish sometimes seems to suggest that there are no degrees in belief—we either hold them or we don't—but certainly we can hold beliefs (or be held by beliefs) more or less strongly, with more or fewer consequences for future beliefs and actions.[4]

This rhetorical relation between beliefs and metabeliefs becomes even clearer when a doctrinal statement of the first-order belief is accompanied by a statement about the second-order belief. For example, in the early 1960s Pope John XXIII supported his advocacy of specific human rights with the assertion of a general philosophical foundation. Noting that every human being had the "right to live, to bodily integrity and to the means necessary for the proper development of life . . . particularly food, clothing, shelter, medical care, rest, and, finally, the necessary social services," the Pope argued further that these rights are "universal and inviolable" (*Pacem*, par. 11, 9). That is, he grounded these rights in "the existence of a moral order which is transcendent, absolute, universal and equally binding upon all" (*Mater*, par. 205). If a later Pope had gone postmodern and renounced the absolutist and universalist second-order beliefs, would not the case for the first-order beliefs in specific human rights have potentially been weakened for at least some Catholics?

All of this is to say (again) that although there are no necessary, logical connections between practice and theory, between belief and metabelief, there are still contingent, rhetorical connections. It is these latter that Fish misses and Rothstein might be bringing to our attention.[5] Now, I must further point out that it is an empirical matter whether Rothstein is right. Is the rhetorical effect of postmodernism—however it is understood—a toleration that makes reactions to fundamentalism less decisive or responses to international terrorism of any kind less effective? I just don't think so.

The disagreement between academic postmodernists and their journalist critics brings up another issue worth noting. Let me make a rather extreme analogy, for which I apologize in advance: fundamentalists are to nonfundamentalists as academic intellectuals are to public intellectuals. What I mean to suggest here is that it sometimes seems as difficult for academic specialists and nonacademic commentators to understand and talk to each other as it is for, say, religious fundamentalists and secular humanists to communicate. In both cases, the academic scholars and the religious fundamentalists make sense of their worlds and talk their talk using special words, concepts, theories, arguments, tropes, narratives, and other pieces of group-specific rhetoric not shared outside their communities. This distinctive rhetoric—a part of their identities constituted by particular shared desires, beliefs, and practices—can seem opaque to outsiders, the nonacademic intellectuals in the one case and the nonfundamentalist public in the other case, even when concerns for similar intellectual or religious issues are held in common.

Of course, my analogy between academic specialists and religious fundamentalists soon breaks down, if ever it worked in the first place. It most immediately breaks down in the United States over the issues of expressive freedom and pluralistic toleration. But it also misfires because academic intellectuals usually see themselves not merely as witnessing to a nonacademic public and certainly not as absolutely condemning (or destroying) that part of the public that does not agree with them; rather, they see themselves or their professions as needing (at some point) to communicate with that public in ways it understands. Some academics take on the role of public intellectual to achieve that goal and to intervene actively in the public sphere in areas both inside and outside their areas of professional expertise.[6] This well-worn issue of the relation between the academy and the larger society is relevant once again in our post-September 11 rhetorical context: What exactly is the relation of academic intellectuals to the U.S. citizen and government responses to September 11—to support for the Patriot Act and the War on Terrorism, for example?

Here we can turn to another recent commentator on reactions to 9/11 events, Edward Said, whose rejection of "false universals" is cited by both Fish and Rothstein, though to very different ends. Rothstein approves of Said's continued belief in "universal principles like 'human rights'" but decries his postcolonial critique of "false universals," those "ideological confections" for legitimating "corporate profit-taking and political power." Fish, on the other hand, ignores Said's advocacy of a certain kind of universalism and simply approves of his rejecting "false universals" because they "stand in the way of useful thinking." Fish explains that universalist appeals to good and evil are rhetorically inadequate. Mantras like "We have seen the face of evil" are at once "inaccurate and unhelpful," according to Fish: "We have not seen the face of evil; we have seen the face of an enemy who comes at us with a full roster of grievances, goals and strategies. If we reduce that enemy to 'evil,' we conjure up a shape-shifting demon, a wild-card moral anarchist beyond our comprehension and therefore beyond the reach of any counterstrategies" ("Condemnation").

Fish's rhetorical advice is part of his more general antifoundationalist critique of various universalisms. He rejects appeals to "abstract universals," whether positive ones such as "fairness" and "individual rights" or negative ones such as "racism" and "hate speech" (qtd. in Olson 131–32). Positive universals are empty and must always be filled in by particular instantiations that are not universal but local, not neutral but interested, not transcendentally general but politically specific. Positive formal universals can never serve the guiding function they claim for themselves: the claim is that "abstractions like fairness, impartiality, mutual respect, and reasonableness can be defined in ways not hostage to any partisan agenda." According to Fish's anti-universalism, any attempt "to define one of these abstractions—to give it content—will always and necessarily proceed from the vantage point of some currently unexamined assumptions about the way life is or should be, and it is those assumptions, contestable in fact but at the moment not contested or even acknowledged, that will really be generating the conclusions that are supposedly being generated by the logic of [universal] principle" (*Trouble* 2–3).

According to Fish, if positive universals are empty, negative universals are nonexistent: "If you could identify hate speech and racism as abstract universals, that would mean that everyone who was rational would be able to recognize and perhaps turn away from instances of them" (Olson 132). Is this the case? Do hate speakers accept the description of themselves as such? Fish answers, no: "They don't think they're speaking hate; they think they're speaking 'the truth.' We think we're speaking the truth. What that means is that hate speech is not the name of a general [universal] mistake; hate speech is the name of a mistake made by people who believe something that you don't believe—or, in fact, believe something that you believe to be evil or dangerous." In other words— words Fish would undoubtedly endorse—the term "hate speech" functions rhetorically like the term "ideology": ideology is what the other group espouses; my group simply speaks the truth. Insofar as ideology, racism, and hate speech refer not to misguided viewpoints but to contrasting rationalities, Fish dismisses sympathetic reeducation of one's enemies and recommends instead aggressive opposition: "These people are not in need of your therapeutic help; they are in need, from your point of view, of being defeated. It's *that* simple. Therefore, what you should try to do is defeat them" (132).

More generally, Fish recommends moving away from universalist vocabularies and asking a different set of questions, empirical questions such as, "What's working? What's not working? What's going to happen if we allow these practices to continue? What's going to happen if certain changes aren't made? Do we want these things to happen? If the answer is 'no,' then there are certain actions we are going to have to take. What are those actions?" (131). These are practical and pragmatist questions, practical in not being based on universalizing theories and pragmatist in making judgments by looking toward the effects of actions. They are also, I submit, rhetorical hermeneutic questions insofar as the judgments made are based on interpretations of past conditions and future probabilities, and those interpretations and resulting judgments are rhetorically enmeshed in the persuasive arguments, enabling tropes, and grounding narratives of the specific times and places of their rhetorical performance. These empirical questions, Fish argues, are quite different from the traditional universalist queries: "Does it correspond to the requirement for fairness?" or "Is it content- or viewpoint-neutral (as if anything ever was)?" (131). Here, Fish makes a political as well as an antitheoretical argument. Not only are universals philosophically empty or nonexistent, they are in the present rhetorical context politically retrograde. Universalist questions "will not serve those who wish to move ahead in general in some progressive way because the content of those terms—'individual rights,' 'fairness,' 'color-blindness'—has now been fashioned by the very agendas that progressives oppose" (131).

In contrast to Fish, Said continues to see political usefulness in the vocabulary of universalism. Fish and Said do agree on the same *negative* point in criticizing "false universals," a rhetorical point about how appeals to "counterfeit universals" are "designed to create consent and tacit approval." These false universals are intended to prevent discussion rather than encourage it. "Ideological confections" such as "*the* West" or "the clash of civilizations" are "deployed not as they sometimes *seem* to be—as instigations for debate—but quite the opposite, to stifle, pre-empt and crush dissent whenever the false universals face resistance or questioning" (Said, "Public" 31). Said thus sees careful, rigorous rhetorical analysis as a primary responsibility of today's intellectuals: "The intellectual's role is first to present alternative narratives and other perspectives on history than those provided by the combatants on behalf of official memory and national identity—who tend to work in terms of falsified unities, the manipulation of demonized or distorted representations of undesirable and/or excluded populations, and the propagation of heroic anthems sung in order to sweep all before them" (34).

These observations by Said were made prior to September 11, but in his comments immediately after the attacks he continued to push the same rhetorical point: "Demonisation of the Other is not a sufficient basis for any kind of decent politics, certainly not now when the roots of terror in injustice can be addressed, and the terrorists isolated, deterred or put out of business. It takes patience and education, but is more worth the investment than still greater levels of large-scale violence and suffering"

("Islam"). Believing intellectuals have an important role to play in that education, Said sounds postmodern when he stresses "the absence of any master plan or blueprint or grand theory for what intellectuals can do, and the absence now of any utopian teleology toward which human history can be described as moving." Given this cultural and political context, Said goes on to suggest a strategy for intellectual participation in the public sphere: "One invents—in the literal use of the Latin word *inventio*, employed by rhetoricians to stress finding again or reassembling from past performances, as opposed to the romantic use of invention as something you create from scratch—goals abductively, that is, hypothesizes a better situation from the known historical and social facts" ("Public" 34). Such rhetorical invention is what Said does when he goes against the postmodernist grain and continues to appeal to notions of "universality" and "human rights." These appeals are what Rothstein notes but Fish ignores (at least in the *New York Times* piece) about Said's work.

In his Oxford Amnesty Lecture a decade ago, Said remarked on Partha Chatterjee's call for "a new universality" and lamented that the dominant formulation of universalism had been produced by "the Western community of nations presided over by the United States" and was based on old forms of political and cultural nationalism. "Now, however, it has given itself an internationalized and normative identity with authority and hegemony to adjudicate the relative value of human rights. All the discourse that purports to speak for civilization, human rights, principle, universality, and acceptability accrues to it" in such a way that "we now have a situation . . . that makes it very difficult to construct *another* universality alongside this one." To achieve an alternative construction, Said calls for "a renewed sense of intellectual morality": "For the intellectual, to be 'for' human rights means, in effect, to be willing to venture interpretations of those rights in the same place and with the same language employed by the dominant power, to dispute its hierarchy and methods, to elucidate what it has hidden, to pronounce what it has silenced or rendered unpronounceable" (*Reflections* 429–30).

Said's belief in universal human rights explains his criticism of one of the postmodern thinkers that Rothstein also criticizes, though again their critiques serve different purposes. For Rothstein, Richard Rorty is simply one of those postmodernists who has "challenged objective notions of truth" and led to the relativism he deplores; but for Said, Rorty is one of those who takes the "ultrapostmodern position" that "human rights are 'cultural things,' so that when they are violated they do not really have the status accorded them by such crude foundationalists as [Said], for whom they are as real as anything else we can encounter" ("Public" 32). But both Rothstein and Said miss important aspects of Rorty's rhetorical pragmatism. Like Fish, Rorty has tried many times to explain why he rejects the charges of relativism supposedly entailed by the anti-objectivism Rothstein criticizes. For example, in his most recent book, Rorty writes, "Insofar as 'postmodern' philosophical thinking is identified with a mindless and stupid cultural relativism—with the idea that any fool thing that calls itself culture is worthy of respect—then I have no use for such thinking. But I do not see that what I have called 'philosophical pluralism' entails any such stupidity.... The difference between pluralism and cultural relativism is the difference between pragmatically justified tolerance and mindless irresponsibility" (*Philosophy* 276).

Said sees appeals to universal human rights as a crucial rhetorical strategy, not only for encouraging understanding but for actively promoting peace and justice throughout the world. Rorty, in contrast, eschews such rights talk insofar as it buys into a "human rights foundationalism" that assumes "the existence of a universal human nature" (*Truth* 170). This essentialist assumption has led to the long "philosophical search for commonality" among different human beings. Pragmatists such as Rorty want us to give up this search for a common, universal human nature. Pragmatists

> think that moral progress might be accelerated if we focused instead on our ability to make the particular little things that divide us seem unimportant—not by comparing them with the one big thing that unites us but by comparing them with other little things. . . . Convinced that there is no subtle human essence which philosophy might grasp, [pragmatists] do not try to . . . rise above the particular in order to grasp the universal. Rather, they hope to minimize one difference at a time—the difference between Christians and Muslims in a particular village in Bosnia, the difference between blacks and whites in a particular town in Alabama, the difference between gays and straights in a particular Catholic congregation in Quebec. The hope is to sew such groups together with a thousand little stitches—to invoke a thousand little commonalities between their members, rather than specify one great big one, their common humanity. (*Philosophy* 86–87)

One might question the practicality of this particularist plan on a global scale, but the rhetorical strategy of redescription of difference in order to achieve toleration and cooperation within and across groups is not unrelated to the kind of rhetorical invention that Said advocates. Said's point, and it is a point well taken, is that redescriptions that leave out the potent terminology of human rights are much less likely to achieve the goals Rorty wants.[7]

But however much Said and Rorty disagree over the usefulness of rights talk, they strongly agree in their shared antireligious secularism. In his response to the 9/11 terrorist attacks, Said not only encourages intellectuals to analyze critically the "political rhetoric" in the United States that "fling[s] about words like 'terrorism' and 'freedom' . . . large abstractions" that "have mostly hidden sordid material interests." He also calls on intellectuals to adopt a "secular consciousness" that needs to be felt in both the United States and the Middle East: "No cause, no God, no abstract idea can justify the mass slaughter of innocents, most particularly when only a small group of people are in charge of such actions and feel themselves to represent the cause without having a real mandate to do so." Cautioning all participants in the post-September 11 aftermath to remember that "there isn't a single Islam: there are *Islams*, just as there are Americas," Said goes on to argue,

> The trouble with religious or moral fundamentalists is that today their primitive ideas of revolution and resistance, including a willingness to kill and be killed, seem all too easily attached to technological sophistication and what appear to be gratifying acts of horrifying retaliation. . . . Instead of getting a wise leadership that stresses education, mass mobilisation and patient organiza-tion in the service of a cause, the poor and the desperate are often conned into the magical thinking and quick bloody solutions, . . . wrapped in lying religious claptrap. ("Islam")

Rorty also sees himself as a secular intellectual. In fact, Rorty has at times used such a self-identification to distance himself from the label of "postmodernist." He writes, "These days intellectuals divide up into those who think that something new and important called 'the postmodern' is happening, and those who . . . think we are (or should be) still plugging away at the familiar tasks set for us by the Enlightenment." Rorty identifies with the politics (if not the metaphysics) of the latter group, who "typically see the secularization of public life as the Enlightenment's central achievement and see our job as the same as our predecessors': getting our fellow citizens to rely less on tradition, and to be more willing to experiment with new customs and institutions" (*Philosophy* 168).

Neither Said nor Rorty has much use for figuring out how to employ religious traditions for contemporary philosophical or political purposes in the public sphere. Both endorse the separation of church and state, structurally separate in democratic and other political formations and rhetorically separate in any debates over public policy. Rorty views religion in public discussions to be a sure conversation stopper, while Said sees religion as encouraging intolerance and exacerbating economic, political, and social injustice throughout the world. Neither considers religious traditions to be much of a resource either for effective redescription of political issues or for rhetorical invention by intellectuals in the public sphere.

Events, Subjects, Truths

In contrast, the atheist French philosopher Alain Badiou has used at least one such tradition (Pauline Christianity) in exactly this way to propose reconceiving universalism in the political debates of the contemporary world. Badiou's immediate comments on the 9/11 attacks resembled those cautions about uncritical patriotism that were made by some U.S. academic intellectuals and then criticized as unpatriotic relativism by some journalists and by Lynn Cheney's American Council of Trustees and Alumni. In an interview, Badiou condemned "the terrible criminal attack in New York in September, with its thousands of casualties" but then added, "If you reason in terms of the morality of human rights, you say, with President Bush: 'These are terrorist criminals. This is a struggle of Good against Evil.' But are Bush's policies, in Palestine or Iraq for example, Good? And, in saying that these people are Evil, or that they don't respect human rights, do we understand anything about the mindset of those who killed themselves with their bombs?" ("Evil" 74).

Badiou raises these questions in creatively rethinking the nature of evil and the truth of universals. I can only hint at the broad scope of Badiou's philosophical project, but I hope I can say enough to suggest the potential rhetorical power of his theory of events and universals. Whereas Rorty argues against notions of universal human rights and Said argues for their political necessity, Badiou separates universalist appeals from rights talk. In several books over many years, Badiou has provided the theoretical explanations that make such rhetorical strategies especially useful for thinking and acting within our post-September 11 present.

Badiou proposes a complex philosophy of the event: an unpredictable event emerges out of a situation, and as the event is named, a truth-procedure develops in response. That truth-procedure includes a commitment to the event, a "yes" to it that constitutes an individual as a subject arising from the event. This commitment to the truth of the event, this fidelity, this faithfulness of the subject is all important. Truth, for Badiou, is not a proposition that corresponds to a preexistent state of affairs; rather, truth is something that happens and must be maintained (a view, I think, similar to that found in the pragmatist tradition). These events, subjects, and truths are of four types: political, scientific, artistic, and amorous. For example, the American Revolution requires the ongoing commitment of a democratic subject for the political truth of democracy to continue; a love encounter requires the persistent fidelity of the loving subject; the Galilean scientific revolution required a paradigmatic shift of belief and practice constituting an experimenting subject; and so on.

To put this another way and more fully, in the beginning was the event, but only after the emergence of the words naming the event and a saying "yes" to it. Something like this paradox drives a central argument of Badiou's provocative intervention into contemporary philosophy. He calls for an end to the End of Philosophy and proposes its new grounding in a return to the antisophistry of Plato, the name given to "the first philosophical configuration" that composed the procedures of truth "in a unique conceptual space." But "return" may be the wrong word, for Badiou's is not the traditional "Back to Plato" exhortation; rather, his philosophy works through the anti-Platonism of the last century and comes out the other side. He does not attempt to recapture a Platonic One but recognizes the suasive force of (what he calls) the "Great Modern Sophistry" and its postmodern championing of Heraclitean multiplicities. However, his metaphysical multiplicity, his "Platonism of the multiple" is not abstractly generalized in some ideal absolute. Instead, it is particularized as "a 'situation,' a state of things, any presented multiple whatsoever" (*Manifesto* 103, 36).

A situation is partly structured by the dominant opinions and knowledges that make "veridical statements" possible. But Badiou reserves the term "truth" for the product of truth-procedures that are initiated by the naming of an event that emerges in a situation: "As long as nothing happens, aside from that which conforms to the rules of a state of things, there can admittedly be cognition, correct statements, accumulated knowledge; there cannot be truth." Truth arises only through generic procedures—truth operations "identifiable as such in their recurrence"—

that "specify and class all the procedures determined thus far which may produce truths (there are but scientific, artistic, political and amorous truths)." These truth or generic procedures emerge after an event that supplements a situation, and this supplement "can neither be named nor represented by referring to the resources of the situation (its structure, the established language naming its terms, etc.)." Rather, it is "inscribed by a singular naming, the bringing into play of an *additional signifier*," such as "the American Revolution" or "the consummate love of my curious life" (my examples, not Badiou's), and it is "the effects *on the situation* of this bringing into play of an 'additional-name' which will weave a generic procedure." Out of the four generic procedures—the scientific, the artistic, the political, and the amorous—comes the specific truths of a situation (*Manifesto* 33–37).

Badiou offers his philosophy of the event as a counter to what he sees as the postmodern relativism of much contemporary philosophy. I cannot take up here my disagreements with Badiou's limited interpretation of postmodernism. I have in other places suggested alternative perspectives on ancient and postmodern sophists that respond to the charges of sophistic relativism.[8] These perspectives include the rhetorical pragmatism I have been elaborating in this essay. What I want to focus on here, however, is Badiou's entirely different tack, a perspective on univeralism that he has recently illustrated through a detailed reading of Saint Paul's epistles.

In *Saint Paul: la fondation de l'universalisme*, Badiou illustrates how the Christian subject is constituted out of Paul's proclamation of the Word. This subject says "yes" to the event of Christ's Resurrection and stays committed to that "yes" through his or her beliefs and practices, attitudes and passions, the truth-procedures of the Christian faith. This committed subject of Pauline Christianity is particular, and the religious truth maintained is singular. However, Paul's Christian subject is both singular *and* universal. As the Apostle to the Gentiles, Paul intended his teachings for everyone; he committed himself to the truth-procedure of preaching the Word to all. Thus, argues the atheist Badiou, the Christian subject is a universal subject, addressed to all thinking beings and assuming all to be thinking beings. This universal subject is unprecedented in history.

It is in this way that Badiou begins to reconceive the role of universalism. Universals are neither pregiven metaphysical absolutes nor simply preestablished ideal commonalities. Rather, they are singular truths emerging out of commitments to historical events, and they involve the rhetorical claim of being addressed to all human beings. The good—political or otherwise—consists of these evental truths, and evil is the obstruction of these truths. Or, as Badiou puts it,

> A Truth is the subjective development of that which is at once both new and universal. New: that which is unforeseen by the order of creation. Universal: that which can interest, rightly, every human individual, according to his pure humanity (which I call his generic humanity). To become a subject (and not remain a simple human animal) is to participate in the coming into being of a universal novelty. That requires effort, endurance, sometimes self-denial. . . . There is Evil each time egoism leads to the renunciation of a Truth. . . . Egoistic self-interest carries one away, risking the interruption of the whole progress of a truth (and thus of the Good). ("Evil" 72)

Of course, such redefinitions of universals don't easily solve all the problems I have been discussing in this essay, problems concerning the contemporary rhetorical scene of post-September 11 debates over religious fundamentalism, academic postmodernism, and the role of intellectuals in those debates. But Badiou's thinking does illustrate one of the ways academic, public intellectuals try to offer new understandings and new vocabularies for discussing problems in the public sphere. In this case, differences among Fish, Rorty, Said, and Badiou about universals point to further critical articulations that need to be made as we come to terms with the political consequences of 9/11. Their public thinking requires us to attend to how the rhetoric of academic theorizing travels across different cultural domains; how different kinds of intellectuals need to address not only the specific logics but also the more general rhetorical effects of their vocabularies and theories; and how passionate commitments to truths and the usefulness of universalist appeals constitute part of that rhetorical terrain. All of this needs to be brought to bear as we explore the limits of tolerance, the necessity of judgment, and the inevitability of action.

Separating Absolutes from Universals

From a rhetorical hermeneutic perspective, an exploration of these issues emerges first from an interpretation of the rhetorical exchanges I have described throughout this essay—the critiques, responses, assertions, citations, and elaborations of Rothstein, Fish, Rorty, and Said in the 9/11 aftermath. I have focused on the significance of the vocabulary of "human rights" and the topoi of "universals." I have suggested that Badiou's philosophy of the event provides an especially suggestive theory for developing further a rhetorical pragmatist take on universalism. In fact, one might say that Badiou's evental philosophy is an ontological supplement to pragmatism, while pragmatism is a rhetorical supplement to his evental philosophy.[9] Evental philosophy gives a historical account of the believing subject posited by pragmatism; it suggests a way to understand the being-in-the-world of the practical agent who has said "yes" to an event to which he or she tries to stay faithful. Conversely, pragmatism gives a rhetorical account of how the believing subject thinks and acts within this commitment to the truth of an event.

The primacy of belief is central to both accounts. At least in one place, Fish (like Badiou) uses Pauline Christianity to elaborate what he terms (unlike Badiou) "the postmodern lesson" that the story we humans enact is "underwritten by nothing firmer or more 'objective' (independent) than the inner conviction of those who live it out." Quoting Paul's Epistle to the Hebrews, Fish notes how we, like Abraham, "act on the basis of a faith that is its own foundation ("On other surety none"): 'By faith Abraham, when he was called . . . obeyed; and he went out, not knowing whither he went'" (Foreword xviii). There is nothing outside our web of beliefs that transcendentally grounds our actions: "No brute data available and perspicuous apart from our belief provides independent warrant for that belief." When that belief meets counterevidence, "you either recharacterize that evidence so that, despite appearances, it becomes a reason for persisting, or you respond by abandoning your faith for another, itself no more securely anchored in public and independent controls, no more *sure*, than the faith you now regard as error" (xviii–xix). Or, as Fish asks and answers elsewhere, how can Christianity (or any set of religious or nonreligious beliefs) be falsified for a believer? Fish argues that

> the central beliefs of Christianity cannot be falsified (or even strongly challenged) by evidence that would not be seen as evidence by those who hold the beliefs. For one party [of non-Christian skeptics], falsification follows from the absence of any rational account of how the purported phenomena (walking on water, feeding five thousand with five loaves and two fishes, rising from the dead) could have occurred; for the other [the Christian

believers] the absence of a rational explanation is just the point, one
that, far from challenging the faith, confirms it. (*Trouble* 268)

Counterevidence is counterevidence only in light of sets of assumptions,
webs of beliefs, ensembles of accepted practices, and so forth; and "no
believer will find his faith shaken by evidence that is evidence only in the
light of assumptions he does not share and considers flatly wrong" (268).
It is within these rhetorical conditions of possibility that a believing
subject thinks and acts as an agent committed to the truth of an event.
Thus, despite their different views of postmodern sophistry and universalist truth, Fish's rhetorical antifoundationalism nicely complements
Badiou's evental philosophy, and vice versa.

Moreover, there might still be a way to salvage a certain rhetorical
pragmatist use for the notion of universality. We can start by separating
"absolutes" from "universals," absolutes as metaphysical concepts from
universals as rhetorical and interpretive productions. Absolutes are
philosophical concepts foundationally, transcendentally, unconditionally
supporting specific judgments. The philosophical tradition that
postmodernism questions usually associates "absolutes" with "universals," as in the encyclicals I cited from Pope John XXIII. As a rhetorical
pragmatist, I'm suggesting a disarticulation, a separation of "absolutes"
from "universals." Universals, in my sense, are not philosophical notions
at all. They are actual or perceived commonalities, empirically not
metaphysically established as rhetorical resources for supporting specific
beliefs and practices at specific times and places. They are socio-historical
singularities rhetorically and hermeneutically determined as common
across different groups. In specific cases of appealing to these contingent
universals, such as promoting peace and social justice or preventing the
killing of innocent civilians, there will always be contingent questions that
are simultaneously interpretive and rhetorical. In a specific case, can a
universal be empirically established as such? And even if it can, can it be
successfully invoked in an appeal based, for example, on socio-psychologi-
cal motives and pragmatic probabilities (others do it, or others found it
effective, or similar reasons)?

Working out these notions of universality to increase their political
viability is an example of what Rorty and Said advocate in calling for new
vocabularies and rhetorical *inventio*. It is also, I think, what Étienne
Balibar has in mind when, in speaking of ideal universality, he says: "It is
a question, not of speaking the established language of politics, of 'playing
the game' according to its well-known rules, but of collectively breaking

through the limits of public communication by means of new language"
(72). Perhaps the rhetorical pragmatist strategy could be even more
precisely characterized as trying to play the political game in new ways
by breaking the customary rules using old words with transformed
meanings.

Ultimately, however, political acts based on contingent universals
will be grounded in the commitment, the fidelity to truth, in Badiou's
sense of that term. What this means in part is that, as horrendously
catastrophic as were the events of September 11, as individually and
collectively significant as were those terrorist attacks, our responses, our
attempts to understand and act in good faith, will be based on other events
of the kind Badiou describes. These are events of universal truth making,
events like the founding of our nation and its call for a universal
democratic subject and, for some of us, events like that embraced by one
Apostle of the Word and his call for a universal believing subject.
Answering such calls acknowledges difference but commits to a truth
addressed to all, a universality that is not found in the past but that will
be made in the future through the very acts of understanding required to
accomplish its hearing.

Notes

1. Rhetorical hermeneutics combines *rhetorical pragmatism* (in contemporary theory debates) and *cultural rhetoric study* (within disciplinary practice and
cultural commentary). See Mailloux, *Rhetorical* and *Reception*.

2. See, for example, Lawrence, and Marty and Scott.

3. See Fish, *Trouble* 279–84. Fish writes, "The thesis, baldly put, is that
anything one believes about a particular matter is logically independent of the
account one might give . . . of how beliefs emerge or of what underlies them or
of what confirms them or calls them into question" (280).

4. When not discussing the effect of theoretical accounts on specific beliefs,
Fish certainly acknowledges the varying degrees of conviction in believers.
Indeed, a believer's depth of conviction is central to Fish's account of whether
and how beliefs are challenged and changed. See, for example, *Doing* 146 and
Trouble 61, 125. Also see Olson 76–84.

5. In a more recent article, which specifically mentions Rothstein's charges,
Fish continues to make his convincing but narrowly logical point: "The claim
that something is universal [believed to be true] and the acknowledgment that I
couldn't necessarily prove it are *logically independent* of each other. The second
does not undermine the first" (emphasis added). This sentence is immediately
followed by Fish's assertion: "Once again, then, a postmodern argument turns

out to be without any deleterious consequences . . . and it certainly does not stand in the way of condemning those who have proven themselves to be our enemies in words and deeds" ("Postmodern" 34).

6. To my mind, Fish too narrowly restricts the use of the label "public intellectual" when he defines such a person as "the *public's* intellectual; that is, he or she is someone to whom the public regularly looks for illumination on any number of (indeed all) issues." He goes on to point out that "as things stand now, the public does not look to academics for this *general* wisdom, in part because (as is often complained) academics are not trained to speak on everything, only on particular things, but more importantly because academics do not have a stage or a pulpit from which their pronouncements, should they be inclined to make them, could be broadcast." Those academics who do get called upon Fish labels "'rent for a day' intellectuals or 'cameo' intellectuals—persons brought in either because they are considered authorities on a particular issue (the media equivalent of an expert witness) or because they hold a position on that same issue that can be theatrically opposed to the position of another well-credentialled professor" (*Professional* 118–19). I think Fish sets the bar a bit too high (and makes his definition unhelpfully restrictive) in thus refusing the name "public intellectual" to most academics who currently speak on public issues to nonacademic audiences through various media.

7. Again, in the case of Rorty, the connections and nonconnections between (poststructuralist or any other kind of) theory and (political or any other kind of) practice need to be carefully analyzed. I have made some initial attempts to do this with Rorty's helpful pragmatist theory and his problematic liberal politics; see "Making" and "Rhetorical."

8. See my introduction and the essays by others collected in Mailloux, *Rhetoric*.

9. I am grateful to Alain Badiou for the first half of this formulation and for additional conversations leading to the second half.

Works Cited

American Council of Trustees and Alumni. "Defending Civilization: How Our Universities Are Failing America and What Can Be Done about It." http://www.goacta.org/Reports/defciv.pdf (14 Oct. 2002).

Badiou, Alain. "On Evil: An Interview with Alain Badiou," Interview by Christoph Cox and Molly Whalen. *Cabinet* 5 (2001): 69–74.

———. *Manifesto for Philosophy.* Trans. Norman Madarasz. Albany: State U of New York P, 1999.

———. *Saint Paul: La fondation de l'universalisme.* Paris: Presses Universitaires de France, 1997.

Balibar, Étienne. "Ambiguous Universality." *differences* 7 (1995): 48–74.

Fish, Stanley. "Condemnation Without Absolutes: Postmodernism and the Reality of Terrorism." *New York Times*, 15 Oct. 2001: A19.

———. *Doing What Comes Naturally: Change, Rhetoric, and the Practice of Theory in Literary and Legal Studies*. Durham: Duke UP, 1989.

———. Foreword. *Justifying Belief: Stanley Fish and the Work of Rhetoric*. Gary A. Olson. Albany: State U of New York P, 2002. ix–xx.

———. "Postmodern Warfare: The Ignorance of our Warrior Intellectuals." *Harper's* July 2002: 33–40.

———. *Professional Correctness: Literary Studies and Political Change*. Oxford: Clarendon, 1995.

———. *The Trouble with Principle*. Cambridge, MA: Harvard UP, 1999.

John XXIII. *Mater et Magistra: Encyclical of Pope John XXIII on Christianity and Social Progress* (15 May 1961). http://www.vatican.va/holy_father/john_xxiii/encyclicals/documents/hf_j-xxiii_enc_15051961_mater_en.html (14 Oct. 2002).

———. *Pacem in Terris: Encyclical of Pope John XXIII on Establishing Universal Peace in Truth, Justice, Charity, and Liberty* (11 April 1963). http://www.vatican.va/holy_father/john_xxiii/encyclicals/documents/hf_j-xxiii_enc_11041963_pacem_en.html (14 Oct. 2002).

Lawrence, Bruce B. *Defenders of God: The Fundamentalist Revolt against the Modern Age*. San Francisco: Harper, 1989.

Mailloux, Steven. "Making Comparisons: First Contact, Ethnocentrism, and Cross-Cultural Communication." *Post-Nationalist American Studies*. Ed. John Carlos Rowe. Berkeley: U of California P, 2000. 110–28.

———. *Reception Histories: Rhetoric, Pragmatism, and American Cultural Politics*. Ithaca: Cornell UP, 1998.

———. *Rhetorical Power*. Ithaca: Cornell UP, 1989.

———. "Rhetorical Pragmatism and the Uses of Literature." *REAL: Yearbook of Research in English and American Literature* 15 (1999): 171–80.

————, ed. *Rhetoric, Sophistry, Pragmatism*. New York: Cambridge UP, 1995.

Marty, Martin E., and R. Scott Appleby, eds. *Fundamentalisms Comprehended*. Chicago: U of Chicago P, 1995.

Olson, Gary A. *Justifying Belief: Stanley Fish and the Work of Rhetoric*. Albany: State U of New York P, 2002.

Rorty, Richard. *Philosophy and Social Hope*. New York: Penguin, 1999.

————. *Truth and Progress*. New York: Cambridge UP, 1998.

Rothstein, Edward. "Attacks on U.S. Challenge the Perspectives of Postmodern True Believers." *New York Times* 22 Sept. 2001: A17.

Said, Edward W. "Islam and the West Are Inadequate Banners." London *Observer* 16 Sept. 2001: 27

————. "The Public Role of Writers and Intellectuals." *The Nation* 17 Sept. 2001. http://www.thenation.com/doc.mhtml?i=20010917&s=essay (14 Oct. 2002).

————. *Reflections on Exile and Other Essays*. Cambridge, MA: Harvard UP, 2000.

PART THREE

POLITICAL PROSPECTS

The Estate Agent:
Stanley Fish and His Trouble with Principles

Terry Eagleton

It is one of the minor symptoms of the mental decline of the United States that Stanley Fish is thought to be on the Left—by some of his compatriots, anyway, and no doubt by himself. In a nation so politically addled that "liberal" can mean "state interventionist" and "libertarian-ism" letting the poor die on the streets, this is perhaps not wholly unpredictable.

Stanley Fish, lawyer and literary critic, is in truth about as left-wing as Donald Trump. Indeed, he is the Donald Trump of American academia, a brash, noisy entrepreneur of the intellect who pushes his ideas in the conceptual marketplace with all the fervor with which others peddle secondhand Hoovers. Unlike today's corporate executive, however, who has scrupulously acquired the rhetoric of consensus and multiculturalism, Fish is an old-style, free-booting captain of industry who has no intention of clasping both of your hands earnestly in his and asking whether you feel comfortable with being fired. He fancies himself as an intellectual boot-boy, the scourge of wimpish pluralists and Nancy-boy liberals, and that ominous bulge in his jacket is not to be mistaken for a volume of Milton.

In a series of audacious bounds, then, we have argued our way from a "radical" antifoundationalism to a defense of the Free World. This leaves Fish in the enviable position of accruing cultural capital to himself by engaging in avant-garde theory while continuing to defend the world of Dan Quayle. A superficially historicist, materialist case—our beliefs

181

and assumptions are embedded in our practical forms of life—leads not only to a kind of epistemological idealism, but to the deeply convenient doctrine that our way of life cannot be criticized as a whole. For who would be doing the criticizing? Not us, since we cannot leap out of our local cultural skins to survey ourselves from some Olympian viewpoint; and not them either, since they inhabit a different culture, one incommensurable with our own. *They* may think that we are raiding their raw materials and exploiting their labor power, but that is just because they have never heard of the civilizing mission of the West. The felicitous upshot is that nobody can ever criticize Fish, since if their criticisms are intelligible to him, they belong to his cultural game and are thus not really criticisms at all; and if they are not intelligible, they belong to some other set of conventions entirely and are therefore irrelevant.

This whole discreditable epistemology rests on a number of errors. In its credulous assumption that any thoroughgoing critique would need to be launched from some metaphysical outer space, it shares the delusion of the liberalism it detests. The only difference is that whereas some liberals used to think that there was such a vantage point, pragmatists like Fish think that there isn't. Nothing has otherwise altered. To imagine that we are either the helpless prisoners of our beliefs or their supremely disinterested critic is to pose the problem in an absurdly polarized form. Here, as usual, Fish's rather stagey relish for the melodramatic theoretical gesture leads him astray. It prevents him from seeing that a certain capacity for critical self-distancing is actually part of the way we are bound up with the world, not some chimerical alternative to it. His case fudges the question of how people come to change their minds, just as it adopts an untenably monistic view of the relations between a specific belief system and particular bits of evidence. It also suggests that we cannot ask where our beliefs come from because any answer to this question would be predetermined by our beliefs.

But the belief that our beliefs are bound up with a historical form of life is itself a belief bound up with a historical form of life. Fish's penchant for the local and partisan, his aversion to human rights and abstract principles, his contempt for what he calls "mutual cooperation and egalitarian justice," his macho scorn for tolerance and impartiality— all this belongs to a very definite advanced capitalist culture, although Fish, in ironic violation of his own tenets, appears to regard such doctrines as universally valid. Perhaps it is Fish, rather than some universalist abstraction called "humanity," who is unable to distance his own beliefs and place them in a broader historical context.

Like most of his compatriots, Fish is not the most cosmopolitan of creatures. The essays in *The Trouble with Principle* deal with racism, pornography, abortion, free speech, religion, sexual discrimination—in fact, most of the stock-in-trade of enlightened U.S. academia. This, on any estimate, is a pressing agenda; but it does not betray the slightest sense that there is anything else in the political universe worth discussing. With typical American parochialism and self-obsession, Fish's book is silent about famine, forced migration, revolutionary nationalism, military aggression, the depredations of capital, the inequities of world trade, the disintegration of whole communities. Yet, these have been the consequences of the system of which the United States is the linchpin for many perched on the unmetaphysical outside of it. Being unable to leap out of your own cultural skin seems to mean in Fish's case having no grasp of how your country is helping to wreak havoc in that inscrutable place known as "abroad." One has the indelible impression that Fish does not think a great deal of abroad, and would be quite happy to see it abolished. He is strenuously opposed to hate speech, but appears utterly ignorant of the structural conditions in his own backyard that give rise to such ethnic conflict. Indeed, he champions the social and economic order that helps to breed the effects he deplores. He is rightly concerned about anti-abortion fanatics, but not, as far as one can judge, about the military, ecological, and economic threat that his country represents for so much of the world. For him as for many of his "leftist" colleagues, a good deal of morality seems to come down to sex, just as it always has for the puritanical Right.

Fish's *The Trouble with Principle*

The Trouble with Principle is a series of polemics against liberalism, and it scores some splendid points against the creed. Being something of a bruiser, and furnished with the ferociously competitive instinct of a small boy, Fish is almost pathologically allergic to cozy pluralism, and he sees shrewdly how it can spring from there being nothing much at stake in the first place. He understands how the procedural formalism of liberal doctrine can trivialize the actual content of passionately held positions, and how its tenderly sentimental equalizing of all viewpoints can mask a callous indifference. Like a traditional "virtue" moralist, he holds that what is at stake in political ethics is the substance of a way of life, not just who gets to determine it. He is alert to the bogus impartiality of a liberalism that has decided in advance what is to count as a viewpoint to be tolerated, and he is agreeably scathing about what he calls "boutique multiculturalism." Unlike many liberals, he does not make the mistake of seeing zero-sum conflict as necessarily destructive. On the contrary, he refuses to varnish the truth that there are a good many important contentions that someone is going to have to win and someone else to lose. Nor does he indulge in the liberal hypocrisy that power is ipso facto a bad thing, an opinion usually maintained only by those who have it. It is true that he might profit from relishing power a little less flamboyantly, but at least he seems to see that whether it is good or bad depends on who is doing what with it in which situation.

On the other hand, as the good liberals tend to say, Fish cannot for the life of him understand how someone can be tolerant and committed at the same time. If one cannot sit loose to one's own convictions, then tolerance can only be a sham. Fish thus detests liberalism rather as a hillbilly might detest the rococo self-qualifyings of a Jamesian New Yorker too pussy-footing and polite to say what he means. For Fish, liberals really have no balls, and his aversion to them seems quite as temperamental as it is theoretical. But tolerance is not just a question of style, and it is perfectly compatible with passionate partisanship. Fish does not see this because he too often thinks of tolerance as a psychological affair rather than a political one. If I am tolerant, however, this does not necessarily mean that I hold my own opinions lukewarmly; it means that I allow you to hold yours as fervently as I hold mine. Indeed, I am quite as passionate about this as you are about your desire to have your own view prevail at all costs. It is not, as Fish tends to suspect, that liberals are eunuchs whereas the engagé like himself are real men. Not all liberals are Laodiceans, and how zealously one holds one's own beliefs will not in itself tell us whether opposing opinions should be censored. Given the strength of my own convictions, I may find it inconceivable that others can hold the views they do, but this does not necessarily mean that I clamor for their suppression. Why she thinks Bill Clinton is a saint is a mystery, but she can broadcast the opinion from the rooftops for all I care. On the other hand, I may have quite a good understanding of what brings some people to be racists, and may well imagine myself feeling the same in similar circumstances, while firmly agreeing with Fish that racists should not be permitted to express their prejudices in public.

Phenomenologically speaking, I cannot imagine what it would be like not to believe that Bill Gates has a somewhat anemic sense of the human soul. But I can imagine the kinds of condition that would compel me to abandon this prejudice, such as his suddenly publishing a novel of such metaphysical magnificence as to put *The Magic Mountain* in the shade. The opposite of tolerance in this respect is not conviction but dogmatism; and since dogmatism means among other things refusing to elucidate the grounds on which one holds one's beliefs, Fish, for whom beliefs would seem as mysteriously given as the planet Venus, is guilty of the offense. When A.J.P. Taylor remarked that he had extreme views but held them moderately, he may have meant, as Fish would be bound to claim, that he did not really hold them at all. He was, after all, being interviewed for a Magdalen College fellowship at the time. But he may have meant that, though he indeed believed what he believed, he did not believe in pushing his opinions down people's throats, or hanging others bound and gagged from the rafters while he hectored them. Fish, by contrast, sees all conviction as necessarily authoritarian, since he imagines that the political institution of tolerance is just a fancy way of not having the courage of one's convictions. And this is the rather sinister side of his sometimes bracing critique of liberalism.

The Trouble with Principle is quite right to insist that there are views that should not be tolerated, and that free speech is thus in any absolute sense an illusion. It is salutary that no one in Britain for quite some time has been able to utter certain sorts of insult in public without running the risk of criminal prosecution. But Fish, with his usual eye for theatrical effect, enlists this for a swingeing assault on the principles of tolerance, impartiality, and mutual respect, as though the fact that they, like any principles, have to allow for important exceptions must necessarily invalidate them altogether. Nor is it anything but sophistry to claim that, since all speech acts are socially conditioned, no speech is really free. This is rather like claiming that since swanning around the Savoy all day is quite as shaped by social convention as laboring in a salt mine, guests at the Savoy are no freer than miners.

Fish dislikes principles because they are abstract, universal, neutral, formalistic, and inflexible. By defining all principle in such sublimely Kantian terms, he engages in his usual custom of straw-targeting his antagonist in order to ensure himself a Pyrrhic victory. Everyone is against *this* kind of principle, just as everyone is opposed to sin. But without certain general principles we would not even be able to identify concrete situations; and when Fish tells us, as though he were telling us news, that abstractions such as justice or equality must be further specified, he is maintaining that it is *these* abstractions that must be thickened up, rather than, say, the principle that all children under six should be tortured. To that extent, at least, he is committing himself to the language of liberalism. On his own view of things, how could he not, since he is a historical product of it?

In any case, once one begins to spell out why one wants to promote certain partisan interests, it becomes notoriously hard to avoid the language of generality altogether. Even Fish's opposition to hate speech must presumably include, somewhere along the line, the fact that the vilified group is a collection of humans rather than a bunch of hollyhocks, if one may employ a term ("human") that some pragmatists find rather distasteful. *The Trouble with Principle* veers accordingly between a tough but implausible case (all general principles are bogus) and a mild but boring one (all principles must be concretely specified, and will alter in the process), to which hardly anyone, least of all Hegel, would take exception. Like almost all diatribes against universalism, it has its own rigid universals: in this case, the priority at all times and places of sectoral interests, the permanence of conflict, the a priori status of belief systems, the rhetorical character of truth, the fact that all apparent openness is secretly closure, and the like.

Fish's appeals to history are almost always gestural. He means by history something like what Henry Kissinger means by it—that is, as far back as he can remember. This is a pity, since if he had a rather richer sense of the past he might recognize that the universalist liberal principles he abhors were once the last word in iconoclasm. In the age of Enlightenment, appeals to difference, specificity, and local interests were often enough reactionary, and claims to universality could topple princes from their thrones. For a true pragmatist, general principles are as general principles do; at some times and places they may be a lot more subversive or emancipatory than at others. And if lots of local cultures find universal principles useful things to adhere to from time to time, as they plainly do, why should a pragmatist like Fish be so universally dismissive of them?

What these essays do, in effect, is what so much postmodern thought does when confronted with a "bad" universality—which is to say, set up a "bad" particularism in its place. They fail to grasp that such militant particularism is just the flipside of the vacuous universalism it deplores, rather than a genuine alternative to it. Stanley Fish is the flipside of John Rawls, rather as tribalism is the terrible twin of globalism, or the view from nowhere is inevitably countered by the view from us alone. In this respect, Fish is a fully paid-up tribalist who, like Slobodan Milosevic, champions a unique people molded by its own peculiar customs and traditions. It is just that to Milosevic these people are known as Serbs, and to Fish as academics. One might even dub him something of a communitarian (several of his objections to liberalism, such as his view of the relations between belief and selfhood, are of this kind), were it not for the fact that he despises all such gooey human togetherness for much the same reasons that one imagines Clint Eastwood does.

Big Fish, Little Fish

In the teeth of all such soppy consensus, Fish is a Hobbesian and Machiavellian who enjoys conflict, believes only in what he can taste and handle, and likes to win. He sees his dislike of universal essences as anti-Platonic, though much of the time this is just a high-toned way of saying that he has the outlook on life of an estate agent. It is unclear how winning and intolerance go together, since you cannot be said to have beaten a rival whom you have tethered to the starting blocks; but it is clear enough how this philosophy, which Fish implicitly recommends as universally valid, fits rather better with being the dean of a U.S. university at the turn of the millennium than it does with being a sixth-century Scottish hermit.

To refer to Fish the Dean, however, is to reveal the fact that there are two Fishes, Little and Big. Little Fish is a saber-rattling polemicist given to scandalously provocative pronouncements: truth is rhetoric, free speech is an illusion, unprincipled behavior is best. Big Fish is the respectable academic who will instantly undercut the force of these utterances by insisting that they are descriptive rather than normative. Far from being radical recommendations, they simply describe what we do anyway without always knowing it, and "theory," the Trumps of this world will be relieved to learn, thus has no effect whatsoever on practice. Antifoundationalism is therefore unlikely to alienate the New York foundations, and Fish can buy his reputation as an icono-clast on the cheap.

Little Fish is in hot pursuit of a case that will succeed in alienating absolutely everyone; he is the cross-grained outsider who speaks up for minorities, and, as a Jew, he comes from one such cultural margin. Big Fish, by contrast, has a consensual, good-boy disdain for rebels, whose behavior is in his eyes just as convention-bound as those they lambast. It is fortunate for this schizoid character that there is a place where aggression and consensus go together. It is known as the U.S. corporation, of which the campus is a microcosm. In academia, you can hammer your colleagues, safe in the knowledge that, since you all subscribe to the same professional rules, it doesn't really mean a thing.

There is an evident contradiction between the self-interested behavior of advanced capitalism and the consensual character of its liberal ideologies. Into this embarrassing gap, *The Trouble with Principle* inserts its mischievous, sub-Nietzschean thesis that we should acknowledge that the God of consensuality is dead and come clean about the self-interest. So far, the system has always resisted this seductive solution to its contradiction, in the belief that hypocrisy was a price worth paying for a few rags of ideological respectability. Fish's work may be one straw in the wind turning an increasingly self-discrediting social order toward this more insolently up-front self-apologia. And if Fish is Nietzschean enough in this, so is he in the eternal recurrence of his writing. He now seems to have written the same book several times over—after you have stated that everything comes down to cultural beliefs, it is hard to know what to do next but to say it again, this time with a few different examples. Perhaps, in order to break new ground, Fish will just have to wait for his beliefs to change, as a man might await the moment when his cell door swings open.

Works Cited

Fish, Stanley. *The Trouble with Principle*. Cambridge, MA: Harvard UP, 1999.

Critical Theory and Political Action

Margaret Kohn

With characteristic bravado, Stanley Fish dismisses theory as irrelevant to matters of practical concern. His writings intervene in wide-ranging debates across multiple disciplines, and he brings to these debates an unusual combination of erudition, clarity, and acumen. His position boils down to two fairly straightforward points: first, he claims that neutral, abstract principles (such as toleration, fairness, and critical thinking) are merely ways of disguising substantive political goals; second, he insists that metacritical insights in general, and his own antifoundationalist conclusions in particular, have no political implications.

At first, Fish's iconoclasm is refreshing to any political theorist who has guiltily doubted whether every textual decentering, aesthetic gesture, and aporia contributes to transformative politics quite as much as some literary critics assume. But Fish's argument poses an important challenge to social theory in general. He insists that both foundationalist and antifounda-tionalist approaches, in different ways, fail to make any meaningful contribution to practice. In other words, political theory is an oxymoron. While it is tempting to dismiss his claim as a mere polemic, it is a challenge that political theorists must be able to answer. In an intellectual climate in which the value of humanistic studies in general and the disciplinary status of social and political theory in particular are under attack, we must be able to explain why theory matters. While this essay briefly considers the political power of universal theory, the primary purpose is to investigate the possibility of critical theory, a mode of conceptual analysis that is anchored in and contributes to particular historical processes. Thus, the goal of this chapter is to challenge Fish's provocative claim that theory has no consequences.

Fish's Antifoundationalism

In his influential essay "Political Theory as a Vocation," Sheldon Wolin poses an important question: Is choosing a theory the same as "choosing something momentous, like a self, or something innocuous, like an 'intellectual construct'?" (1075). When I first read that essay in the dark days of graduate school, I found the phrase "momentous, like a self" to be profoundly moving because it reminded me of a remote time in college when studying philosophy shattered a whole edifice of assumptions and certainties about personal identity, shared responsibilities, and social structures. Inspired by new texts and new arguments, I started to question my moral intuitions. It was a time when identity seemed both precarious and powerful and when ideas were absolutely crucial to the process of self-fashioning. Hazy and perhaps idealized as the memory of that time is, it motivates my defense of political theory as a (pro)vocation.

Fish's dismissal of theory initially appears straightforward. While he claims that theory "produces nothing," he also concedes that principles do have a certain rhetorical power (*Trouble* 4). In other words, his answer to Wolin's query would be that choosing a theory is more like selecting a wardrobe: clothing hides or accentuates particular attributes, projects a certain image, but is never constitutive of the self. Theory may serve as a ruse, an artifice, or an accouterment but never as a roadmap or a guide for the perplexed.

Fish argues that universal theorizing is a contradiction in terms, in that theory is unable to transcend its own situated political context and therefore can provide no neutral, objective analysis of political problems.[1] The trouble with principle is that in the absence of any Archimedean point from which to evaluate concrete problems, theory becomes a fraudulent attempt to disguise its own particular values in universalist language (see *Trouble* 1–15). Fish concludes that "our convictions and beliefs cannot be grounded in any independent source of authority and validation, that is, in any neutral principle, impartial algorithm, master imperative, rule, sacred text, unimpeachable authority, and so on" ("Reply" 925).

There are two problems with this first component of Fish's argument. First, it appears that he is creating something of a straw man by collapsing all of theory into one particular approach—universalist, transcendental theory—that has by now been largely discredited and abandoned. Even John Rawls, by far the most influential proponent of the kind of defense of liberal neutrality that Fish objects to, has long since modified his claims. In "Justice, Political Not Metaphysical," Rawls admits the difficulties involved in imagining an unencumbered self behind a veil of ignorance, free from the influences of experience, culture, and identity. Instead, he suggests that the veil of ignorance is a heuristic device that could help clarify the principles and practices of a liberal, democratic society (224).

Today, many liberals defend their views not in terms of universal neutral principles but as pragmatic arrangements for achieving societal consensus (see, for example, Galston 99–105). If my undergraduate students are any indication, this is how many citizens understand the liberal framework. In "Vicki Frost Objects," Fish defends a Christian fundamentalist who argued that the public school's secular curriculum violated the free exercise (of religion) clause of the First Amendment. My students agreed that Fish was right: the idea of neutrality was a fraud. A public school curriculum based on "critical thinking" does indeed foster values—pluralism, toleration, revisability—that emerge out of and sustain a particular worldview. While acknowledging that neutrality and toleration only extend to a limited set of views defined as "tolerable" (excluding, for example, the tenets of fundamentalist religion), the students felt that the curriculum was defensible—but in quasi-communitarian rather than liberal terms.

In a democratic polity, a collective endeavor like public education must reflect the values and priorities of the majority; at least in the contemporary United States, a moderately diverse curriculum would be acceptable to the largest number while alienating the fewest. Even parents who would not define themselves as liberal would have a motive to support it. From the perspective of rational choice theory, the members of any group would prefer a curriculum that defined their beliefs as true and the alternatives as false. But each group would also prefer Lockean (that is, limited) toleration to public policies that persecuted its views as blasphemy. While the doctrine of toleration contains implicit limitations and exclusions, these are more benign than open persecution. Even if fundamentalist Christians cannot veto a "secular humanist" curriculum in the public schools, they can still run private schools, churches, and associations with little interference.

In the absence of any clear majority, liberalism is the rational choice. It may be a myth, but it is, perhaps, a salutary one.

Fish is correct in insisting that illiberal views are not tolerated by theories of toleration, but this theoretical point needs to be enriched by political analysis. Most people—Marxists, deep-ecologists, fundamentalists—possess a variety of different, sometimes conflicting values. Along with salvation, they may also desire peace, stability, career advancement, and social justice. Liberal principles are just one possible mechanism for compromise. Despite its own founding mythology, liberalism did not emerge out of abstract reasoning; it was born, like the proto-liberal Thomas Hobbes himself, against the backdrop of religious wars, with bloodshed and cannons booming in the background. Hobbes insisted that the first priority of the individual was self-preservation and that the social contract was a way to set limitations upon the otherwise vast destructive potential of the human desire for glory, recognition, domination, and certainty. It is, of course, impossible to eliminate all conflict, but it is possible to mitigate it by establishing shared norms. In a slightly less dramatic fashion, many Americans continue to reach the same conclusion today.

To the degree that Fish plays the role of a gadfly, constantly reminding liberals of the inevitable imbrication of principle and power, he makes an important contribution. He is absolutely right that the self cannot be imagined in isolation from its substantive commitments and experiences. No heuristic device or conceptual framework or principle stands above the fray and outside of politics. But intervening in politics requires that we provide reasons to persuade our adversaries, and, yes, it requires principles and concepts that link together otherwise apparently unrelated facts and experiences. This is what Fish himself does when he engages in political debate. In *There's No Such Thing as Free Speech*, Fish defends affirmative action on the basis that it is a principled strategy to achieve a goal rather than just arbitrary discretion:

> What justice requires is not that each case be decided on its own merits (whatever that would mean) but that any decision reached in a particular case follow some rationally defensible set of considerations. It would be reprehensible if the decision were flatly arbitrary, traceable to no logic of selection whatsoever, but so long as there *is* a logic of selection, and one that could be justified with reference to a moral and educational vision, the individual inequities it yields will in an important sense be principled. (72–73)

And what principle will affirmative action reflect? Fish relies upon fairness, but a fairness that he acknowledges privileges the claims of some at the expense of others, a fairness with casualties. While Fish, like his opponents, relies on general principles, he does so with greater attentiveness to their contested nature, their costs and exclusions. The question of fairness is only raised when there are rival visions, conflicting interests, and mutually exclusive claims on scarce resources. It only arises in hard cases. According to Fish, "The amount of unfairness in the world can never be eliminated or even diminished; it can only be redistributed as in the course of political struggle one angled formulation of what it means to be equitable gives way to another" (73).

Does this mean that fairness is nothing but a way of disguising self- (or group) interest?[2] Not exactly. It is hard to imagine how Fish, a white male who has flourished under the older system of exclusions, would benefit from affirmative action. In fact, he tells us that he once lost a deanship based on the (legitimate) criteria of diversity. So his defense of affirmative action arises out of the conviction that it is fairer—or, more precisely, that the world would be a better place—if his egalitarian, historically contextualized approach to fairness were operative. Of course, the invocation of fairness by itself settles nothing because what divides the two sides are differing substantive views of what fairness really is. As an example of such a substantive view, he proposes egalitarian (as opposed to meritocratic) criteria. Yet, a paragraph later he claims that "all the other abstractions" (equality, justice, autonomy, diversity) are as empty as the concept of fairness ("Reply" 925). Or, rather, they are *either* empty and meaningless pretensions (when used by opponents), or they are substantive norms embedded in particular worldviews and legitimately marshaled in actual struggles (when used by Fish).[3]

There is nothing wrong with having principles, even defending them passionately, while acknowledging that they are contestable and constructed. What troubles me is the related conclusion that theory does not matter, that there is no point in reflecting upon, critiquing, and transforming these principles even though they serve as an unavoidable framework for political conversation and action. On the one hand, Fish says that principles should be rationally defensible; on the other hand, he dismisses as irrelevant the attempt to defend them. Since Fish acknowledges the rhetorical power of principles such as equality and fairness, it is impossible to avoid discussion about the meaning and applicability of these terms. If substantive, embedded norms are a fundamental part of political struggle, then they must also be challenged and defended, defined and delimited, transformed and reimagined as they are invoked in diverse situations. Fish himself does this when he insists that equality and fairness make no sense when abstracted from particular historical conditions.

So, it would seem that the issue might be a semantic one. What Fish calls "practice," I still want to call "theory."[4] Or, more precisely, I contend that theory cannot be completely separated from praxis, nor can it be dismissed. A term like "equality" would be an empty abstraction if invoking it did not always involve some claim about equality vis-à-vis particular salient features. Invoking a norm such as "equality before the law" poses the question of how it is possible to minimize the impact of manifold social inequalities such as race, gender, nationality, education, and class in the courtroom. The solutions adopted thus far—from the reasonable woman standard in sexual harassment cases to the obligation to appoint public defenders—are informed by a contestable (but also defensible) understanding of equality.[5] Not only do they bring us slightly closer to realizing the illusive goal of equality, they also transform our understanding of what equality is. Theory and practice are intrinsically linked: no theory is unencumbered by local concerns, and no reality is accessible independent of preexisting interpretive frameworks. While the two dimensions are not the same, they are constantly transforming one another.

Socialized in an intellectual tradition that draws on Marx, Nietzsche, and Foucault, most contemporary theorists understand their work to be embedded in disciplinary practices and structured by historical contexts. For Fish, this may be a correct understanding of the production of knowledge, but it still is not theory. He claims that once supplemented by local historical concerns, "theoretical terms are no longer theoretical in the claimed sense of guiding practice from a position outside or above it" (*Trouble* 287).[6] The problem is that most theories do not claim such an Archimedean viewpoint. It is puzzling that Fish defines theory as something that he himself has so compellingly proved cannot exist. While he devotes his formidable intellectual talents to proving the spectral nature of a ghost, he leaves it to others to unravel the relationship between theory and practice.

What Is Theory?

How do we arrive at what Fish calls our beliefs and commitments, our judgments and our politics? As William Galston puts it, "If the end justifies the means, what justifies the end?" (103). Fish implies that there is no meaningful answer to that question. For Fish, judgments are based on intuitions and only retrospectively justified by reasons. He insists that the "desires come first and last, and the principles, appropriately tailored, piece out the middle" (*Trouble* 161). His judges seem to inhabit a world of smug certainty, and perhaps we all do most of the time. But what happens when our certainties dissolve, when there is some complexity or tension that tests the limits of received wisdom or that is situated on the margins of the admittedly vast terrain of prejudice and self-satisfaction?

In the guise of critique, Fish actually reinforces the unsustainable distinction between principles and substantive positions (see *Trouble* 8). If I argue that affirmative action is fair because it counterbalances existing white privilege, am I articulating a substantive position or a principle? Now, suppose that my interlocutor says that it is not fair because there is no way to be sure that those who benefit from the remedy are the same people who suffered the harm. I respond that we must look at the problem of racism as a structural one: individuals who benefit from affirmative action will also serve as role models, mentors, and community leaders, thereby diffusing their individual benefit across a minority group. This conversation strikes me as a typical political discussion, and I am not sure at what point the dreaded line to abstract principle has been crossed. What starts out as a debate about affirmative action becomes a discussion of the nature of fairness. The two dimensions are intertwined yet distinct because the more expansive understanding of fairness can be used in subsequent discussions of different topics. I doubt that political argument can take place without appeal to these sorts of general concepts. Invoking a principle like fairness is not the end of political debate but the beginning. It provides a framework for discussing what fairness is and how to achieve it.

This meaning of the term "theory" becomes more confusing when Fish names "originalism" and "strict construction" as examples of the ostensibly neutral principles that provide post-hoc rationalizations of prior decisions (see "Theory Minimalism"). If these are examples of theory, then the operative definition cannot be something akin to the Platonic forms or Rawl's original position. Fish's entire case hangs on this point, since he acknowledges that "local hermeneutics," rules of thumb that are reliable most of the time, do matter. What he rejects is theory, which he identifies exclusively with "general hermeneutics," "a procedure whose steps, if they are faithfully and strictly followed, will 'always yield correct results.'" He goes on to say that strict construction is an example of general hermeneutics ("Consequences" 88). But strict construction of the constitution only tells the practitioner what kinds of questions to ask, what sorts of evidence to privilege; it does not aspire to some general, universal solution independent of reality. For example, in constitutional law a justice has to decide whether to privilege the way a word or concept was used at the founding or the way it is used today. The reasons for making this determination in one case will guide one's decision in the next. This does not mean that the outcome of any given case can be predicted by a constitutional theory. Even a judge convinced that the framers' intent is the correct standard may find that the framers themselves were conflicted and left certain provisions intentionally vague as a way to build consensus. Given the complexity of human action, our intrinsic capacity for creativity and learning, and the opacity of the human condition, it is hard to imagine any procedure that will always yield correct results.

Strict construction is a local hermeneutic. It is a name for general rules internal to the particular practice of constitutional interpretation that emerged in the context of other guiding doctrines like *stare decisis*. Theories like "semantic originalism" or "the living constitution" are ways of approaching the relationship between the constitution and contemporary conflicts. They are rules of thumb that help judges decide what the constitution requires in cases in which judicial precedent and political practices have not yielded a convincing solution. When a judge has to decide a difficult case, political preferences, theories of interpretation, and internalized understandings of the duties of the bench will collectively determine his or her decision; most of the time the resolution will not be reducible to just one of these factors. This is why judicial behavior is not predictable; there is sometimes unanimity across ideologically diverse courts, and individual judges transform their views based on their experiences on the bench.

The process of political judgment on the part of the citizen, however, is very different. We are not bound by precedent or professional norms, and our decisions are not subject to higher scrutiny. Are we guided by theory? In "The Politics of Nostalgia," J. Peter Euben explains how people are "driven to theorize by the need to make sense of a world that suddenly appears out of joint as they themselves come to feel displaced in it" (59–61). He tells the story of Peg, a mother from Iowa who lost her son to friendly fire in Vietnam:

> Peg not only became politicized; she simultaneously became "theoreticized" in the sense that the loss of her son generated a

passion to find meaning in his death by asking increasingly com-
prehensive questions about the nature of our public life. Naturally
enough the questions began with a demand for details about his
death. But they soon expanded in scope into questions about the
Vietnam War and war in general, about patriotism and democratic
accountability, and eventually to questions about American political culture and political realism. (60)

So, Fish is right that the most random events of life such as a divorce, a
text, a devastating loss, a trip to an unfamiliar place can be the occasion
for a fundamental transformation of values. But whereas Fish takes this
existential fact as evidence that theory does not matter, the opposite is the
case: in these moments of disruption and disorientation, theory becomes
important. So long as common sense continues to function, there is little
reason to reflect on the structures and meanings that underlie our shared
world. But in times of crisis, individual or collective, these certainties and
assumptions break down and we must engage in the painstaking process
of discarding them, reinvigorating them, or replacing them.

Critical Theory

Can theory provide any guidance in times of crisis? If we grant that theory
is not something universal, unchanging, and context-transcendent, can it
still make a meaningful, distinctive contribution to political judgment?
Most social and political theorists would say yes. In the absence of a
convincing account of human nature, god, or history to serve as a stable
foundation, theory becomes concerned with the constitution, structure,
and exercise of power. It involves reflection on the ways we legitimize
and criticize these processes. Legitimation or critique, however, always
implies some standard of evaluation. What if the standard of evaluation
is not yet formulated but exists in practice in a protean form? The task of
critical theory is to articulate a conceptual framework that better reflects
existing normative aspirations and political possibilities. This is not
utopian, at least not in the etymological sense of the word: far from being
no (*ou*) place (*topos*), the critique emerges out of the tensions in social
experience. Critical theory emphasizes that theory can draw attention to
submerged or confused intuitions embedded in existing practices.

An analogy from Thomas Kuhn's *The Structure of Scientific Revolutions* illustrates this point quite well. Kuhn recounts a psychological

experiment in which the subjects were asked to identify a series of playing cards (63–64). The deck that was used, however, included anomalies such as red spades and black hearts. At first, the subjects had no trouble fitting the unusual cards into their preexisting conceptual categories. For example, they identified the black four of hearts as either a heart or a spade. After increased exposure to the anomalous cards, some subjects became confused and troubled, and eventually most recognized the need for new conceptual categories. It would have been interesting to have compared the subjects' responses had they been told in advance that all decks are not the same and that some rogue states color their hearts black. While the experiment did not take this next step, it seems plausible to surmise that the subjects would have identified the cards almost immediately.

The task of critical theory is to recognize the black hearts and to find a vocabulary to describe them. More generally, critical theory attempts to provide concepts that allow people to see their social and political world in new ways. To suggest that profit is actually surplus labor rather than return on investment makes the economic world look very different. One common criticism of this strategy is that it relies on an untenable assumption about true and false consciousness, an epistemological dualism that rejects widely shared convictions as mystification. But the truth or falsity of social categories is itself a product of a system of social meanings, such as the system that Marx called "bourgeois ideology." Within the system of classical economics, it makes sense to call surplus labor "profit." The point is that there is another possible way of creating meaning from the same set of institutions and practices. Marx did not try to prove that classical economics was false; instead, he revealed how its truths reflected and sustained particular interests, the interests of the ruling class. Since opposing economic interests already pitted workers against owners, a new set of concepts was able to interpret reality and guide action. This idea of "knowledge-constitutive interests" is one of the cores of critical theory (see Habermas, *Knowledge* 296–329).

Axel Honneth defines critical theory as a normative critique that is embedded in social processes and that is "dependent upon the quasi-sociological specification of an emancipatory interest in social reality itself" (255, 256). In other words, critical theory emerges out of and transforms social and political practice. It is unapologetically partisan. Whereas Fish insists that a theory contaminated by politics is, by definition, no longer a theory, the Frankfurt School maintains that there is a necessary interconnection of the two components.[7]

Critical theory has two dimensions. It involves an immanent critique of existing practices and a reflection on transformative possibility. The first dimension is easiest to explain. The method of immanent critique as practiced by Marx was an effort to contrast the normative self-understanding of bourgeois society with the consequences of bourgeois practice. For example, he revealed how the legal freedom of exchange within the marketplace was based on sustained violent dispossession of labor power and served to reproduce relations of structural dependence. The task of immanent critique is not to juxtapose an ideal to existing reality; instead, it reveals traces of an underlying emancipatory possibility through a thorough interrogation of actual practices (see Benhabib 34).

Critical theory also encompasses a transformative dimension. "The intellectual side of the historical process of emancipation" is not simply that of commentator or cheerleader; theory must reflect upon social processes and apply such knowledge to help solve existing problems of practice (see Horkheimer 188–243). According to this vision, theory is the sedimentation of a past process of interpretation crystalized in a form that is usable in the present. Critical theory highlights the tensions between the overall framework and the perspective of individual action. Individuals often experience social structures as comparable to nonhuman, natural processes. Critical theory attempts to develop a new set of concepts that reveal rather than reify the interests that underlie and sustain these seemingly natural structures (Horkheimer 207–08). Theory provides a language and set of concepts that organize experience in such a way that the appropriate course of action becomes more transparent.[8]

Critical Self-Consciousness and Political Change

For Fish, critical theory simply is not theory: "Once supplemented, however, theoretical terms are no longer theoretical in the claimed sense of guiding practice from a position outside or above it; such filled-in terms will be *internal* to the practice and have force only for those who already move within the practice's assumptions and norms" (*Trouble* 287). But what about theories that claim to guide practice from inside? This would seem to be the only possibility, given that Fish (and many others) believe that it is the human condition to be permanently situated in webs of meaning of our own making. Can we still understand the structure and function of different regions of the web, even from the inside?

At least since Marx, much attention has been devoted to *Ideologiekritik* or what I called immanent critique above. This tactic has by no means been the exclusive possession of Marxists. In fact, a version of *Ideologiekritik* has become the central preoccupation of poststructuralists inspired by Michel Foucault's genealogical method. According to Foucault, genealogy is a history of the discursive frameworks that structure contemporary practices. It excavates modern forms of knowledge/power in order to uncover the contingency of their foundations. Genealogy reveals today's certainties as an early epoch's contested possibilities. By breaking the discursive lock of dominant forms of knowledge, Foucault's followers (myself included) hope indirectly to open up the conceptual space for a new politics. While genealogy and immanent critique are not the same, they both try to reveal the way that principle disguises power.[9] According to Fish's logic, they are both based on the myth of critical self-consciousness. It is this "characteristically left error of assuming that an insight into the source of our convictions . . . will render them less compelling" that Fish seeks to expose (*Doing* 395). According to Fish, the insight that contingent interpretive constructs underlie our perceptions does not change our perceptions, nor does it diminish the intensity of our commitments.

Fish gives two reasons why this "critical self-consciousness" does not change anything (*Trouble* 233–38). He argues that the operative power relations are what matter, not perceptions. Recognizing contingency does not make us desire change, much less make transformation more possible. I take this to mean something like the following: after reading Pierre Bourdieu's *Distinction*, a young scholar may realize that her appreciation of Thai food and Indian tapestries actually reflects her desire to distinguish herself from her petit-bourgeois origins without exceeding her limited budget. This realization, however, does nothing to change her taste in food and décor, let alone her modest income. Nor does it cause her to question the academic values and identity into which she has been socialized. Fish also insists that the idea of critical self-consciousness relies on an objective standpoint of critique. He criticizes Bonnie Honig and Chantal Mouffe for arguing that power is ubiquitous while naively believing that this insight will somehow diminish its effects (*Trouble* 234).

While the first argument has some merit, the second is less compelling. To reiterate a point that I made above, if there is no Archimedean point outside of politics, then you unavoidably must assess and transform political structures based on internal standards. To deny this possibility would be to deny politics itself because it would imply total paralysis, a world in which there is neither thought nor action. Even without a privileged standpoint, our theories can help us to see new things, recognize connections, highlight tensions or inconsistencies, persuade (or identify) adversaries, and mobilize allies. Situated actors constantly engage in political argument. They use principles to try to convince others to share their views, thereby creating a viable group capable of collective action. There are numerous examples throughout history of groups that have become mobilized after finding a shared vocabulary to express moral intuitions that members had thought were the product of isolated experiences. In order to create counterhegemonic meanings and identities, individuals must present reasons why the hegemonic ones are unsatisfactory. One way to do this is to show that the dominant ideals of freedom or merit are actually structured to serve the interests of a particular class or race or gender. Such unveiling and critique can serve as a motivation for action.

Fish's mistake is that he focuses on the *general* point that every claim to truth is actually an exercise of power. The political power of theory does not come from a *general* defense of antifoundationalism; it emerges out of a whole series of *particular* interventions that denaturalize specific beliefs. For example, the realization that the hegemonic understanding of freedom and equality is the product of class interests did inspire many bourgeois intellectuals (and workers for that matter) to become active in the socialist movement. When we find out that truths we once held to be self-evident, such as women's inferiority to men, may actually be the narrow self-interest of a particular group, we are one step closer to challenging them. Of course, there are many occasions when denaturalizing received wisdom does not transform our convictions. I suspect that Fish's claim that theory does not matter is partially inspired by the widespread hypocrisy of intellectuals whose personal and even political lives seem to contradict their theories. We all know the Marxist who helps crush graduate TAs' unions and the pluralist who runs the most sectarian conferences and journals. But to grant that many factors intervene in the complex process that translates conviction into action does not mean that principle does not matter. Human nature is very complex and our convictions are embedded in deep-rooted identities, habitual practices, desires, and interests that cannot simply dissolve into thin air. While there is no formula dictating the outcome of political and moral transformation, denaturalizing the dominant assumptions is often a first step. The claim that all truths are the products of prior struggles over power may be a cliché without political consequences, but only because the abstract formulation by its very nature is anemic. The value of genealogy lies in the detailed analyses of particular regimes of power.

In *Doing What Comes Naturally*, Fish challenges the approach to critical theory taken by academics inspired by the Frankfurt school. He grants that the negative enterprise of immanent critique is coherent but concludes that the positive component is beset by an irresolvable contradiction. If critical theory is to escape the "illegitimate and imposed limitations of the prevailing modes of thought" and overthrow them, it must be guided by a theory that is itself formulated in terms of existing mystified consciousness (448). The only alternative would be to claim that theory can completely transcend the context of its own production, an idealist claim that critical theory rejects. Different strands of critical theory have dealt with this conundrum in different ways: Adorno turned to art, Habermas to language, Benjamin to forgotten historical artifacts. According to Fish, each asserts the existence of "mysterious (that is, genealogically impossible) activities and agents" with an "unimaginable capacity of standing apart from the 'prevailing realm of purposes'" (449–50). But herein lies the difference between poststructuralism and critical theory. Critical theorists sustain an ambivalent regard for reason, even while exposing its implication in processes of domination.

Adorno and Habermas have both presented arguments for privileging certain bases for criticism and consensus. In *Aesthetic Theory*, Adorno suggests that the work of art can open up a domain of experience in which domination is not the primary relationship to the outside world. Aesthetic activity confirms the possibility of a noninstrumental approach to nature and society. Habermas' discourse ethics is a more familiar solution to the same problem. He argues that the mode of social integration achieved through speech and intersubjective agreement (the lifeworld) differs from the instrumental rationality of the system. Neither of these solutions is completely satisfying, especially if art and communication are theorized as intrinsically free of power. But they do point to domains that might nurture resistance in particular historical locations.

Perhaps Fish's skepticism emerges from an untenable worldview, a tendency to see the system as a totality that requires the ability to "stand apart" in order to acquire insight. Given that modern individuals inhabit multiple subject positions and cultural locations, however, it is hard to envision a social totality. Critique emerges from tensions and contradictions within a system. Total domination and systematicity are illusory, given the intrinsically human capacity for action and invention. Between the Scylla of determinism and the Charybdis of idealism, critical theory understands human freedom as the capacity to interpret social and historical texts as tools for improving our shared world.

Fish is right, however, to point out that changing our ideas is not the same as changing reality. The realization that it may not be natural "to truck and barter" does not make capitalism go away. It does not necessarily undermine the power of capitalism at all. Different institutions and structures are more or less resistant to change. In some domains like personal identity, a new theory of subjectivity can have direct consequences (although, of course, there are still deep-rooted psychic barriers and social sanctions). Other structures, like capitalism, are less directly affected by individual transformations in consciousness. The disruptive effect of aesthetic experience or theoretical insight, by itself, is not political. Challenging ourselves and our certainties is futile if it does not culminate in action, especially collective action. To celebrate critical self-consciousness as an end in itself is a typical intellectual conceit. Critical theory recognizes that intellectual analysis by itself is fairly impotent. Only in conjunction with existing social forces will theory have political consequences. Theory is part of the process of self-clarification internal to political processes. While critical theory does not aspire to an objective, bird's-eye view of social movements, it does draw upon the resources of history, including intellectual history, to identify processes and to clarify goals.

The Convergence of Theory and Rhetoric

The final question to be resolved was already raised above: has this debate been largely semantic? At first it seems that the answer is yes, given that Fish himself acknowledges the necessity of invoking embedded principles, which he defines as "strong moral intuitions as to how the world should go combined with a resolve to be faithful to them" (*Trouble* 9). But to dismiss the issue as "merely semantic" is to underestimate the power of words. Rhetoric matters. By insisting that theory does not matter, Fish is teaching that we do not need to reflect systematically upon our moral intuitions.

Theorizing is necessary because of the distinctive character of legal, moral, and political knowledge. In "Denis Martinez and the Uses of Theory," Fish recounts a conversation between a baseball player and his coach in order to illustrate that theory has nothing to contribute to playing ball. But legal theory is not like baseball. In baseball there are stable unchanging rules of the game and clear standards for victory. It does not matter whether a successful player says that Jesus or the tooth fairy guides his swing; a home run is a home run. The same is not true in law, ethics, and politics, where the reasons provided are the basis of legitimacy. As Ronald Dworkin put it, "Denny Martinez never filed an opinion" (382). Law, by its very nature, is a matter of interpretation; it involves explaining how to apply general rules to settle disputes. The solutions to the disputes also transform the rules. In a legal system governed by the common law tradition of *stare decisis,* interpretations become part of the law itself.

While judges literally have to file an opinion, citizens implicitly do something similar. When a troubling controversy or decision emerges, they have to revisit the basis of their own moral and political judgment and to "write" a new account that resolves the tension between the old values and the new dilemma. Influential political theorists from the past provide models of ways to examine, strengthen, and challenge our moral intuitions. Compelling analogies can also help illuminate political and moral dilemmas. Through theory, past struggles over meaning can shed light on contemporary problems. More often, theory can demonstrate the inadequacy or contingency of hegemonic concepts and assumptions. The problem is that Fish frames the choice in terms of black and white: principles are "either empty—without content and therefore incapable of giving guidance to anyone in any direction—or they are already filled with the imperatives of one or another substantive norm and provide guidance of exactly the kind they supposedly outflank—partisan, interested guidance" ("Reply" 925). Where do his "strong moral intuitions" fall in this schema? If they fall into the latter camp, how should we understand the process of developing, explaining, challenging, and changing these intuitions?

In *Emancipation(s)*, Ernesto Laclau suggests a third alternative. Like Fish, Laclau believes that abstract universal principles are "empty signifiers" that have no transcendental, unchanging meaning independent of particular substantive agendas (34). At any given moment in time, however, an abstract principle like "freedom" or "justice" does have a determinate content that is the product of the traditional usage of the word. Yet, because of its abstract formulation, the principle, what he calls the "universal," also exceeds any particular content. It expresses a broader aspiration as well as a given set of policies or preferences. Because of this dual structure, it is constantly vulnerable to destabilization, to new attempts to transform the meaning. In the arena of politics, the rhetorical and theoretical dimensions converge. The arguments that we use to persuade others come to influence our subsequent normative intuitions. Furthermore, as new groups appropriate concepts like rights or democracy in service of more inclusive political agendas, they are performing a rhetorical feat. They are strategically wielding the tools of moral and political discourse while at the same time transforming the concepts themselves.

Notes

1. Fish writes that there is "no principle not already inflected with substance" and that there is "no substantive agenda that is not (in the appropriate non-neutral sense) principled" (*Trouble* 14).

2. According to Fish, "It is not that 'acting impartially' is an impossible form of behavior indistinguishable from other forms; it is rather than 'acting impartially' is an activity whose shape is a function of a partisan and therefore potentially challengeable ('you think *that's* evidence?') conception of what such an activity is" (*Doing* 439).

3. To cite just one of many examples, Fish refutes the argument that affirmative action is reverse discrimination, stating that "the reasoning works only if the two practices [Jim Crow and affirmative action] are removed from their historical contexts" (*Trouble* 30). This is very similar to the argument between Socrates and his interlocutors in the *Republic*. Is justice simply a way to disguise the will of the powerful? Does justice require treating everyone the same or appropriately responding to their differences? While the name of Plato and his theory of the forms is often invoked as the paradigmatic example of abstract, universal theorizing, many scholars of ancient thought have concluded that the Platonic dialogues actually dramatize the limitations and demonstrate the impossibility of a metaphysical approach to political theory.

4. At times, Fish seems to dismiss all theory; at other moments, he specifies that his target is only a particular kind of theory. In questions and answers after his presentation of "Theory Minimalism" at the School for Criticism and Theory in July 2000, he stated that only universal, context-transcendent claims should count as theory.

5. Kathryn Abrams relies on the work of Susan Estrich to show how theoretical arguments about the epistemological privilege of the male experience could have important legal consequences. The challenges to objectivism helped modify the legal standards employed in cases dealing with rape and sexual harassment.

6. In another recent essay, he again defines a theory of interpretation as "some general account of the process such that anyone persuaded of it would have some notion of what to do—how to proceed, how to make decisions or evaluate evidence" ("Interpretation").

7. I am using the term "critical theory" broadly. While inspired by the Frankfurt School, my understanding of the terms also draws on Marx's method of immanent critique and Foucault's notion of genealogy. For an excellent discussion of the similarities and differences between the Frankfurt School and Foucault, see McCarthy (43–47).

8. While the link between critical theory and the socialist movement conjures a whole host of controversial associations with Soviet style communism and the Marxist theory of history, the fundamental relationship between theory and practice applies to other historical and ideological contexts.

9. There are both important similarities and differences between critical theory and Foucault's genealogy. At the risk of overlooking important differences among Frankfurt School theorists as well as different stages in the intellectual trajectory of key figures like Adorno, we can outline certain elements that critical theory and genealogy share: the claim that reason is embedded in history and therefore implicated in power; a method of critique that investigates the historical constitution of apparently universal forms of authority; a conception of subjectivity that can never be opposed unproblematically to a world of independent objects; a turn to aesthetics as an alternative basis for freedom. The primary difference between critical theory and Foucault's genealogy is that the former maintains a greater emphasis on the emancipatory potential of context transcendent norms (see McCarthy 43–74).

Works Cited

Abrams, Kathryn. "The Unbearable Lightness of Being Stanley Fish." *Stanford Law Review* 47 (1995): 595–614.

Adorno, Theodor. *Aesthetic Theory*. Trans. C. Lenhardt. London: Routledge, 1984.

Benhabib, Seyla. *Critique, Norm, and Utopia: A Study of the Foundations of Critical Theory*. New York: Columbia UP, 1986.

Dworkin, Ronald. "Pragmatism, Right Answers, and True Banality." *Pragmatism in Law and Society*. Ed. Michael Brint and William Weaver. Boulder: Westview, 1991. 359–88.

Euben, J. Peter. "Politics of Nostalgia," *Vocations of Political Theory*. Ed. Jason Frank and John Tamborino. Minneapolis: U of Minnesota P, 2000. 59–90.

Fish, Stanley. "Consequences." *The Stanley Fish Reader*. Ed. H. Aram Veeser. Oxford: Blackwell, 1999. 86–113.

———. "Denis Martinez and the Uses of Theory." *Doing* 372–98.

———. *Doing What Comes Naturally: Change, Rhetoric, and the Practice of Theory in Literary and Legal Studies*. Durham: Duke UP, 1989.

———. "Interpretation is Not a Theoretical Issue." *Yale Journal of Law and the Humanities* 11 (1999): 509–15.

———. "A Reply to J. Judd Owen." *American Political Science Review* 93 (1999): 925–30.

———. "Theory Minimalism." *San Diego Law Review* 37 (2000): 761–76.

———. *There's No Such Thing as Free Speech, and It's a Good Thing Too*. New York: Oxford UP, 1994.

———. *The Trouble with Principle*. Cambridge, MA: Harvard UP, 1999.

———. "Vicki Frost Objects." *Trouble* 153–61.

Foucault, Michel. "Nietzsche, Genealogy, History." *The Foucault Reader*. Ed. Paul Rabinow. New York: Pantheon, 1984. 76–100.

Galston, William A. "The Trouble with Fish." *The Public Interest* 189 (2000): 99–105.

Habermas, Jürgen. *Knowledge and Human Interests*. Trans. Jeremy J. Shapiro. Boston: Beacon, 1971.

———. *The Theory of Communicative Action*. Trans. Thomas McCarthy. Vol. 2. Boston: Beacon, 1984.

Held, David. *Introduction to Critical Theory: Horkheimer to Habermas*. Berkeley: U of California P, 1980.

Honneth, Axel. "The Social Dynamics of Disrespect: On the Location of Critical Theory Today." *Constellations* 1 (1994): 255–69.

Horkheimer, Max. "Traditional and Critical Theory." *Critical Theory: Selected Essays*. New York: Continuum, 1992. 188–243.

Kuhn, Thomas S. *The Structure of Scientific Revolutions*. 3rd. ed. Chicago: U of Chicago P, 1996.

Laclau, Ernesto. *Emancipation(s)*. London: Verso, 1996.

McCarthy, Thomas A. *Ideals and Illusions: On Reconstruction and Deconstruction in Contemporary Critical Theory*. Cambridge, MA: MIT P, 1991.

Rawls, John. "Justice as Fairness, Political Not Metaphysical." *Philosophy and Public Affairs* 14 (1985): 223–51.

Wolin, Sheldon S. "Political Theory as a Vocation." *American Political Science Review* 63 (1969): 1062–82.

Extirpating for Fun and Profit

H. Aram Veeser

Stanley Fish's thirty years as a seventeenth-century scholar have made him a surprisingly insightful commentator on Islamic fanatics, born-again Christians, doctor-killing anti-abortionists, and politically correct multiculturalists. Not only is he a fundamentalist himself, but he makes a pretty good philosophical case that the rest of us are fundamentalists, too; it's just that some of us don't know it.

Fish is a postmodern casuist and controversialist, made from a seventeenth-century mold. His diction reawakens dark memories of that less pallid time, when heaven and hell seemed just around the next campfire and when fire itself conjured thoughts of heretics at the stake. He considers freedom of speech to be a damaging myth, and when he warns First Amendment advocates against "honoring the means above the ends and cutting the heart out of your moral vision," one is back in the sanguineous world of Jacobean tragedy, where "The Burning Babe" was a favorite poem, where a young cavalier was likely to enter, stage left, his rapier bearing his lover-sister's heart (in *'Tis Pity She's a Whore*), and where a good frontispiece was a gashed heart below a set of bleeding eyes (Richard Crashaw's "The Weeper" in *Carmen Deo Nostro*). Beyond his taste for Grand Guignol, Fish believes that words lack fixed meaning, and that is another part of his Reformation heritage. Casuistry—the art of wrenching meanings—introduced wordplay and an often tortured logic that desperate souls might use to ameliorate pressures and wriggle between the contradictory, sometimes fatal demands that the politics of religion placed on individual conscience. Words under such pressures have all the stability of squirming puppies, and Fish, who defines and respecifies keywords each time they appear, likes to play dogcatcher. A typically tautological sentence begins, "If the difference is funda-mental—that is, touches basic beliefs and commitments ..." (*Trouble* 66). His major concepts often come shrink-wrapped in their own definitions, as with "antifoundationalist theory hope" or "self-consum-ing artifacts" (the title of his book that was a finalist for the National Book Critics Circle Award). Reading him begins to resemble moonwalking: you cover a lot of ground but don't get very far.[1] Milton's prose has been described as that of a man jumping up and down in the same place, and Fish has inherited the style as well as the substance.

Fish has grown into his controversialist's role. Once known chiefly among English professors specializing in seventeenth-century studies, he has expanded his range, and today, whenever the public worries about political correctness, moral relativism, or academic freedom, Fish is available for comment. With frequent op-eds and a monthly shoptalk column in the *Chronicle of Higher Education*, Fish has followed his own advice to other critics: if you want to do work that resounds beyond the academy, get out of it. Now that he is out there, he has become something of an exiguous figure—too pro-status quo to be a Jeremiah, too academic to be a New York intellectual (besides, he lives in Chicago), too versatile for single-issue identification (he's not *the* Palestinian or *the* post-feminist). In a high-profile series of public debates, the conservative author Dinesh D'Souza attacked political correctness while Fish de-fended it. In a series of *New York Times* op-ed articles, Fish analyzed the fallacies of popular biography, examined the trial procedures at the first Rodney King hearing, condemned Alan Sokal's hoax perpetrated on the editors of *Social Text*, and justified the flip-flopping of Democrats and Republicans as they pursued and then condemned legal challenges to the presidential election of 2000. He has attacked devotion to principles; questioned the validity of such words as *fairness*, *equality*, and *merit*; condemned freedom of speech; called for censorship; lauded accountants who bend financial rules; and, in short, pressed us to take every measure that is "hostile to the interests of adversaries." He has taken up an array of topics, but if you put all his editorials and appearances together with his monthly *Chronicle of Higher Education* column, Fish emerges as having a single coherent message: we are all fundamentalists, but only some of us know it.

Fundamentalism and Exclusion

Fundamentalists believe. They believe strongly enough to act on their beliefs, and are, consequently, extremists. They believe so strongly that they act against those whose contrary beliefs they deplore. These exclusionary tendencies are not, needless to say, the characteristics usually associated with liberals, those twenty-first-century heirs of John Locke, J.S. Mill, and F.D.R. Yet, it is Fish's radical thesis that liberalism—even the liberalism of Mill's "On Liberty"—excludes, forbids, censors, silences, deports, imprisons, and indeed executes every bit as effectively as do its fanatical adversaries. His book *The Trouble with Principle* offers an illustration:

> Michael Walzer provides a concise example at the beginning of his book *On Toleration*. "I won't have much to say," he says, "about the arrangements that get ruled out entirely—the monolithic religious and totalitarian political regimes." That is, he won't have much to say about those forms of thought indifferent or hostile to the tolerance that is his subject. (162)

It pleases Fish to catch Walzer in this sleight of hand.[2] Walzer stands in for all liberal thought when he excludes, in advance, under the banner of tolerance and inclusiveness all who oppose his premise. But that failure of evenhandedness is nothing against liberals because "judgment without partiality" is "not an option for human beings and is available only to gods and machines." Fish finds it potentially self-entrapping that deep-thinking liberals can remain unaware of their own illiberal and intolerant behavior. Wishing to remain "fair," they can be bluffed into denying their own deeper convictions.

Fish is the first to acknowledge his own intolerance. Comparing himself to one noteworthy liberal, Fish writes that "Richard Rorty wants to continue the conversation of humankind. I want to end it" (qtd. in Veeser 5). Perhaps his intellectual identity as a displaced seventeenth-century pamphleteer (like Milton) explains his moral, epistemological, and aesthetic stance.

First, he has a fundamentalist morality and epistemology that derive from his scholarship on the sixteenth and seventeenth centuries. By "fundamentalist morality," I mean that he believes that we all have unshakable beliefs, even and especially those who believe in pluralism, equal time for all sides, all-inclusiveness, and multiculturalism—all of which he contends are impossibilities. By "fundamentalist epistemology," I mean his notion that we can change our minds only by trading in one belief for another. He has written a series of prize-winning books and essays about England's own heyday of fundamentalism, extremist retaliation, religious wars, and hypnotic belief—a set of topics that modern liberals would call superstition, fanaticism, and ignorance but that Fish treats with sophistication and, yes, empathy. Empathy in the sense I intend it has its very sharp edge and functions chiefly to manipulate one's opponents. Unlike other pundits, he is steeped in the classical traditions of controversy, and he thus brings an uncommon skill-set to the op-ed page.

Second, he has a fundamentalist aesthetic. He finds beauty and excitement in the ways literary authors reason and argue about fundamental issues—issues like belief, faith, salvation, and damnation. He jokes about discovering that all the Christian humanists at Yale were Jews, but now even kabbalists seem nonplussed by his fascination with sophistry and with the intricate faulty reasoning of others. Many reviewers seemed puzzled by his latest book on John Milton, with its tellingly functionalist title, *How Milton Works*. Their reservations were that Fish lacks the "very fine sensibility" that is required to read Milton well (Pritchard) and that he "does not care much for the poetry of Milton's poetry" (Vendler). They and a brace of lace-curtain Miltonists approach Fish the way Martha Stewart might enter a post-punk Long Island City squat. The obvious riposte is that Pritchard and Vendler lack the imagination to see the poetry in Milton's spiritual politics.[3]

Fish's Reformation and seventeenth-century background has helped to make him a major public intellectual. Straddling the early modern and postmodern eras, he revives a rich tradition of intellectual activism, combining his talents as controversialist and casuist and bringing along an indispensable premise, that of the true believer. Everyone in the seventeenth century was a fundamentalist, he contends. He considers belief to be single and unified; thus, he attacks interdisciplinary studies, pluralism, and critical self-consciousness.

These attacks began just as postcolonial studies and its attendant themes of split subjectivity, bi- or multinationalism, and critical self-consciousness began to acquire academic prominence. This sociological fact raises a question about the motivations behind Fish's monist epistemology. Ostensibly directed at public-sphere liberals and right-wingers, Fish's assault on ambivalence also touches elite, academic, postcolonial critics whose premise is the splitting of the subject of enunciation, the "non-dialectical middle, a structure of jointed predication," and postcolonial mimicry (see Bhabha). For *Interventions*-reading postcolonial theorists no less than school of education multiculturalists, double consciousness is a fundamental fact of life. Conferences, journals, and classes on these topics are a growth industry at the most prestigious universities, and one must ask why, as the consummate professional, Fish is not more welcoming.

Controversy and casuistry—both terms come from England during the Protestant Reformation, the locus of Fish's major scholarly achievement. Controversialists appealed to the people and circumvented Church authority, and controversial pamphlets (thanks to Gutenberg) initiated a novel populism. The Protestant Reformation and the ensuing religious wars encouraged printing, and vice versa: the vast majority of publications through the seventeenth century were religious in nature. The pamphlet wars democratized the political culture. Christopher Elwood writes,

> From the onset of the controversy over the eucharist in the mid-1530s, Catholic leaders had been extremely critical not only of Reformed interpretations and arguments but also of their habit of appealing to public opinion. By discussing complex and delicate theological matters in vernacular writings designed for a mass readership, they seemed to be placing the resolution of theological differences in the hands of an audience hardly equipped for the task. Without rescinding their condemnations of the Reformed tactics and despite a certain distaste for writing in French on theological issues, Catholic writers eventually were forced to adopt the very strategy Protestants had pioneered. By the early 1560s the need to stem the tide of Protestant propaganda successes provoked an extraordinarily large number of Catholic responses, in vernacular pamphlets and treatises, to the by now familiar Reformed claims regarding the Mass and the Holy Supper. (113)

French Catholic pamphleteering spiked between 1556 and 1561, by which time Catholics and Protestants combined were publishing one hundred documents each year. The English battle of the texts was no less intense. William Tyndale, the translator of the first English Bible, was burned at the stake for heresy by Catholic authorities, while James Bainham, a lawyer, was interrogated, tortured, and burned at the stake by no lesser a personage than Sir Thomas More, all because he refused to abjure his Protestantism. They were hardly alone: Thomas Bilney and many others went to the fire.[4] Verbal warfare flared for the next one hundred and thirty years, leading up at last to the overthrow of monarchy in England (Ben Jonson satirizes it in the figure of Zeal-of-the-Land Busy, a Puritan hypocrite, and in the game of vapours, which is "every man to oppose the last man that spoke: whether it concern'd him, or no"). Milton was the pamphleteer who most eloquently justified the execution of Charles I.

Casuistry and controversy flowered together in the poisonous soil of excommunication and absolutism. The controversy between Protestant and Catholic casuists turned into an all-out paper war. Also known as case divinity and practical theology, casuistry is "a method of adjudicating the claims of self and law" (Brown 1; see Patey 56). Catholics who were asked to swear obedience to an excommunicated monarch used casuistry to determine whether they should betray their faith or their king, endured damnation or persecution.[5] Disreputable offshoots of casuistry, such as equivocation and mental reservation, sometimes make us forget that it had its aesthetically spectacular modes, that agonizing internal debate sometimes took the highly structured and artful forms of Herbert's poetry, Bacon's essays, and Donne's meditations. "The seventeenth century can justly be called the Age of Conscience," writes an eminent cultural historian: "Certainly, there has been no period in English history when men and women were subjected to so many religious and political conflicts of duty and allegiance or responded to them in so intensely scrupulous a fashion" (Thomas 29, 44–45).

Many of the poets and writers studied by Fish were indebted to the casuistical tradition, a tradition that gave them a method for passionate reasoning (see Slights and Zagorin). The intellectually demanding poetry of John Donne was a perfect example. According to the author of a fine book about Donne's casuistry, "Resistant to fixed prescriptions and totalizing doctrine, casuistry assumes that the meaning of a text— whether legal, biblical, literary, etc.—is contingent and unstable" (Brown 12). Casuists extended these proto-deconstructionist insights to law. Consequently, they recognized that the literal interpretation of law is not always just. "It is not the bare letter of the law that wise men should stand upon," wrote the casuist Bishop Joseph Hall, "but the drift and intention of the law" (qtd. in Brown 5). Fish goes further and contends that the purpose of a law is to invite its own interpretation and therefore its self-demolition. But Bishop Hall would certainly receive the grade of "A" in any legal theory course taught by Stanley Fish.

Fish and the Popular Press

The typical pattern in Fish's journalistic writing is first to describe a rule or convention, and then to see how far it may be transmogrified to attain a higher good. It's a bit embarrassing now, after Enron, but Fish has written in his *Chronicle* column that deans should take the rules lightly and feel free to shift designated funds: "To be sure, this is often 'against the rules,' but the rules can be stretched and bent by resourceful accountants (they should be courted at every opportunity) . . ." ("Golden"). Like the casuist who warns against too slavish an obedience to the letter of the law, Fish abjures the letter of the university budget in order to achieve more essential university goals. Creative accounting has no flavor of crime, from this point of view; it is rather a demolition of false external forms, brazen idols really, that violate the truth of the spirit.

The formulas and rituals of academia can be elaborate, not to say feudal, and Fish knows by long experience in the university milieu that one must thoroughly understand false external standards in order to stretch them properly. He enumerates arguments in such a way as to deflate them. These are the twelve specious arguments against affirmative action, he will point out, or those are the four misguided complaints about postmodernism. A small but representative instance comes when he describes his superiors' reaction to his relentless empire-building at the University of Illinois in Chicago, where presidents, chancellors, and chief financial officers "will begin to think things like 'there's no end to these demands,' 'this is more than we bargained for,' 'what have we gotten ourselves into,' and 'enough is enough'" and will begin "to say things like 'let's take a pause'" ("Staying"). "This is the 'heckler's veto' argument, firmly rejected by a succession of Supreme Court decisions," he will say, exposing the sleazy rationale used after 9/11 to dismiss an Arab professor ("Is Everything").

Only an excellent lawyer can unmake the law, and given Fish's fundamentalism it would have to be a canon lawyer. A majority of Fish's op-ed essays and *Chronicle* columns identify a conventional pattern and then proceed to analyze its flaws. It's often a humorous process, but not always. Under the humorous heading might belong the formulas for offering, accepting, and refusing academic jobs: "You might think that the word 'and' should be changed to 'or'—accepted or declined—for, after all, doesn't it have to be one or the other? Well actually, no" ("Were"). Unlike the olden days, when a letter of one paragraph arrived in the mail, nowadays a protracted three-way courtship ensues, involving tests of love and requests for start-ups, centers, and even, in one case, a chimpanzee. In other *Chronicle* shoptalk pieces, we learn about other rules, patterns, and rules of thumb: the ritual character assassinations performed by higher-education reporters; the Golden Rule for academic deans (tell the truth, tell it early, and tell it often, "stopping more often than the Ancient Mariner"); the rituals of granting leaves-of-absence to faculty who have accepted (provisionally) other jobs; the typical three-stage pattern of a university trying to do something big (stage one, "sending a message": make flashy appointments; stage two, signaling that "we're not a flash in the pan": continue to make even more appointments in still other departments; stage three, "staying the course": convince now-weakening administrators of the five-year rule—namely, that it takes five years of sustained effort to build a base). All these works are designed to amuse as well as inform.

More formulas are exposed in a tragicomic, I-don't-know-whether-to-laugh-or-cry piece that details the characteristics of unhappy departments: "You know it's an unhappy department if its bylaws are longer and more complicated than many of the articles department members write" ("Probably"). Lengthy bylaws resemble what Milton calls idolatry: the substitution of external props for essential matters—or, as Fish puts it here, "procedural questions stand in for the substantive issues that are never allowed to surface." Idolatry governs the departmental merit-pay committee, where the external, false, and brazen external measure of the good is "a 'price list' of activities, awarding so much for a book, so much for a refereed article, so much for an unrefereed article, so much for a footnote, so much for an appearance at your daughter's third-grade class." Well, that's objective and fair, isn't it? No, Fish replies. "There is a perverse economy to this procedure, which assures that the scorecard of everyone's failures and humiliations—along with the successes that spread pain evenly to those who haven't had them—can be publicly displayed and given their precise monetary value down to the last penny" ("Probably"). Here, the objective rules deploy to inflict pain and humiliation without allowing the real conflicts between faculty ever to achieve resolution.

Under the heading of serious op-eds come those about conventions and rule-bound actions that threaten to destroy enterprises that deserve to live. In this group fall the essays about Rodney King, terrorism and postmodernism, the Sokal hoax, affirmative action, and academic freedom. In the King piece, one of his earliest *New York Times* op-eds, Fish discovers a trope that is common to three then-contemporary battles:

Rodney King's effort to win a settlement against the Los Angeles Police Department; environmentalists' battle to save the habitat of the piping plover; and black construction workers' suit to gain access to Philadelphia's historically white building trades. All three ran up against powerful defenses that won by dividing and subdividing history until it had no historicity left. The LAPD defense slowed down and segmented the tapes of the King beating, asking the jurors frame-by-frame, "Was *this* an excessive use of force?" Lumber outfits demanded to be shown just one plover that they had killed. Philadelphia construction companies wanted to see just one black who'd been denied work because of race. Fish shows rather brilliantly that isolation and segmentation work to erase sequence and history—the cumulative effects of thirty-two blows, the aggregate effects of deforestation, and the long-term disadvantages wrought by hundreds of years of segregation and exclusion. In each instance, the lawyers for the LAPD, lumber companies, and construction trades cynically used an apparently neutral and decent-sounding principle: the idea that proof of injury demands an intending perpetrator and an identifiable victim. The principle frustrates justice.

Fish's acquired Puritan distrust of external "neutral" principles and absolute laws enables him to see something that no other commentator could see: "No amount of *external* policing" can produce inward virtue, and "conceiving the law as an external check" will produce only an ambivalence, a split between inner and outer selves (*Doing* 400, 401). The disastrous outcomes will include deforestation, an all-white construction industry, and no relief for Rodney King. By naming and publicizing the strategy of breaking things down into ahistorical units, he may—who knows?—be helping to stop that practice.

People who fail even to master the formulas of their respective trades are the saddest cases. The fundamentalist in Fish loathes those who lack a sense of vocation and who desperately appeal to universal standards, appeals that strike his ears as magic incantations. In his piece about the uproar over the sex conference held at SUNY New Paltz in 1997, it is the university president who is reduced to supernatural invocations. By Fish's account, the conference was a pallid academic affair, but its title, "Revolting Behavior: The Challenges of Women's Sexual Freedom," caught the attention of New York's Governor George Pataki and some conservative university trustees. A mudslinging exchange between them and the institution's president followed. Fish condemns both sides as knaves and fools: on the knave side, the meddling trustees, led by Governor Pataki; on the fool side, New Paltz president Roger Bowen. The governor and the trustees are out of touch with academic matters, including scholarly interest in sex and the body, and seized the opportunity to make a cheap political killing. The governor condemned sadomasochism, Fish writes, and where will that courage take him next—to denounce the common cold? The college president foolishly defended his conference as free speech rather than establishing the value of what was actually said. Fish tells Bowen what he should have done: "When one SUNY trustee, Candace de Russy, complained that the conference 'had absolutely nothing to do with the college's undergraduate mission,' the college president, Roger W. Bowen, should have replied either, 'Yes it does, and here's why,' or, 'You're right, and I made a mistake.'" ("School"). This is, I think, perfect. Fish shows that, instead of doing his job, Bowen went on about academic freedom "and then added, as if to assure everyone that he knew trash when he saw it, that he 'personally found several of the planned panel topics to be offensive.'" Fish objects to the craven use of *offensive* ("a known weasel word"), but he objects even more to Bowen's reverential and irrelevant appeal to academic freedom. Bowen had confused "genuine judgment with the invocation of some magic phrases." Understand *magic* as another word for *idolatrous* and we have a further example of the Miltonic casuist in action.

Fish has nothing against principles so long as we don't actually believe in them. His autopsy of the 2000 presidential election discovers a savory instance of such opportunism. At first, Democrats threatened to mount a legal challenge and Republicans declared that it would be undemocratic to move the political contest to the courts. As soon as a recount seemed to put victory within Democratic reach, the two sides switched positions. Republicans mounted a legal challenge to stop the recount, and Democrats "insisted that the people and not the courts" should be allowed to decide the election. Fish considers this a crisp illustration of the trouble with principles:

> The rhetoric of both parties has been full of words like "principle" and "process" that make an implicit claim: we are not asking for what favors our side but for what is required by a nonpartisan standard of fairness. But the agility with which the two sides switched positions shows that each is really looking for the argument that has the best chance of furthering its interests. ("High-Minded")

Fish applauds this unprincipled use of principle. It illustrates his point that the principle follows the politics, not the other way around. It's not the opportunism but the embarrassment over it that is objectionable. Each party believes that its candidate deserves to win and should make any arguments that will achieve that end. The Democrats and Republicans may appear to be hypocritical, but they are not.

Democrats and Republicans are, in brief, fundamentalists, and it is apparent when they choose substance over principle. "They have their eyes on the right goal: not the implementation of a procedure that will be fair to everyone—there is no such procedure; that's why we have politics—but the victory, at least for four years, of the ideas and politics they think are essential to the health of the nation." Democrats and Republicans are essentially or fundamentally committed to a goal, and principles will not stand in their way. Fish is all for this kind of fundamentalism: "If a candidate believes in an agenda, he should pursue it politically, without rest and without apology (although apologies, if strategically offered, can be a means of pursuing it)" ("High-Minded").

Fish contends that liberals simply fail to understand the first thing about fundamentalism and that this profound imaginative failure leads to mistaken presuppositions and errors of judgment, providing no way to anticipate the adversary's next move. He differentiates himself by showing real respect for fundamentalists (they've earned it because at least they know that they believe in something). The born-again Christian mother Vicki Frost gets a respectful hearing from Fish—though not from the pluralist judge of her case—when she sues to keep her children from being taught about other religions (see "Vicki"). One month after 9/11, Fish was ready to grant that the Twin Tower hijackers had courage ("'cowardly' is not the word to describe men who sacrifice themselves for a cause they believe in"). And he corrected those who condemned the attacks on moral grounds: "Invoking the abstract notions of justice and truth to support our cause wouldn't be effective anyway because our adversaries lay claim to the same language" ("Condemnation"). And they bear other similarities to the United States, which has its own share of chiliastic visions and sectarian strife:

> What is the difference between the confident pronouncements that the Al Qaeda brand of Islam is a deviant one and the excommunications and counter-excommunications of Catholics and Protestants, and within Protestantism of Baptists, Anglicans, Lutherans, not to mention Jehovah's Witnesses, Seventh-Day Adventists, Mormons, and Mennonites? Merely to pose

these questions is to realize that the specification of what a
religion is and the identification of the actions that may or may
not be taken in its name are entirely *internal* matters.
("Postmodern").

He is exactly right about the attempts of an Ashcroft or a Rumsfeld to
adjudicate between versions of Islam. It is silly, he says, to seek universal
terms that would be persuasive to everyone—no such terms exist. He
even quotes his erstwhile rival, Edward Said, to the effect that "false
universals" should be rejected. Rather than dismiss the hijackers as
"irrational" (another such false universal), "the better course is to think
of these men as bearers of a rationality we reject because its goal is our
destruction" ("Condemnation").

If fundamentalism is rational, then rationality is a fundamentalism.
Academic freedom is "an orthodoxy and a faith," Fish writes. But he is
untroubled by liberals' religious cast of mind, no different in its intensity
from various Shi'a and Taliban theologies. He is troubled only that liberal
faith sets itself up as antifaith and is a religion that denies it is a religion.
Freedom of religion in a liberal regime means denial of religion: "It's a great
move whereby liberalism, in the form of academic freedom, gets to display
its generosity while at the same time cutting the heart out of the views to
which that generosity is extended" (*Trouble* 40, 41). Liberalism offers
religion a seat at the seminar table and commands it to stay seated. Religion
may sit there to be discussed, analyzed, and reasoned with, but it cannot
walk out and enact its own postulates: marry its two wives, attack its
infidels, murder its abortionists, commit its suttees. Religion must approach
liberalism softly, with (Fish says amusingly) the diffidence of a host
offering hors d'ouerves to her guests. Fish knows better, his imagination
well-stocked with images of Bainham and Tyndale writhing at the stake,
and of Milton's employer Cromwell, sword in hand, driving the Members
out of Parliament. Liberalism energetically pursues, meanwhile, its own
fundamentalist agenda. Fish produces no end of examples to prove that
we're all exclusionists.

That's hardly news. What's new is the demonstration in all Fish's
venues that liberal mainstreamers have the same jealous desire to win
absolutely: the "proponents of doctrinaire agendas" want to win; they
"want to occupy, and be sovereign over, the discursive space, and expel
others from it. And *this* academic freedom will not permit (it wants to win,
too, and does by exiling from its confines any discourse that violates *its*
rules)" (*Trouble* 40). That's okay by Fish. All he objects to is academic

freedom's embarrassment at its own exclusionism and the ensuing urge to cut out its own heart:

> It all sounds fine and highly moral, but in fact it displaces morality by asking you to inhabit your moral convictions loosely and be ready to withdraw from them whenever pursuing them would impinge on the activities of others, . . . to suspend those very urgencies that move you to act in the world, and to regard them as no different than the urgencies of your enemies. (41)

Sounding very much the minor prophet of the Old Testament—talking about enemies, group survival, and martial valor—Fish actually functions as a coach in a grim halftime locker room. Thus, he is to be found telling demoralized readers of the *Times* or *Harper's* or the *Chronicle* that it is "not so clear why you would be so willing to allow what you deplore to flourish" and that we are "wrong to think that inclusion, of a truly capacious kind, is possible. All that is possible—all you can work for— is to arrange things so that the exclusions that inevitably occur are favorable to your interests and hostile to the interests of your adversaries" (44).

Support your local fundamentalism, he urges, and take no guff from those who try to principle you out of it; they have their own agenda. The burden of his wrath falls on multiculturalists, who are exaggerated liberals and thus even more prone to quail before manipulators brandishing principles such as colorblindness, equality, freedom of speech, and meritocracy. He has written that multiculturalism is a logical impossibility because its commitment to celebrating all cultures will exclude believers in monoculture. Would-be multiculturalists make the Walzer move and eliminate from the realm of moral consideration all those who believe in racial superiority, the immorality of homosexuals, and the natural right of men to govern women. He writes, "Liberal neutrality and multiculturalism are both engines of exclusion trying to fly under inclusive banners" (*Trouble* 44). He urges them to face the facts, to embrace their own fundamentalism, and, onward ho, to ban pornography and the Ku Klux Klan, suppress neo-Nazis, silence Holocaust deniers, and, indeed, go after all things disagreeable and forget about fairness and freedom of speech. In doing so, he assures us, "you will not be compromising the First Amendment; you will be honoring it by performing the act of censorship that was implicit in it from the beginning" ("Fisheye"). So, you will be fulfilling the First Amendment by banning speech. This pyrotechnic piece of sophistry caps the Fish performance.

Fish and the Public Sphere

"Extirpating" is in the title of this chapter, and it is a word forever tied to the topic of censorship. There is no such thing as free speech, Fish argued in 1994, and nothing in his journalism suggests any change of mind. His passage on censorship and extirpation begins with a reading of Milton's *Areopagitica*, an essay that Fish tends to cite in every discussion of free speech and the First Amendment. Toleration, unregulated publication, books as the lifeblood of a precious spirit—these stirring ideas fill *Areopagitica*, named after the highest judicial court of Athens. Milton intones with force and poetry the original anticensorship mantras—thus does a seventeenth-century political pamphlet remain the most potent literary endorsement of unrestricted speech and publication.

Fish demonstrates, however, that Milton's *Areopagitica* actually *condemns* freedom of speech and press. As Milton approaches his denouement, he pulls up short to make a reservation, and that reservation ends up taking back every untrammeled liberty he has just granted:

> I mean not tolerated popery, and open superstition, which as it extirpates all religious and civil supremacies, so itself should be extirpate . . . that also which is impious or evil absolutely against faith or manners no law can possibly permit that intends not to unlaw itself. (qtd. in *There's* 103)

The pleasures of this passage for Fish are many. It annihilates a sacred cow worshiped by free-speech liberals. It rejects freedom of expression and reserves to itself the right to judge precisely which forms of speech and action should be prohibited. Its violent imagery—*extirpate* as in "root out, exterminate, or totally destroy a class, sect, or nation; . . . render extinct"—injects force and passion (*Oxford English Dictionary*). When Milton leaves his idealist generalities and gets down to cases, he's as exclusivist and bloody-minded as Slobodan Milosevic.

Fish traces this bloodline of passionate conviction in order to connect Milton with us, just as he wants to connect the frames of the Rodney King video. For most people, Fish's yearning for continuity and his faith in a unified, uninterrupted history are reassuring. Most of us prefer to believe that the past sorts itself into a coherent story with clear lines of cause and effect: smoking leads to cancer, overeating to obesity, hard work to success. Fish embraces rules of thumb or common sense, and it is the bedrock of his advice to other deans and college administrators. His belief in a coherent historical narrative provides a comforting ballast to his somewhat less conventional views, such as his view that words have no fixed meaning, that rules should be stretched by resourceful accountants, that law acquires its shape from efforts to bend it, and that freedom of speech means imposition of censorship. These counterintuitive maxims seem to come right out of *Brave New World*, where we learn that ignorance is knowledge and weakness is strength. A general readership who suspects maxims like these will have its confidence restored by Fish's conventional view of history. Television-watching Americans believe that life is a story.

Of course, there are a few Americans, often French-trained ones, who believe otherwise. Migrant intellectuals from the Indian subcontinent or South and Latin America, the Caribbean, Africa, and elsewhere have infiltrated the professorial ranks. And they, like gay and lesbian scholars, feminists, African-Americans, and members of other marginalized groups, have entered the profession on their own terms, often with their own approach to history. And that approach is a view of history as multiple or fractured, of the double-consciousness born of exile or segregation, of incomparably different cultural experiences, of a heightened experience of racial and national difference. Fish can no more accommodate his narrative to these ideas than Milton could accommodate Catholicism or Walzer could accommodate monolithic religions and totalitarian regimes. Fish cannot account for multiple and hybrid histories because that would be like an English barrister, whose stock of arguments must be drawn from case law that goes back to the Magna Carta, attempting to cite as precedent Mughal-dynasty property disputes or Ming emperors' decisions on torts. Fish simply rules out these other historians, these historians of others, before he even begins to argue his case.

Fish is thus himself dependent "on an exception that literally carves out the space in which expression can then emerge." Freedom of expression depends on a prior act of censorship because "without restriction, without an inbuilt sense of what it would be meaningless to say or wrong to say, there could be no assertion and no reason for asserting it" (*There's* 103). Permission to speak gains its distinctive outline only against the possibility that such permission may be withheld. So, too, Fish's hoary commonsensical view of history requires, for its existence, the proximate threat of its own annihilation in order to live. Just as tolerance law carves out its own space by excluding "popery and impiety," or *On Toleration* thrives by excluding ayatollahs and dictators, so too does Fish's fundamentalism exclude the hybridity and double-consciousness crowd.

Fish's attempts to extirpate ambivalence and self-doubt have their very attractive effects. He embarrasses and corrects the muddle-headed President Bowen and teaches him to stop defending the First Amendment and start defending his academic mission and colleagues. He punctures free-speech absolutism and upbraids judges who by worshiping free speech fail to stop the KKK and skinheads. He continues to expose the cynical appeal to fairness that shields Rodney King's attackers and permits the Philadelphia construction trades to keep the profits of two hundred years of segregation and racism. These are not inconsiderable achievements.

People tend to believe, however, that while Fish's wordplay may be radical, his politics are not. Terry Eagleton has consistently urged that view, saying that Fish's innovation has been "to hijack an apparently radical epistemology for tamely conservative ends" ("Estate"). But I think that Eagleton has things the wrong way around. Fish's public-sphere attacks on freedom of speech and the press, on bogus impartiality, colorblindness, equality, merit, and all such magic words, on administrator-speak and antifundamentalism, look very radical compared to the usual pundit monotone. It is only when he considers the new wave in academia—the Bhabhas, Maillouxs, Robbinses, and Spivaks—that the conservative fit comes upon him. These scholars and their views have to be swept off the board, ruled out in advance by his anticosmopolitan intolerance for ambiguity and his skepticism that cultures and vocabularies can overlap. He laughs at those who believe that they can critique their own ideas or who experience divided loyalties. But we have to forgive him his intolerance. It carves out the space in which he can continue to speak.

Fish's emergence as a public intellectual thus compels us to invert the received opinion that he's epistemologically bold and politically supine. I would contend that he offers one of the most highly politicized accounts of Milton and the other English Renaissance poets. Fish takes up their work precisely where it is grittiest, where they lend the heightened form of verse to big issues of salvation, damnation, and redemption. Nurtured on these classical examples, Fish brings unusual erudition and passion to his journalism. Who besides Fish would alert the readers of the *Chronicle* ("Stop") that Robert Burton, in his book *The Anatomy of Melancholy*, has much to tell us about reporters from the *Wall Street Journal*; or warn college deans ("Probably") that, by sharing power, they risk falling into the weakened state of the Avignon papacy? More substantially, Fish values whatever is contentious in the work of Milton, Donne, and Herbert, and he dangles before us the attractive possibility that our contentions can be poetic, too. He alone is reviving the tradition of Swift by showing how the foul rag-and-bone shop of our squabbles can be transformed into the golden song of Byzantium. Just as he alerted academic readers that Milton was repeatedly trapping them and making them fall for the wrong rhetoric, he is now alerting *Times* readers that the cultural and political right is trapping them by making them fall for magic words like *equality, fairness*, and *merit*. His sophisticated debunking of legal formalism bears fruit in the public domain when he is able to prove that a similar formalism has produced the shame-culture of department salary committees, Bowen's misguided free-speech defense, and the fatuous higher-education-speak of "benchmarks" and "best practices." Finally, his Machiavellianism, acknowledged in *The Trouble with Principle*, enables his tongue-in-cheek praise for Democrats and Republicans who blandly adopt and abandon their principles at need.

Outside the public sphere, on the edges where Fish correctly believes professors dwell, the stakes and the game are both quite different. And at this level, Fish's positions seem potentially self-serving and weak. His casuistical style and repetitive argumentation serve to recenter the academic debate in a now unrealistically narrow tradition. With ambivalence and hybridity moving to the center stage of academic humanities research, a continuist and organicist version of history and narrative will no longer advance the debate. His ultramontane insistence on a discredited historicism has to be regarded as his ticket into the popular press. And from the point of view of specialists who are developing new ways of writing subaltern and alternative histories, that is exactly where Fish and his outmoded historicism belong. In fact, he has already begun to move away from the purely academic matters that have occupied and benefited from his attention. His decision to leave full-time teaching, become a full-time university administrator, and, most important, begin to write for newspapers and magazines, hints that he envisages for himself a role larger than that of a specialized scholar.

Of course, Fish has been famous for saying that scholarship and political agendas should be kept rigidly apart. As late as 1995, in his book *Professional Correctness*, he insisted that interpretive literary work should content itself with pleasure and avoid politics. He summed up his view in a coda: "The academy—Love it or leave it" (2). His views may not have changed, but his location has. Fish is for the time being still in the academy, but he has one foot out the door.

Notes

1. Terry Eagleton has been insistent on this issue, contending that Fish is "doomed to write the same book over and over again" and that he "now seems to have written the same book several times over" ("Death" 6; "Estate" 11). But this may be Eagleton's rationale for himself having written the same review several times over.

2. This is the same Walzer who wished to exclude Palestinians from the world of moral concern (in his book *Exodus and Revolution*)—a wish for which he received a sound drubbing by Edward Said. See "An Exchange" and Said.

3. See Pritchard, Kermode, Vendler, Nuttall, and Leonard. High-stakes pamphleteering and propaganda, raised to an art form, are Fish's speciality, but they are not to everyone's taste, and critics were puzzled, to put it kindly, by his latest Milton volume, with its attention to "De Doctrina Christiana" (he claims to have settled the question of authorship); *Aereopagitica*; "An Apology against A Pamphlet"; "Of Reformation"; "The Reason of Church Government"; "Of Prelaticall Episcopacy"; "The Doctrine and Discipline of Divorce"; "The Readie and Easie Way"; "Modest Confutation"; "Tetrachordon"; and, in short, to Milton's finest works of politico-religious controversy. To have charged that Fish neglects "the sensuous, expansive side of Milton" (Kermode), or to charge that he "does not care for the poetry of Milton's poetry" (Vendler), or to call "absurd" Fish's view of Milton as "monist, authoritarian, obscurantist, a completely closed mind" (Nuttal), is to wish that Fish had written a different book. It is also to blind oneself to the poetics of controversy, argument, and passionate belief. Of *that* poetics, Fish is the true connoisseur.

4. Bainham was burned in 1531. See Greenblatt 74–75.

5. See Smuts, and Keenan and Shannon.

Works Cited

"An Exchange: Michael Walzer and Edward Said." *Grand Street* 5 (1986): 246–59.

Bhabha, Homi. "Postcolonial Criticism." *Redrawing the Boundaries: The Transformation of English and American Literary Studies*. Ed. Stephen Greenblatt and Giles Gunn. New York: MLA, 1992. 437–65.

Brown, Meg Lota. *Donne and the Politics of Conscience in Early Modern England*. New York: Brill, 1995.

Eagleton, Terry. "The Death of Self-Criticism." Rev. of *Professional Correctness:*

Literary Studies and Political Change, by Stanley Fish. *Times Literary Supplement* 24 Nov. 1995: 6.

———. "The Estate Agent." Rev. of *The Trouble with Principle*, by Stanley Fish. *London Review of Books* 2 Mar. 2000. http://www.lrb.co.uk/v22/n05/eagl01_.html (15 Oct. 2002).

Elwood, Christopher. *The Body Broken: The Calvinist Doctrine of the Eucharist and the Symbolization of Power in Sixteenth-Century France*. New York: Oxford UP, 1999.

Fish, Stanley. "Condemnation without Absolutes: Postmodernism and the Reality of Terrorism." *New York Times* 15 Oct. 2001: A19.

———. *Doing What Comes Naturally: Change, Rhetoric, and the Practice of Theory in Literary and Legal Studies*. Durham: Duke UP, 1989.

———. "Fisheye: A Sneaky Kind of Censorship." *Across the Board* 37.8 (2000): 10.

———. "The Golden Rule." *Chronicle of Higher Education* 21 Sept. 2001. http://chronicle.com/jobs/2001/09/2001092101c.htm (15 Oct. 2002).

———. "The High-Minded Fight Over Florida." *New York Times* 15 Nov. 2000: A 29.

———. *How Milton Works*. Cambridge: Harvard UP, 2001.

———. "Is Everything Political?" *Chronicle of Higher Education* 29 Mar. 2002. http://chronicle.com/jobs/2002/03/2002032901c.htm (15 Oct. 2002).

———. "Postmodern Warfare: The Ignorance of Our Warrior Intellectuals." *Harper's* July 2002: 33–41.

———. *Professional Correctness: Literary Studies and Political Change*. Oxford: Clarendon, 1995.

———. "School for the Scandalous." *New York Times* 21 Nov. 1997: A35.

———. "Staying the Course." *Chronicle of Higher Education* 4 Jan. 2002. http://chronicle.com/jobs/2002/01/2002010401c.htm (15 Oct. 2002).

———. "Stop the Presses." *Chronicle of Higher Education* 24 May 2002. http://chronicle.com/jobs/2002/05/2002052401c.htm (15 Oct. 2002).

————. *There's No Such Thing as Free Speech, and It's a Good Thing, Too.* New York: Oxford UP, 1994.

————. *The Trouble with Principle.* Cambridge: Harvard UP, 1999.

————. "Vicki Frost Objects." *Trouble* 153–61.

————. "Were It Not for My Wife (or Husband, Partner, Mother, Dog, or Flower Garden)." *Chronicle of Higher Education* 26 Apr. 2002. http://chronicle.com/jobs/2002/04/2002042601c.htm (15 Oct. 2002).

————. "You Probably Think this Song Is about You." *Chronicle of Higher Education* 1 Mar. 2002. http://chronicle.com/jobs/2002/03/2002030101c.htm (15 Oct. 2002).

Greenblatt, Stephen. *Renaissance Self-Fashioning: From More to Shakespeare.* Chicago: U of Chicago P, 1980.

Keenan, James F., and Thomas A. Shannon. *The Context of Casuistry.* Washington, DC: Georgetown UP, 1995.

Kermode, Frank. "Cross-Examining Milton." Rev. of *How Milton Works*, by Stanley Fish. *New York Times Book Review* 24 June 2001. http://query.nytimes.com/search/full-page?res=9502E5DF1631F937A15755C0A9679C8B63 (15 Oct. 2002).

Leonard, John K. "Did Milton Go to the Devil's Party?" Rev. of *How Milton Works*, by Stanley Fish. *New York Review of Books* 18 July 2002: 28–31.

Nuttall, A.D. "Everything Is Over before It Begins." Rev. of *How Milton Works*, by Stanley Fish. *London Review of Books* 21 June 2001. http://www.lrb.co.uk/v23/n12/nutt01_.html (15 Oct. 2002).

Patey, Douglas Lane. *Probability and Literary Form: Philosophic Theory and Literary Practice in the Augustan Age.* Cambridge: Cambridge UP, 1984.

Pritchard, William H. "Fish Contemplating a Bust of Milton." Rev. of *How Milton Works*, by Stanley Fish. *New England Review* 22.4 (2001): 177–85.

Said, Edward. "Walzer's *Exodus and Revolution*: A Canaanite Reading." *Grand Street* 5 (1986): 86–106.

Slights, Camille Wells. *The Casuistical Tradition in Shakespeare, Donne, Herbert, and Milton.* Princeton: Princeton UP, 1981.

Smuts, R. Malcolm. *Culture and Power in England, 1585–1685*. New York: St. Martin's, 1999.

Thomas, Keith. "Cases of Conscience in Seventeenth-Century England." *Public Duty and Private Conscience in Seventeenth-Century England*. Ed. John Morrill, Paul Slack, and Daniel Woolf. Oxford: Clarendon, 1993. 29–56.

Veeser, H. Aram. Introduction. *The Stanley Fish Reader*. Ed. H. Aram Veeser. Malden, MA: Blackwell, 1999. 1–9.

Vendler, Helen. Rev. of *How Milton Works,* by Stanley Fish. *The New Republic* 30 July 2001: 35–37.

Zagorin, Perez. *Ways of Lying: Dissimulation, Persecution, and Conformity in Early Modern Europe*. Cambridge: Harvard UP, 1990.

Professional Distinction

Evan Watkins

Published in 1995, Stanley Fish's *Professional Correctness* antagonized a lot of people. With the reception of *Professional Correctness* and with Fish's departure from Duke University, the end of the 1990s seemed also to mark an end to Fish's representative status. Up to that point, he had not only been a major figure in a discipline; he had also appeared as one representatively crucial embodiment of connection between the discipline's intellectual direction and its institutional position within major research universities in the United States. Arguably, others may have filled either one of those two slots more compellingly than Fish, but no one else combined them as he did or made them even as remotely interdependent in the same way as he could. Thus, *Professional Correctness* caused trouble in part because it seemed so out of step with emergent intellectual directions in English—not just critically challenging or acerbic or playing the pragmatist to whatever current idealism was around, but fundamentally out of step—and in ways Fish hadn't been before. For many, the assumption of his support for their new directions was no longer tenable. It's been nearly a decade, however, since Fish delivered the lectures on which *Professional Correctness* is based, and returning now to those arguments makes it much easier to avoid the did-he-or-didn't-he-betray-his-commitments questions. It's correspondingly much more difficult, however, to avoid the disciplinary issues he raises. Things have changed for English studies in the university, and in ways that for me make *Professional Correctness* disturbingly relevant.

"English" seems to be the discipline at stake for Fish, but it's really literary study that is the center of his discussion. As Gary Olson and others have commented, rhetoric and composition as an intellectual endeavor and writing instruction generally don't factor into Fish's account of disciplinary practices, even though they have always accounted for a huge percentage of student credit hours and FTEs and increasingly account for a great deal of intellectual energy and ferment. It is literary study, however, that for Fish establishes the distinctiveness of English as a discipline; and, more specifically, it's the interpretive process of determining what literary texts *mean*: "The short (and methodologically unhelpful) answer is that the purpose of literary interpretation is to determine what works of literature mean; and therefore the paradigmatic question in literary criticism is 'What is this poem (or novel or drama) saying?'" (*Professional* 25). The pursuit of meaning, as he acknowledges parenthetically, can involve multiple and often competing methods. And while the "paradigmatic question" may be a question of meaning, the appropriate answer, he suggests later, must always be indirect: "Something must always be left over, unaccounted for, open to still another turn of the interpretive screw; were this not so, the work could be said to have engaged in totalizing—in telling (or claiming to tell) the truth about the world once and for all—and thereby forfeited its right to be called 'literary'" (34).

Nevertheless, the distinctness of literary studies, what differentiates it from other disciplines across the university spectrum, is the pursuit of meaning in *literary* texts—that is, those texts that among other things encourage an infinitely prolonged process of interpretation. And that, of course, was the source of most of the trouble for a great many of those in attendance at the Nineteenth Alabama Symposium on English and American Literature in 1993, where Fish presented most of the themes that were later developed into *Professional Correctness*. The essays collected in *English as a Discipline; Or, Is There a Plot in This Play?*— work that emerged from the Alabama conference—clearly reflect the criticisms aimed at Fish. What was most troubling for some was the emphasis on "the literary" in ways that would seem to re-aestheticize literature, taking it out of the everyday world of social relations while at the same time precluding serious attention to a whole range of other texts, the texts of popular culture in particular. For others, the more serious problem was the conclusion Fish drew from his premise of distinctiveness—namely, that working as a literary critic in a university discipline was not in itself political work. For example, in his "Afterthoughts" in

English as a Discipline, Paul Lauter remarks that creating a binary opposition between political work and the interpretation of meaning "obscures what we actually do both in figuring out what a poem 'means' and in carrying out political work" (184).

It is possible to agree with Lauter (and I do) that figuring out meaning and carrying out political work isn't an airtight binary without, however, taking still a further step in the linkage. At the risk of an immediate oversimplification, what strikes me in rereading this collection now is the rather remarkable faith shared by so many literary critics that textual meaning and social effects can be necessarily and causally connected. For all the discussion of extending or breaking the boundaries of literary studies and politicizing its practices that went on in the 1980s and well into the 1990s, I recall very little that suggested that political work might require doing something else altogether than figuring out meanings. The idea seemed to be that the figuring had to be done in very different ways than had been done in the past, and that it had to operate on very different texts, but the interpretive process was only a means to a larger end in any case. Once meanings could be refigured, the social effects would follow—by the exercise of the corresponding "self-awareness," or whatever—and if these were not the desired effects then it was because you hadn't quite yet plumbed the mystifications of the meanings.

This is a gross oversimplification, of course, but one that usefully throws into relief Fish's contrasting assumption that the only direct and necessary effect of interpreting literary texts is to establish the disciplinary distinctiveness of literary studies. In other words, for Fish interpretive constructions of meaning and the effects that actually follow are connected only within a contingent circularity—in this case, the differential institutional process by which disciplines realize a certain distinctive "immanent intelligibility," a term that features significantly in Fish's argument. He remarks in his introduction to *Professional Correctness* that this argument is completely consistent with his earlier work, and whether this is entirely true or not, the consistency is nowhere more evident than in his emphasis on "immanent intelligibility." The term is a reminder that epistemological issues have always been at the forefront of his understanding, whether his immediate concern is the interpretation of a given literary text, the most arcane reaches of theory, or the institutional circumstances of literary studies. In "Them We Burn: Violence and Conviction in English Departments," his response to the papers presented at the Alabama symposium, Fish remarks tellingly, "Of course, someone is immediately going to challenge me and say, 'Well, we do lots of things around here; how can there be one kind of thing that we do?' But that's to grab the wrong end of the epistemological or indeed disciplinary question" (162). The adjectival interchangeability of "epistemological" and "disciplinary" should explain a lot. It shouldn't really come as a surprise to find the "gateway" into *Professional Correctness* located at the identification of the intelligibility of literary studies—how do we know that we know we're in the field of literary studies and not another field?

That gateway, however, should also alert us as readers to the fact that the argument is being carried out at another level than most of the criticisms advanced in *English as a Discipline* and elsewhere after the publication of *Professional Correctness*. This isn't really an argument about the excision of politics or the hazards of abandoning Milton's texts for *Friends* episodes, or the dubious virtue of giving lots of NPR interviews, or even the issue Northrop Frye struggled to define toward the end of his career: what knowledge is most worth having. It is, again, about how you know that you know you're in the field of literary studies and not another field. And as a result, the question addressed to self-professed "political criticism," for example, isn't whether political criticism is a good or bad thing, or whether it's good politics or bad politics, but, rather, what it could tell us about the status of our knowledge of where we are. Needless to say, the answer for Fish is "not much," but this reply shouldn't at all be taken as a reason to imagine that Fish would have us all renounce politics in our roles as literary critics. It's simply that neither renunciation nor affirmation bears on the question.

Gary Olson's critique of Fish in *Justifying Belief: Stanley Fish and the Work of Rhetoric* usefully recognizes that Fish has constructed his argument so that "it is difficult to disagree with his position *if you take those arguments on the terms that he sets out*" (29; Olson's emphasis). For Olson, however, the context of those terms is Fish's emphasis on the literary at the expense of ignoring how the discipline of English also includes rhetoric and composition: "That is, the structural makeup of Fish's arguments is such that so long as we grant his context (literary studies), his contentions are unassailable. . . . The key to Fish's argument is the term *literary*" (30). To some extent, of course, the recognition of the literary as "key" is true enough. Fish openly admits his veneration of the process of interpreting literary texts and claims much would be lost if we abandoned that process for something else. I've tried to suggest, however, that for the purposes of his argument the importance Fish assigns to literary studies is a function of a "context" that is relentlessly epistemological. I would, then, modify Olson's statement to read something like the following: so long as we grant the primacy of his epistemological context, his contentions are perhaps not completely unassailable but at least extremely difficult to dispute on the grounds of anything—rhetoric and composition or otherwise—having been "left out," because by definition the aim of epistemological inquiry isn't empirical exhaustiveness but, precisely, how to establish the intelligibility (or not) of whatever turns up. Thus, it was a mistake on Fish's part not to have recognized that rhetoric and composition has "turned up" big time in English for some time, a point I'll return to in a moment. But this mistake doesn't affect his determination of the parameters of importance assigned to epistemological issues. The larger question would seem to involve the adequacy of epistemology as a disciplinary description. If indeed you "grab the wrong end" of the epistemological stick, have you simultaneously and necessarily, as Fish implies, also gone wrong in your understanding of English as a discipline?

Phrased this way, however, the question lends itself all too easily to an inquiry long familiar to readers of Fish: his process of teasing out the epistemological assumptions implicit in assertions about the direction and value of literary studies—a task Fish gleefully turns to right away in "Them We Burn," no less than in the larger frame of *Professional Correctness*. As always for Fish, the conclusion is to maintain the distinctiveness of literary studies, to recognize that unless literary studies can differentially establish an identity in relation to the other enterprises with which it institutionally coexists, it may not be able, as Fish bluntly states, to "sustain a challenge to its usefulness" (162). That is, the inquiry finally isn't undertaken in order to convict his targets of incoherence or inconsistency (although that's, of course, an inevitable byproduct that leads in turn to the hostility his recent work has received), and even less to demonstrate that they have illicitly grounded their politics or their collapsing of disciplinary boundaries or whatever else in an unconscious demonstration of epistemological intelligibility and distinctiveness. The problem lies in a failure to recognize that the grounding when it occurs is completely *licit*; were it not, nothing whatsoever would follow from the effort. Epistemology, in other words, doesn't project a description of the discipline at all. It's simply what we have to do in order to have a discipline to describe—or exhort, or change, or indeed affect anything. It's how we know that we know there is a distinctive disciplinary identity, and how those in other disciplines recognize the distinctiveness of our practices.

This reasoning explains why Fish worries what he does throughout *Professional Correctness*. Whether it's the political claims of New Historicism, the interdisciplinary ambitions of cultural studies, or the attempt to achieve the visibility and influence of public intellectuals, the danger remains the same: an indiscriminate blurring of disciplinary distinctiveness at the risk of losing academic respectability or institutional position. Thus, despite what some of his critics have charged, it doesn't seem to me that Fish has any real interest at all in disciplinary boundaries per se, and certainly not in policing specific limits. As he remarks over and over, distinctiveness in any case is always relative to the contiguous disciplines within the institution. As disciplines change, identities obligingly alter as well, sometimes from within and sometimes in response to change by their immediate disciplinary contacts. What Fish worries is not this contingent and ongoing process, but rather the potential in the various movements and directions he discusses to prompt an exit from that process, to disconnect practices from the professional contexts of "the academic guild."

In the near decade since *Professional Correctness* was published, there have been a great many debates about what has happened in English studies during that decade. There is no longer the same breathless anticipation about the newest theoretical inflection, but the fate of "theory" isn't clear at all. For some, it has been abandoned, its political implications at best co-opted and at worst deliberately eliminated from positions of power within the discipline. For others, theory has simply undergone a healthy mutation from the high-level abstractions of the 1970s and 1980s into multiple specific locations, and thus now has become thoroughly a part of virtually every area and ensemble of practices in English. Area studies programs have disappeared in some schools, but in others they have become standout separate programs rather than being folded into English or some other discipline. Thus, depending on one's own position, either the gains of the past three decades have been rolled back to accommodate a return to some aestheticized apolitical fastidiousness barely masked by a patina of rapidly aging theory jargon, or theory did its work so successfully that it now belongs everywhere and has in fact undergone a valuable transformation as area studies (particularly women's studies, African American studies, and ethnic studies) rewrote it into differentially useful specificities.

These and a number of other debates continue; as usual in an academic setting, nothing is more difficult than discerning what just happened. It strikes me, however, that there is still another way to describe what has been going on within English since Fish first elaborated the arguments of *Professional Correctness*. Generalizations are always suspect given the immense range and variety of English programs in colleges and universities, but it does seem plausible to suggest that on the whole the discipline has behaved pretty much as Fish suggested it should. New Historicism certainly didn't transform English into a political wing, and in any case it always resembled an older aesthetic criticism far more closely than any discernible political program. Cultural studies may still claim some serious interdisciplinary or occasionally counterdisciplinary ambitions, but in 2003 those rhetorics encounter corroborating echoes not only from administrators, but also from serious scholars in a number of different disciplines. Through a perspective like Fish's, this doesn't mean that disciplines are disappearing at all, only that their distinctive identities—as always—are changing. And cultural studies in some ways seems to have anticipated some of those changes. For a number of scholars, that may imply it has been institutionally co-opted, for others that it now has a better chance to be more effective. And while there are scholars in English who continue to be visible as public intellectuals, in an increasing number of circumstances that visibility is as likely to be a matter of fundraising as it is speaking out on the major issues of the day, for fundraising from a great many different sources, usually in ways that involve alumni, has become a crucial part of the work of English department administrators and senior faculty in order for a department to prosper.

In sum, I would suggest that there are some good reasons to believe that the dissolving of boundaries that concerned Fish in *Professional Correctness* has not materialized. This isn't meant to suggest that what a number of scholars and critics have anticipated as a massive "return to literature" has occurred, nor does Fish's own argument imply that such a return is necessary for disciplinary distinctiveness. My point is that while it is plausible to describe a recent history of English studies in terms that suggest that the discipline continues to follow out the conditions of "immanent intelligibility," the *position* of English in the university nevertheless has been changing in a number of ways. In an argument like Fish's that puts such a premium on the differential distinctiveness of a discipline, the failure to consider positional relationships among disciplines is a telling omission.

This is the point where Fish's lack of attention to how English as a discipline includes not only literary studies but also rhetoric and composition becomes crucial. On the one hand, rhetoric and composition has come to occupy much more of an intellectual center in many departments in ways that intersect directly (if often uneasily) with the elements of literary studies that Fish identifies as crucial to disciplinary distinctiveness. On the other hand, one significant reason for the recent dramatic growth (as witnessed by recent hiring patterns) in composition in particular has to do with the fact that composition far more directly than literary studies occupies two crucial boundary zones: between English and other university disciplines; and between tenure-track/tenured professors, and graduate teaching assistants, lecturers, and temporary instructors. Whether or not the "immanent intelligibility" of English has altered or dissolved—and I would argue that it hasn't—the position of English within the university has changed, and not entirely for the better by any means. These boundary zones register the changes in all their complexities. Had Fish been paying more attention to composition studies, I think these changes would have already been difficult to miss.

Despite his reiterated claim in *Professional Correctness* that disciplinary identities are differentially relational, Fish seems singularly uninterested in positional relations among the disciplines or in the claims disciplines make on each other within their institutional structure. The relations that *do* interest him are between what goes on in English and what goes on in the larger culture generally. In part, this has to do with his targets of critique; New Historicism, cultural studies, and the idea of the public intellectual all focus on these relationships as well. I have never agreed completely with Fish's contention that the connections between academic work in English and "the outside" are so attenuated as to be almost nonexistent in our culture at this time. Nevertheless, Fish's argument seems to be a useful corrective to the often wildly exaggerated claims about connection, and it is a valuable reminder that the effects of academic work in English studies register first within the discipline and secondly (because disciplinary identity is relational) within the ensemble of disciplines in the university. Given Fish's much stronger insistence on the absence of direct lines of connection to "the outside," however, the lack of attention to disciplinary relations explains a great deal about the limits of his overriding epistemological emphasis on the "intelligibility" of literary studies.

Responding to a series of claims made in *Knowledges: Historical and Critical Studies in Disciplinarity*, a collection of essays about the contingencies of disciplinary constitution, Fish writes in *Professional Correctness*,

> The fact that a self-advertised unity is really a grab-bag of disparate elements held together by the conceptual equivalent of chicken-wire, or by shifting political and economic alliances, or by a desire to control the production and dissemination of knowledge, does not make the unity disappear; it merely shows what the unity is made of, not that it isn't one. . . . So long as it is even temporarily established, the unity of a discipline has a material existence and therefore has material effects that no analysis can dispel. (74)

This seems to me to be true enough, but the corollary is that the "intelligibility" of a discipline also has a material existence, and likewise one that analysis in itself can neither dispel nor establish. Its material existence is established first of all by the complex of *positional* relations with surrounding fields of study. The point Fish himself makes often enough in other contexts applies here as well: one can claim whatever one wants about what one does, but unless those claims are corroborated in some way or another through the positional identity that emerges from within an ensemble of often quite complicated relations, the claims are nothing more than a kind of Platonism.

For Fish, however, disciplinary intelligibility must finally depend instead on the immanence of an endlessly self-referential justification. That is why, as one of his chapter titles has it, "literary criticism is like virtue." It's a story you tell over and over among yourselves: "Moreover, it is hard, if not impossible, to tell that story to those who do not already know it, or, rather, are not already living it" (113). Richard Rorty, he suggests, "makes the same point when he rejects the idea that 'humanities departments should have aims'—goals external to their own obsessions—and counsels us simply to think of departments as oases for 'a bunch of wayfaring pilgrims who happened to take shelter in the same inn, or in the same section of the stacks'" (114). That's really all one can say in justification, Fish concludes, ending the argument by citing the Gershwin line, "Nice work if you can get it" (114). Nevertheless, since as Fish himself admits this account of justification is "in fact a refusal of its demand," the argument must have a coda: but can you get it? Fish writes, "The question acknowledges what everybody knows, that the academic literary enterprise is under siege, and that in an age of shrinking budgets and demands for accountability, a justificatory rhetoric that remains internal to the profession may be, to say the least, counterproductive" (115).

This seems to me a perfect setup to initiate a quite different discussion of the material resources required to sustain the "intelligibility" of a distinct disciplinary set of practices and the "wayfaring pilgrims" who wish to inhabit the discipline. And it seems at first to be where Fish is headed: "What do we say to those not of our party without whose approval and material/political support that living could not be made?" The next sentence, however, suggests otherwise: "What do we say to the *public*, that generalized body that wants, not unreasonably, to believe that the cultural activities it sustains have a benign relationship to its concerns and values?" (115–16). What follows is then an argument about the idea of "the public intellectual" that for the most part develops exactly the same pattern as the arguments about New Historicism and cultural studies. I don't mean to overlook the obvious sense in which "public support" in some generalized, abstract sense is necessary not only for English studies but even more importantly for the institution of the university. Yet, Fish probably knows in more specific detail than anyone that the material resources to support an English department don't come *directly* from "the public" at all. Students don't bring tuition monies to the department staff assistant; legislators don't drop off checks at the department office after the final budget session closes. Resources arrive mediated through the labyrinthine complex of the academic institution with its currencies of FTEs and SCHs and its channels of committees and administrative hierarchies, all of which also help organize and express the positional relations among disciplines in the university.

In short, both the material resources for a department and the "intelligibility" of a discipline have immediate reference to the same ensemble of relations, whether that ensemble is articulated in financial or conceptual terminologies. This is not to say that the two articulations are perfectly coterminous by any means. Anyone working in a university should know better. But just as disciplinary distinctiveness only emerges in the context of surrounding disciplines, so too do material resources. At the limit of Fish's epistemological inquiry, however, these considerations disappear into something we might think of as the psychological consolations of epistemology. That is, all the emphasis on conditions of knowledge, on how we know that we know what discipline we're in, is finally suspended at the moments when for Fish it seems most necessary to deliver the subjective incentive for engaging in that inquiry in the first place as well as the reward for having engaged it: do what you do and take pleasure in it; stop trying to be something completely different from what you are.

I don't take that to be fatuous therapy at all. Like endlessly apologizing after every action, constantly trying to appear anything but an academic in English studies working in an academic institution is at best a complete waste of time, perhaps matched only by the hubris of trying to load everything in the world into the practice of being an academic in English working in an academic institution. But even if Fish were right that direct connections between academic work in English and "the outside" are tenuous to the point of nonexistence, a university is not only itself a massively public institution; it also exists in an immense network of connections to all kinds of "outsides." And being an academic working in English necessarily commits you to some positional role in the complex of university disciplines, both materially and conceptually. It's as much a part of "what we do around here," to borrow Fish's familiar refrain, as interpreting *Paradise Lost.* In an age of "shrinking budgets and demands for accountability," as Fish puts it, let alone all the other shifts taking place in higher education generally, not playing that positional role for all it's worth is also a refusal to do the politics that matter first and most immediately for both our students and ourselves.

Fortunately, however, Fish's practice in these matters is far better than his epistemology would seem to allow. If you don't like his epistemology, you can of course argue with it. But if you don't like his politics you have to do it differently, in the specific context in which you find yourself.

Works Cited

Fish, Stanley. *Professional Correctness: Literary Studies and Political Change.* Oxford: Clarendon, 1995.

———. "Them We Burn: Violence and Conviction in the English Department." Raymond 160–73.

Lauter, Paul. "Afterthoughts." Raymond 182–86.

Olson, Gary A. *Justifying Belief: Stanley Fish and the Work of Rhetoric.* Albany: State U of New York P, 2002.

Raymond, James C. *English As a Discipline; Or, Is There a Plot in This Play?* Tuscaloosa: U of Alabama P, 1996.

The Consequences of Holocaust Denial

Michael Bernard-Donals

The series of public lectures in which Stanley Fish took on the ultra-conservative Dinesh D'Souza, and the fireworks that resulted, coincided with the near-apotheosis of the political right in the United States (culminating in the Republican landslide in the congressional elections of 1994).[1] The rise of that conservative tide gave succor to a number of far-right fringe groups, not least of which were the militias that became visible with Timothy McVeigh's bombing of the Murrah Federal Building in Oklahoma City, and the Holocaust denial movement that became emboldened enough to appear on television talk shows and to buy advertising supplements in campus newspapers around the country. In 1996, perhaps bolstered by the smugness of those on the lunatic fringe, David Irving—the intellectual front man for Holocaust denial—sued Deborah Lipstadt, who had written in her book *Denying the Holocaust: The Growing Assault on Truth and Memory* that Irving was (in the words of Martin Broszat) a "Hitler partisan wearing blinkers," and who thought of himself as "carrying on Hitler's legacy" (Lipstadt 161). Irving claimed that she had libeled him, ruined his reputation, and distorted the facts. Lipstadt's title suggested that Irving wasn't only a bad historian, but that he—like the Holocaust deniers she catalogues in her book—was chipping away at truth, at the reality of the events of the Shoah. This was too much for Lipstadt, and she launched a strong defense.

It was too much, also, for Fish, but for apparently different reasons. Since the publication of *Doing What Comes Naturally*, he had been telling members of the literary critical community that there's no such thing as a transparently principled position: we're encumbered by beliefs and ideological positions, so any ground we stand on shifts depending upon the circumstances, making appeals to truth, or to unmediated events of history, illegitimate. In his debates with D'Souza, Fish extended this criticism to the notion of academic freedom and censorship, making the case that academic institutions, no less than other ideological communities, are encumbered by beliefs and practices that are local to those communities, and so any defense of academic freedom on the grounds that the institution is a place of free and open—not to say objective— debate is preposterous. So, on the matter of Holocaust denial, Fish makes the same point: that Lipstadt's appeals to the inherent validity of evidence and the deniers' (as well as historians') appeals to free speech and academic freedom are equally flawed because each rests on a notion that there is such a thing as unmediated reality and that narrative accounts of it are stronger or weaker depending upon their ability to hew close to that reality.

In this essay, I want to make a case both for and against Fish in his public pronouncements about the Holocaust, and in particular his sense of the stakes involved in the *Irving v. Lipstadt* case. He's right to suggest that it's difficult, if not impossible, to make a case against Holocaust denial on the grounds of academic freedom or the self-evidentness of evidence. But because Fish situates his arguments about history and interpretation squarely inside intellectual and academic communities— something Lipstadt refuses to do—his point about the consequences of the deniers' manipulations of history (that "the battle [against them] has already been won") misses the fact that the deniers have a profound effect not only on history but on history's agents, and that those agents include survivors, survivors' families, and people of goodwill for whom historical forgetfulness (or the falsification of history) is injurious. In short, Fish's sense of "academic freedom" misses the strong link between disciplinary work and the reality that underpins it; in this case, it's the historical reality of the Holocaust that, whether he likes it or not, exerts a severe strain on any narrative accounting of it.

Words and Deeds

It's worth examining the main strands of Fish's argument against Holocaust denial and their connection to other debates because they make clear the stakes involved in his case against Irving and also—perhaps counterintuitively—against Lipstadt herself in her defense of historical truth. Those strands include Fish's complaints that appeals to free speech are naive, and the related claim that they are naive because they insist upon an unsustainable distinction between speech and action (words and deeds). Fish also argues that academic work, regardless of the broader claims intellectuals might make for that work, cannot function as an engine of social change, and so any claim that a historian might make for his or her work is devoid of social force (or, in Fish's terms, consequence). The problem with history in particular, Fish argues, is that it is an examination of events and a narrative accounting of those events, and the historian's storytelling function pulls the rug out from under any claims he or she might make about having all the facts. So, Fish will claim, anyone who wants to suppress hate speech on the grounds of historical precedent (the Holocaust happened; lynchings happened; violence against women happens) or intellectual integrity (the deniers are bad historians) will fail. On the other side, those who defend the deniers on the grounds of free speech will also fail because speech has consequences inside of communities; there is no free speech as such, only rhetorical utterances that serve a particular purpose for a well-defined set of interlocutors.

The argument against the notion of "free speech" is most compactly and cogently argued in the much-cited "There's No Such Thing as Free Speech, and It's a Good Thing, Too." Comparing Canadian laws regulating speech to the First Amendment of the U.S. Constitution, on the basis of which many campus speech codes were struck down or withdrawn by university officials in the 1990s, Fish makes the point that the establishment of colleges and universities doesn't rest on their ability to foster independent ideas; he claims that "all educational institutions rest on some set of beliefs" and so any such institution confronted by speech that one of its members feels is offensive or degrading has to balance the harm that speech might do to the institution's principles or beliefs against the harm of curtailing such speech (*There's* 107–08) . Fish cites Benno Schmidt's *Wall Street Journal* essay on speech codes as indicative of the failure of logic in the First Amendment position: "when the goals of harmony collide with freedom of expression," freedom must be "the paramount obligation of an academic community" (108). Fish notes that the phrase "an academic community" is a dead giveaway, and he argues that there is no such thing as context-less speech, or speech that is free from constraint; an academic institution's belief that speech in and of itself should trump offensive versions of it is a situationally specific belief, a belief that institutions are or should be value neutral.

Fish takes this position a step further in his argument against Rodney Smolla, who tells us in *Free Speech in an Open Society* that a faculty member at a college or university is free to provide "bona fide academic opinions" on matters of race, or any other matter, "even though most people of goodwill and good sense on the campus would find the opinions loathsome" (qtd. in Fish, *Trouble* 77). It is the tension between the "bona fide" academic opinion and the opinion held by those of goodwill that most concerns Fish, and he applies it to the case of *Collin v. Smith*, in which Frank Collin, leader of the National Socialist Party of America, sued the village of Skokie, Illinois for passing ordinances that would have prevented the NSPA from demonstrating in a village densely populated by survivors of the Holocaust and their families. In striking down the ordinances, Judge Wilbur Pell, writing for the majority, says that to deny the NSPA to demonstrate its views would be tantamount to "ideological tyranny," this in spite of the fact that "the proposed demonstration would seriously disturb, emotionally and mentally, at least some and probably many of the Village's residents" (qtd. in Fish 81, 82). Fish calls this position for what it is—one in which good people are convinced, on the principle of free speech, to do nothing—and makes clear that "pornographers, Holocaust deniers, and cross-burners are not for free speech but for pornography, the denial of the Holocaust, and the intimidation of minorities." Fish argues that it is better for people of conscience to forget about principle and instead argue on policy grounds: "that is, on the grounds that you think it is good and right" (90, 89). To deny the Holocaust may, on free speech grounds, be a "bona fide" argument, but it is not good and right.

The other problem with the Skokie decision is that it distinguishes between verbal wrongs and physical or psychological ones, a distinction Fish tells us doesn't hold up (but that causes problems for his argument against Irving and Lipstadt later on). Judge Pell's sense that the NSPA demonstration would do psychological harm to survivors is evidence that some forms of speech aren't just words (as in "sticks and stones may break my bones . . .") but are in fact deeds, and the problem here is that because the fetish that the First Amendment has made of speech trumps those words that might cause harm, harms are "finally not taken seriously" (82). The assumption by Pell—and by others who take free speech as an umbrella that would allow the American Nazi Party to march through a group of Holocaust survivors, or for them to defend Hitler—is that "speech-induced harms, unlike the harms caused by physical assault, are relatively minor, barely skin-deep inconveniences for which a ready remedy is available in the form of counterspeech" (83). Fish doesn't go on to tell us at this point whether he sees this as a useful remedy to Holocaust denial, but he does make clear that liberals who use this argument to defend forms of speech that they themselves find disagreeable or offensive are engaging in a "rhetoric of regret" that leads to passivity or resignation.

The line that First Amendment fetishists draw between words and ideas on the one hand and deeds on the other derives from the *Chaplinsky v. New Hampshire* case of 1942, in which the court held that there are certain words that are simply meant to incite violent reaction, and that these "fighting words" are "likely to provoke the average person to retaliation, and thereby cause a breach of the peace" (qtd. in Fish, *There's* 105; see also Fish, *Professional* 36). The problem, as Fish makes clear, is that one person's breach of the peace is another's pabulum ("every idea is an incitement to somebody"), and the strong line drawn between garden-variety speech and fighting words becomes blurred at best and useless at worst. The *Collin v. Smith* case makes the matter more complicated: Hitler apologists like the NSPA and Holocaust deniers more generally may only be expressing an idea, but that idea ("the Holocaust was not the Holocaust") might logically be considered fighting words to Holocaust survivors. But while the idea may be odious and psychologically injurious, it is still an idea protected by the First Amendment. Cases such as *Collin v. Smith* and *Chaplinsky v. New Hampshire* put a tremendous amount of pressure on the freedom of speech fetishists and show the need to find another criterion for deciding which expressions of an idea— pornography, the National Man-Boy Love Association, Holocaust denial—ought to be suppressed and how.

I would go even further, however, and ask something Fish only hints at: are utterances like Holocaust denial really "effusions of essentially free minds" (*Professional* 36) calculated to have a reasonable effect? If the line between words and deeds is blurry when we're dealing with utterances that are simply expressions of an idea ("every idea is an incitement to somebody"), it gets even blurrier when dealing with words whose consequences are not easily traced back to their (rational) cause. It's one thing to say, as several Holocaust deniers have said, that their case is reasonable and their conclusions are based on a consideration of evidence. Whether serious or not, such statements are clothed in the rhetoric of reason, whereby evidence is gathered, data synthesized, and conclusions reached. It's another thing to start out with the intention, in Lyotard's terms, of producing a damage, and this is precisely what the marchers through Skokie seem to have had on their minds. One of Frank Collin's groupies made the following statement of the planned march:

> I hope [the Jewish residents of Skokie] are terrified. . . . I hope they're shocked. Because we're coming to get them again. I don't care if someone's mother or father or brother died in the gas chambers. The unfortunate thing is not that there were six million Jews who died. The unfortunate thing is that there were so many Jewish survivors. (qtd. in Fish, *Trouble* 80)

Fish sees this statement as producing a reasonable (if unconstitutional) effect: the passing of ordinances to prevent the march. I see it as a calculated attempt to produce a response that would be altogether unreasonable, one that has nothing to do with discourse, or rational discussion, or the changing of minds.

The Consequences of History

Consequences like these are a tricky business for Fish, particularly when it comes to what Richard Rorty would call "abnormal discourse," language that seems to work against the considered norms of a culture, a discourse community, or a discipline. As he's been saying at least since the publication of *Doing What Comes Naturally*, the work of literary theory and of the academic more generally has few if any consequences in the broader social arena. While the university may be the site for pathbreaking work in the fields of law, or history, or cultural studies, and while this work may have real consequences for how these fields do their work, the paradigm shifts that take place in those fields have consequences only for members of those fields. Fish's point in "Being Interdisciplinary Is So Very Hard to Do" and "Looking Elsewhere: Cultural Studies and Interdisciplinarity" is that the legal scholarship of Anita Hill or Catherine McKinnon (or Stanley Fish) has very little bearing or influence upon their politics or the effect they have in the political arena. And the formula works the other way around as well: the political work of a Catherine McKinnon or Anita Hill has little bearing on their credentials, let alone their work, in legal studies. While First Amendment lawyers draw a line between protected speech and that which veers dangerously close to action or incitement, on this score it's Fish who draws the line, this time between the work of the historian or legal scholar and the broader consequences of that work: "[T]he wish that lies at the heart of literary academics, the wish to be consequential in ways larger than those made available by the discipline as it is practiced every day in classrooms" is at best silly, and at its overreaching worst it is "megalomaniacal" (*Professional* 87).

As I say, such consequences are a tricky business, because when it comes to Holocaust denial, much of the work of keeping it contained outside the academy takes place *inside* the academy. Deborah Lipstadt, regardless of her pronouncements in the pages of *Hadassah Magazine*, is a trained historian; David Irving, despite his pronouncements before skinheads, is also a well-regarded historian of military history (though clearly not of the Final Solution). Robert Jan van Pelt and Richard Evans, two of the expert witnesses who testified before the court in the *Irving v. Lipstadt* trial, spent a great deal of their time poring over Irving's books and the documents he and others worked with, and they wrote sprawling reports on what they found. The work of these historians and scholars would seem, at least on the face of things, to have been "consequential in ways larger than those made available by the discipline" not because these scholars made political pronouncements or called Irving a liar in court (though Evans clearly did just that), but because their work seems once and for all to have put the lid on David Irving the "historian" if not his anti-Semitic and racist followers on the lunatic fringe. The language Irving uses in his books on Hitler, and the language used by writers for the *Journal of Historical Review* (the "historical" journal published by the Institute of the same name, the organ of the denial movement in the U.S. and Britain) is discipline-specific and clothed in scholarly garb. But it could not be more consequential, both to survivors and their families, as well as to other people of goodwill and good sense.

Connected to Fish's narrow view of the consequences of academic work is his equally narrow—or, rather, equally flat—sense of history and the work of the historian. Fish cites George Bush the elder, who in 1991 lashed out at the U.N. resolution equating Zionism with racism and who claimed that the equation "is to twist history and forget the terrible plight of Jews in World War II and indeed throughout history" (qtd. in Fish, *There's* 60). Fish worries that it's just this "forgetting of history" that has allowed the right to make its case against, among other things, affirmative action policies by ignoring the history of segregation, exclusion, and brutality that has produced the need for such policies in the first place. Historical forgetting enables anti-affirmative action proponents to call the policies it disagrees with "reverse racism" and thereby puts "racism" and "affirmative action" on the same historical plane. But such an equation is possible "only if one considers the virus of racism to be morally and medically indistinguishable from the therapy we apply to it" (61). There is for Fish—as there is for most historians—a clear and palpable distinction between an event (here, those events that are taken, collectively, as racist actions) and a narrative meant to make those events legible to those of us living in history (here, the equation made possible by the forgetting of history and the replacement of the phrase "affirmative action" with "reverse racism").

In his argument with new historicism, Fish makes the distinction between fact and event clearer still. He grants, with the new historicists, that history is textual; but he is not willing to grant their corollary point, that the textuality of history means that matters of historical fact cannot be settled:

> The belief that facts are constructed is a *general* one and is not held with reference to any facts in particular; particular facts are firm or in question insofar as the perspective (of some enterprise or discipline or area of inquiry) within which they emerge is firmly in place, settled; and should that perspective be dislodged (always a possibility) the result will not be an indeterminacy of fact, but a new shape of factual firmness underwritten by a newly, if temporarily, settled perspective. (*There's* 248)

Challenging the coherence of the narrative on which the evidence of history is arranged does not change the evidence itself, nor does it change the facts that are suggested by that evidence. But the challenge does force us to reconsider and perhaps rearrange those facts according to the challenger's narrative.

Two things must be made clear here: first, the work of challenging the coherence of the narrative must be rigorous and must proceed within established procedures and traditions of inquiry; second, the arbiters of the disagreement will be those engaged in the "enterprise or discipline of an area of inquiry," which, in the case of Holocaust revision and denial, would seem to fall squarely to historians. Facts are facts; paradigms are another matter. Fish ultimately comes down on the side of good old-fashioned historians against the New Historicists, and with Howard Horwitz he tells us that disputes about history aren't epistemological but empirical: they're arguments over "evidence and its significance" (qtd. in Fish, *There's* 253). The challenges to the historical events that comprise the Holocaust are settled in the court of history and cannot be settled with reference to the events themselves; and those challenges may have consequences for how we see history but not, for example, how Jews understand their place in a Europe that still shows the aftereffects of the Final Solution, or how we remember those events (see 255).

Fish is disdainful of those who, like Elizabeth Fox-Genovese, see history as not simply a body of texts and a strategy of interpretation (that is, those who don't see history as textual), but as "what did happen in the past—of the social relations and, yes, 'events' of which our records offer only imperfect clues" (qtd. in *There's* 245). Fox-Genovese's point about history isn't all that distant from Louis Mink's, who writes that after all historiographical options have been considered, "the conviction returns that the past is after all *there*, with a determinateness beyond and over against our partial reconstructions" (93). Mink might suggest that Fish's paradox—that a history is made and that history happens—cannot be solved but that we "oscillate" between its two irreconcilable poles. Pierre Vidal-Naquet, one of the strongest voices against Holocaust denial on both the left and the right, acknowledges Fish's subjectivist position but nonetheless insists that "beyond [discourse], or before this, there is something irreducible which, for better or worse, I would still call reality" (qtd. in Ginzburg 86). The difficulty in Fish's position is that there is very little room left in history for those events or aspects of events that seem to defy a narrative accounting of them but that are nonetheless identifiable and that nonetheless have very palpable and sometimes destructive effects on both the witnesses who see them and those who hear their testimonies. Fish sees history as the work of historians, sees its effects as fairly narrow and well-defined, and sees its discourse as more or less reasonable and rational. The problem with the Holocaust, and with those who—like David Irving and Bradley Smith (the author of the Committee for the Open Debate on the Holocaust's supplements to campus newspapers)—would revise it into something else or argue (or wish) it out of existence, is that they're not willing to confine themselves to the historical enterprise, nor are they willing to engage in discourse or, if they are, use a discourse that amounts to "fighting words," arousing not rational counterarguments but the irrationality of hostility and anger.

Holocaust Denial and Academic Freedom

Fish's extensive essay on the problem of Holocaust denial ("Holocaust Denial and Academic Freedom") is in some respects familiar territory, since it argues—much like the essays that have appeared in his other books—that appeals to historical truth, like appeals to academic freedom, are equally flawed because both seem to insist on some position of authority (verifiable historical reality, the free marketplace of ideas separate from base motives) that simply doesn't exist.[2] To say that Deborah Lipstadt has once and for all quieted the voices of deniers because she's finally proved the events of the Holocaust is just as preposterous as saying that the deniers should have their say because they should be granted academic freedom: "If the standard of validation [of the facts of the Holocaust] is the establishment of a truth that is invulnerable to challenge, no one, including Lipstadt, could meet it" ("Holocaust" 504). Fish argues that there ought to be some other, less severe standard that depends on the careful, methodologically sound scrutiny of evidence and the narratives inside of which it makes sense. It works just the same way with academic freedom: it isn't the freedom to say or do anything in the name of intellectual pursuit, "allowing 'new ideas' to flourish willy nilly until time and the marketplace separated the wheat from the chaff"; academic freedom is just that, *academic* freedom—that is, particular to those practices and enterprises recognized as such by the community of academics (518).

Placed together, these arguments serve as a useful antidote to grand claims for history and academic freedom. But they ignore a nuanced understanding of history, particularly the history of what could be called a "limit event" (the Shoah), that has been established in the last several years by those working on just such events. According to such an understanding, history is broader in its effects, and those effects are far less reasonable and predictable (they are much more radically particular), than Fish would have it. While history and forgetfulness might seem to be at odds (we do ourselves a disservice by forgetting events that, like the Holocaust, we might rather not remember at all), the events of history are *inevitably* lost to memory, and they are lost at precisely the point at which they are witnessed. Historical work produces a narrative that makes sense of the events' detritus, their aftereffects. But historical events affect witnesses and documentary and evidentiary leavings, and those effects aren't always reasonable, rational, or easily subsumed to the narrative that drives them. The revision or denial of history—marches through towns like Skokie, the demonstrations in front of campus newspaper offices that have accepted the CODOH's circulars questioning the occurrence of the Holocaust, or a libel suit like the one David Irving filed against Deborah Lipstadt and her publisher—is itself an event that leaves traces in the historical narratives built to contain it and that has effects that aren't easily confined to the law courts or the historical archives.

Fish says of the *Irving v. Lipstadt* trial that the books and other accounts written about it all seem to have in common the idea that what was at issue in the trial was not "the accuracy of a particular historical account, but the honor of history itself and even the honor of Truth" and that, in a provocative phrase, Irving "is a perpetrator of crimes against epistemology" (499). The problem with Lipstadt's assertions isn't that she's wrong, but that she's right for the wrong reasons. It would be one thing for her to say that she's right and Irving's wrong because his understanding of the evidence is in error and his arrangement of those facts, because they are in error, leads to unsupportable conclusions. But she doesn't say this, according to Fish. Instead, she begins from the premise that "any argument denying or diminishing the Holocaust is specious and that the so called evidence it invokes is not really evidence at all but strained rationalization and downright fabrication" (500–01).

But, in fact, Lipstadt's defense against Irving has little to do with making statements on behalf of History or Truth and has everything to do with the evidence that Irving and other historians have adduced. A good deal of the testimony taken in the *Irving v. Lipstadt* trial establishes not the truth of the account Irving has provided of Hitler, the Final Solution, or even the bombing of Dresden (on which he has also written), but his manipulations of the evidence. In one instance, Lipstadt's lawyer brings Irving's attention to a memo written by Himmler, which Irving says is part of the evidence that exonerates Hitler from any part in the Final Solution. In the memo, Himmler provides notes for a phone conversation with the general in charge of the concentration camp system; Irving writes that the phone call amounted to an order to prevent Jews from being liquidated in December 1941. The order, according to Irving, was, "Jews are to stay where they are" (qtd. in Evans 208–09).[3] But the memo actually reads "the administrative leaders of the SS are to stay where they are." So we do not have an argument, as Fish would have it, over the matter of "historical truth" here; what we have here instead is the manufacture of evidence, evidence that says what it says and around which contexts of whatever nature can be built to provide whatever historically pertinent account of the Final Solution one wants to build. But Irving tried here, and at countless other points in the trial where he was caught in the same sorts of blatant lies about evidence, to simply make something up out of thin air.

So it is hard to see how Fish can reach the conclusion about historians, particularly those involved in the Lipstadt trial, that "neither party reaches its conclusion by sifting the evidence on the way to determining the truth of the matter; rather, each begins with a firm conviction of what the truth of the matter is, and then from inside the lens of conviction receives and evaluates (the shape of the evaluation is assured) the assertion of contrary truths" ("Holocaust" 501). Not only is this patently unfair to the way most historians work, it is particularly unfair to Lipstadt and her lawyers in her defense against Irving. Fish says of historical evidence that it "doesn't just sit there unadorned and unencumbered asking for your independent evaluation" but rather resides "in the midst of a structure (of belief and conviction) that precedes it and colors one's reception of it" (502). Fair enough.

But there are enough instances in the Lipstadt trial that make it plain that structures of belief are not at issue. One piece of evidence that Richard Rampton brought to the court's attention late in the Irving trial concerns the latter's association with racist groups in the United States. In a written interrogatory, Irving denied up and down—as he had done in the past—that he'd had any association with a white-supremacist group called the National Alliance, and he denied in particular that he had attended any meetings of the group. After Rampton produced a letter of invitation to Irving from the Alliance and an entry from Irving's diary describing the meeting, Irving became testy, saying, "There is not the slightest reference either in that diary entry or in any other diary entry to the NA or the National Alliance which confirms what I said about having had no knowledge of them" (Guttenplan 250). Rampton then read a further entry in the diary:

> "Drove all day to Tampa, phoned Key West, etc. etc. etc. Arrived at the Hotel Best Western at 4:00 pm. Sinister gent with pony tail was the organizer. Turned out the meeting here is also organized by the National Alliance and the National Vanguard Bookshop. Well attended." Now, Mr. Irving, do you want to revise the answers you have just been giving me? (250)

While it is certainly the case that this evidence—Irving's diary and the letter of invitation on National Alliance letterhead—doesn't "just sit there," Irving's lie does.

There are indeed multiple narratives that might account for the evidence left from the Final Solution, for the countless memos, lists, speeches and other documents produced by the SS, the Wehrmacht and the Order Police. And there are multiple narratives, too, that might account for the evidence left of Irving's work in archives, for his meetings with racist groups and his travels and phone conversations. But that evidence has a materiality to it. As Fish says in an earlier work, "If you set out to determine what happened in 1649, you will look to the materials that recommend themselves to you as the likely repositories of historical knowledge and go from there. . . . You and those who dispute your findings (a word precisely intended) will be engaged in empirical work" (*There's* 253); the work of establishing the textual nature of the history that the evidence seems to suggest is a different sort of work entirely. But it's this latter sort of work, I think, that Fish associates with Holocaust deniers and those who would stand against them; what the *Irving v. Lipstadt* trial has shown over and over again, however, is that what's at issue isn't the historical accounts produced of the evidence—the matter of the "truth" of the Holocaust's occurrence or non-occurrence—but of the evidence itself and of its durability.

Denial, Memory, and the Witness

It is the evidence's durability—its materiality, the fact that it simply cannot speak for itself—that leads us to try to draw lessons from that evidence, to construct narratives that make sense at some level. That the Final Solution and the destruction of Jewish culture in Europe seem to make no sense from the very beginning makes the job of historians of the Holocaust that much harder; the evidence leads to a narrative of utter unreality, one that seems so contrary to human reason that the denial of those events on the grounds that they are too unreasonable to contemplate might in the end seem easier than accepting them. To paraphrase Yehuda Bauer's question, how could the most civilized nation in Europe contrive to eliminate an entire people in a systemic and scientific way? (14). But it is the evidence's durability that seems to exert pressure on the narratives that would seek to explain them. Fish takes Michael Shermer and Alex Grobman to task for seeing the work of the historian as, in their words, "the combined product of past events and the discovery and description of past events" (21). Fish worries that "[a]ccording to this language, events exert a pressure on their own discovery and co-operate, in a way that remains unspecified, with the task of describing themselves" ("Holocaust" 509). Well, not exactly. What Shermer and Grobman, along with Fox-Genovese, imply is that history (and historical work) is constrained by reality, which, according to Amos Funkenstein, is "beyond the modes of narrative, the mythopoetic intensity of the narrator, the intervening subconsciousness and superego," which is "never isolatable yet all pervasive" (34). The real—both the material dimension of the world that affects individual memories and the affective and counterrational element of the individual memories themselves—"escapes our control, [and] forces itself upon us whether or not we welcome it," but it is also "that which we make relevant, construct, manipulate" (Funkenstein 35). Historical work shows the impingements of the real and tries hard to gain some control over them. Historians write to produce in the reader a sense of what was recollected by the original witness and collected in the material evidence. But what the witness saw, and the materiality of the evidence, are beyond the modes of narrative ("the event," reality as it impinges upon us and our conventions of thought and language); and though the event impinges upon us, it may or may not be narratable, though it is most certainly visible as it works against the grain of the narrative of collective memory. Fish is right: evidence doesn't just sit there unencumbered; but neither does it easily fit any one of the narrative accounts built to subsume it into history, whether it is the account of a Deborah Lipstadt, or a Christopher Browning, or the amateur historian named David Irving.

This is why, in spite of National Socialism's "arguing away" of the facts of Jewish citizenship, or the fraudulence of the *Protocols of the Elders of Zion* and of Holocaust deniers everywhere, the impingements of the real (the reality of the gas chambers, of anti-Semitism, and of the destruction of the Shoah) will ultimately disturb the narrative of denial and show the revisionists for the liars they are. Their "arguments" make sense of the crimes of the Final Solution that are otherwise not sensible or rational: "Many of us say that the Nazi crimes were 'incomprehensible,' that the sheer limitless inventiveness in degradation and killing of that regime defy all our historical explanatory schemes. . . . Precisely this incomprehensibility of the crimes makes their denial into a much more rational account of a possible world (better than ours) in which people act out of rational, or at least predictable motivations" (Funkenstein 47). But individual memory—that which is out of reach of the rational—"shines through" and affects that rational, collective narrative. The effect of the event stands in the way of this sort of "diabolical worldmaking," preventing it from becoming an arbitrary concoction altogether removed from what happened. Though this reality is something outside the narrative that is brought to bear upon history in order to adjudicate accountings, it is nonetheless also embedded into the accountings themselves.

And, yet, it is individual memory that seemed to be entirely missing from the *Irving v. Lipstadt* proceedings. In summing up the trial, D.D. Guttenplan writes,

> And so we take refuge in history, in documents, in facts—cool, detached, silent, precise. . . .
>
> But witnesses, memories, *testimony*—all that was left outside the courtroom. And that seems to me cause for regret.
>
> Witnesses are always partial. Memory is by definition selective. And testimony—not the sworn responses of expert witnesses, but the still-vivid responses of people whose history is lived, not studied—can be treacherous. (307–08)

While Fish (and I) would disagree with Guttenplan's sense of facts as "cool" or "detached," it is the witnesses who do, in fact, seem oddly absent both in the *Irving v. Lipstadt* trial and also in Fish's account of the problem of Holocaust denial. Fish tells us repeatedly that historians do their work "by telling a story that fits with the stories we already know to be true and telling it in ways that corresponds to our by now intuitive and internalized sense of how one connects the dots between observations on the way to a conclusion" ("Holocaust" 510). This "fit" is achieved by hewing closely to the practices and protocols established by historians whose work is more or less conventional and that has effects inside the academy, whose "freedom" Fish sees as specific not universal. The argument that Irving was unjustly prevented from purveying his version of events in the Nazi Reich because as an academic he was simply doing what academics do is corrupt; he was justly prevented from purveying that version because he was not hewing to those conventional methods of inquiry that make a historian a historian.

But what about witnesses, real people, like those survivors in Skokie who would be harmed by a neo-Nazi march through the city, or like those who saw what they saw in hiding and in the camps but whose reality is impugned by those like Irving whose academic credentials are in shreds but who nonetheless tell a certain tale and have a ready audience? Individual witnesses—as well as individuals whose encounters with the events of the Shoah either as secondhand witnesses or as "people of goodwill and good sense" or as those so troubled by its tropes and images that they, like Binjamin Wilkomirski, come to identify with its horror—have a real stake in *Irving v. Lipstadt* and the phenomenon of denial. And the deniers themselves, particularly those unlike Irving who have no claim upon history and who have no other stake in denying the Shoah except their racism and anti-Semitism, must also be accounted for, and their work must be explained in terms broader than the purely disciplinary and academic. Fish is right to say that Holocaust denial, as a phenomenon, can't be allowed on the grounds of academic freedom because what the deniers are doing is not academic work, and he's right to say that their ideas cannot be promulgated on the grounds of free speech because what they're selling is not the context-less expression of an idea. And he's right also to suggest that if we want to do away with the deniers, one way to do this is simply to tell them "that they have not met our criteria for being considered seriously and that we are sending them away" ("Holocaust" 524). Lipstadt "made the bastards pay" by dissolving Irving's reputation as a historian. But denial isn't only about history and about how one responds—through law or through discourse or through other rational, political means—to false claims. "Denial hurts people," Raul Hilberg told Guttenplan before the trial, and therein lies an aspect of Irving's pronouncements about Hitler or the CODOH's insinuations about what really went on at Auschwitz that is a byproduct of the blurred line between words and deeds (302). It isn't so much that "every idea is an incitement to somebody" but that in the case of Holocaust denial there are real harms—harms to memory and to being—that "are finally not taken seriously" either by those clinging fast to the First Amendment or by those who, like Fish in this case, want to see the consequences of work done by historians and faux-historians alike as bearing only on Lipstadt, Irving and their circle (Fish, *There's* 106; *Trouble* 82).

Guttenplan is right: "Irving does represent a real danger," whether or not he's been rendered toothless (and certainly now penniless) by the British courts (298). Deniers really do assault memory, as is implied in Lipstadt's title. During a *Donahue* show taped in 1994, the deniers David Cole and Bradley Smith shared a stage with Michael Shermer and a camp survivor. At one point, the producers showed a clip of Dachau, and in what Shermer hoped would be a rational discussion of the relation of what we know about the Holocaust to what we have heard, he referred to the claim (now known to be, in all likelihood, untrue) that soap was mass produced from the remains of dead Jewish inmates. The survivor, Judith Berg, insisted, "It was true. They made lampshades and they cooked soap. It's true" (Shermer and Grobman 113). In response, Shermer tried to explain the difference between reassessment of facts and the wholesale denial of history, but Smith quickly accused the survivor of lying. From this point things got ugly, and Berg shouted, "I was seven months there. If you are blind someone else can see it. I was seven months there," to which Smith replied "What does that have to do with soap? No soap, no lampshades. The professor [Shermer] says you're wrong, that's all." The eyewitness' very real suffering, and her confusion of her own memories with those of others', became conflated: it doesn't matter at all that she was there and that what she had to offer by way of evidence was both heartfelt and unquestionably verifiable. Her "mistake" was enough for Smith to discount her testimony altogether, regardless of the event that that testimony clearly indicates (though perhaps failed to represent clearly), and the historian's explanation was seen as the hairsplitting of the base casuist.

It is finally memory on which denial has its most profound and damaging effect: not history, not academic freedom, not "the truth," but the events of the Shoah that reside in the memories of those who were there and—more and more through the projections of history and of fiction and of images—those who weren't. The battle has already been won, Fish tells us, because "the vast majority of mainstream researchers support Holocaust affirmers and reject Holocaust deniers," and I'm taken by the way Fish ends his essay: if all else fails in fighting off the deniers' lies, "make the bastards pay" ("Holocaust" 511). But if the battle's been won by the historians, it's precariously unresolved in the much larger field of memory because denial hurts people by filling the silence that inevitably comes from the "damage" of denial with the deniers' false but apparently plausible explanation of the destruction of central European Jewish culture. The Holocaust really is a limit case in which the testimonies that bore the "traces of the here's and now's" and the documents that "indicated the sense or senses of facts" have been destroyed (Lyotard 57). The witness, as much as the historian, is charged with "breaking the monopoly over history granted to the cognitive regimen of phrases" and must lend an ear "to what is not presentable under the rules of knowledge" (57). Our job is to find a way to write that allows what is impressed in memory but lost to language and to "evidence" to have an effect on history; and it may require a language other than that of history to do so.

In the end, I think Fish's point about Lipstadt and some of those who are working against Holocaust denial is right—namely, that when they make claims for historical "truth" they're going too far. I also agree with him that "academic freedom" is squishy ground on which to silence the deniers. But I'm not sure that this is, in the end, just an argument about history or about the force of language and reason. Though his writings about Holocaust denial, particularly his Seegers Lecture, function as a strong rebuttal to the deniers' arguments, they don't go to the heart of why the deniers should be able to make their case in the first place, and they fail to consider arguments from witnesses—problematic as they might be—that might provide a stronger rebuttal still. One reason for this may be that the work of history is more complicated, and has broader implications, than Fish's presentation of it suggests. True, the historian follows lines of inquiry, and based on documentary and testimonial evidence the historian finds a convergence of that evidence that seems to explain a preponderance of it under a controlling if sometimes complicated narrative. But accounts of it are stronger or weaker in part because of the story they *don't* tell as much as for the story that they do; the survivor on *Donahue* may have provided a weak account of her experiences in the camps because of her error regarding the soap supposedly produced in Dachau, but her insistence on the fact that she saw what she saw, despite its inability to tell us precisely *what* she saw, provides another kind of evidence, in another kind of language, that has nothing to do with reasonableness, or the conventions of history, or the archival work that sustains it. Bradley Smith's denial of the witness' memory, and his willingness to provide an alternative narrative in the face of her inability to respond to charges of falsification, has a real historical effect on those for whom the work of the historian matters little and barely registers on the radar.

Fish, I think, would agree with Louis Mink's conviction "that the past is after all *there*, with a determinateness beyond and over against our partial reconstructions," and that even in the face of reconstructions of it in all sorts of narratives, it nonetheless makes itself apparent, though perhaps not rationally so. This, finally, is the deniers' strongest foundation, as well as the historians' predicament; as Vidal-Naquet constantly reminds us, the historian *writes*, and that writing is neither neutral nor transparent. The difficulty is finding a way for that "historical discourse [to be] connected—by as many intermediate links as one likes—to what may be called, for lack of a better term, reality" (110–11). Though historians will continue to marshal evidence and build a strong narrative account of history, that work still won't be enough to counter the deniers, since this is just one more argument based on yet another reconstruction of evidence that is itself often suspect and is susceptible to the same doubt as any other argument. And it will be hard to find stronger, more plausible arguments until we're better able to see the complexity of the circumstances that foster a skeptical disbelief—in its political and cultural variety and contradiction—in the deniers themselves. I'd like very much to believe, with Fish, that whether they know it or not, historians have already won the battle against denial and have made a strong case that the Holocaust is "after all *there*." But if we leave it up to historians and other scholars, and it is left to the rest of us to "make the bastards pay," we may need to find alternate means, and alternative languages, to make sure that the silence inherent in memory isn't filled with lies that accrete until they become real.

Notes

1. Fish's side of the debates, staged in 1991 and 1992, are published in *There's No Such Thing as Free Speech, and It's a Good Thing, Too*.

2. The argument has been delivered, in various incarnations, in lectures on campuses across the country, including the University of Wisconsin at Madison. At Valparaiso University's Law School, it was given as the "Seegers Lecture," which was subsequently published in the *Valparaiso Law Review*.

3. The memo reads in full:

> Besuch bei Schwarz.
> Koksagys.
> Verwaltungsfuhrer der SS
>   haben zu bleiben.
> Lappenschuhe u. Finnenstiefel

In the third and fourth lines, Irving has changed the "h" to a "j," the "a" to a "u," and a "b" to a "d," thus rendering it "Juden zu bleiben," the Jews are to stay where they are. Irving tried hard during his testimony to suggest this was an honest mistake having to do with the sloppiness of Himmler's handwriting (though Himmler's handwriting is fairly clear according to Evans, a historian who has seen the relevant documents), and he tried to ignore the fact that "Juden zu bleiben" is ungrammatical (whereas "haben zu bleiben" is perfectly grammatical).

Works Cited

Bauer, Yehuda. *Rethinking the Holocaust*. New Haven, CT: Yale UP, 2001.

Evans, Richard J. *Lying about Hitler: History, Holocaust, and the David Irving Trial*. New York: Basic, 2001.

Fish, Stanley. "Being Interdisciplinary Is So Very Hard to Do." *Profession 89* (1989): 15–22.

————. "Holocaust Denial and Academic Freedom." *Valparaiso University Law Review* 35.3 (2001): 499–524.

————. "Looking Elsewhere: Cultural Studies and Interdisciplinarity." *Professional Correctness: Literary Studies and Political Change*. Oxford, Eng.: Clarendon, 1995. 71–92.

————. *Professional Correctness: Literary Studies and Political Change*. Oxford, Eng.: Clarendon, 1995.

————. *There's No Such Thing as Free Speech, and It's a Good Thing, Too*. New York: Oxford UP, 1994.

————. *The Trouble with Principle*. Cambridge: Harvard UP, 1999.

Funkenstein, Amos. *Perceptions of Jewish History*. Berkeley: U of California P, 1993.

Ginzburg, Carlo. "Just One Witness." *Probing the Limits of Representation: Nazism and the Final Solution*. Ed. Saul Friedlander. Cambridge, MA: Harvard UP, 1992. 82–96.

Guttenplan, D.D. *The Holocaust on Trial*. New York: Norton, 2001.

Lipstadt, Deborah E. *Denying the Holocaust: The Growing Assault on Truth and Memory*. New York: Free P, 1993.

Lyotard, Jean-François. *The Differend: Phrases in Dispute*. Trans. Georges Van Den Abbeele. Minneapolis: U of Minnesota P, 1988.

Mink, Louis O. *Historical Understanding*. Ithaca: Cornell UP, 1987.

Shermer, Michael, and Alex Grobman. *Denying History: Who Says the Holocaust Never Happened and Why Do They Say It?* Berkeley: U of California P, 2000.

Vidal-Naquet, Pierre. *Assassins of Memory: Essays on the Denial of the Holocaust*. Trans. Jeffrey Mehlman. New York: Columbia UP, 1992.

PART FOUR

AFTERWORD

One More Time

Stanley Fish

Let's begin by getting the guilty pleas out of the way. First, I plead guilty to many (although not all) of the crimes Terry Eagleton accuses me of. I am, as Eagleton says, a Hobbesian, and in several senses: I teach Hobbes regularly. I share his distrust of abstractions (which he derides as "absurd speech"). I am drawn to his account of the conventional nature of our judgments and reckonings. I find the deflationary mode of his writing—his way of letting the air out of a moral vocabulary he finds empty and refashioning it in material terms—congenial. (Eagleton no doubt means to suggest something darker by the kinship he asserts, but I shall let that pass.)

I am also guilty of not being on the left (although the right has no interest in claiming me). I can't see why it matters, but for the record I am what used to be known as a Skip Jackson-Bobby Kennedy democrat— fairly progressive on social issues, fairly conservative on economic issues, and decidedly conservative on foreign policy issues. This means, as Eagleton also says, that I am "not the most cosmopolitan of creatures." I travel abroad rarely, and my knowledge of what is happening in Europe, Asia, Africa and Latin America is pretty much limited to what I learn from newspapers, magazines and TV documentaries. Accordingly, I do not write about or comment on international issues. I confine myself to matters of which I have some knowledge—the American academy, the nature and history of professionalism, the theory and history of disciplines, sixteenth- and seventeenth-century English Literature, Freud, literary theory, legal theory, philosophy of language, contract law, first amendment jurisprudence, affirmative action, the jurisprudence of church and state, anglo-American liberalism, university administration, the teaching of composition, American television shows. This is a relatively long list, but, as I acknowledged in the preface to *Doing What Comes Naturally*, I bring to its items a small set of (obsessive) concerns, and so Eagleton is certainly onto something when he accuses me of writing the same book over and over again. (The materials and even the centuries change but my interrogation of them almost always traces out the same patterns.)

Eagleton, however, misses the mark when he lists my "scandalously provocative statements"—"truth is rhetoric, free speech is an illusion, unprincipled behavior is best"—and when he reports that I mount an all-out "assault on the principles of tolerance, impartiality, and mutual respect, as though the fact that they . . . have to allow for important exceptions must necessarily invalidate them altogether."

To take the last point first, my argument is not that abstractions like tolerance, impartiality, and mutual respect are *invalidated* by exceptions to them, but that they are *constituted*—made operational and doable—by exceptions. That is, they exist only in the form made available by the (prior) exceptions and do not exist in the strong or pure form often assumed by those who recommend them. Consider, for example, mutual respect, a habit of mind and practice that requires that you not make the differences (racial, ethnic, religious, political, cultural, sexual) you might have with some persons into a reason for excluding them from the conversation, or restricting their speech, or refusing them a hearing, or deporting them from the country. No one, however, who invokes mutual respect means *all* differences; mutual respect will always be exercised in the context of the more general difference (presupposed and in place) between those you take seriously and therefore respect even when you disagree with them and those whom no one (at least in your view) should take seriously (maybe creationists, or tobacco scientists, or out-and-out racists, or postmodernists, or people who think rap is better than Beethoven). Thus, Amy Gutmann and Dennis Thompson, two of our contemporary apostles of mutual respect, distinguish between those whose views we respect and those whose views we merely tolerate. (We won't kill them, because that's not the kind of thing we do, but neither will we invite them to our conferences or publish them in our journals.) This still leaves Gutmann and Thompson with a lot of people to whom they can show mutual respect (and there would be a real difference between their behavior and the behavior of strident dogmatists), but the mutual respect they show will have been shaped, will have the form and scope it has, by virtue of the *prior* decision—via the mechanism of the distinction between respecting and merely tolerating—*not* to respect some people. And that decision will not have been an encroachment on, or a diminution of, mutual respect; rather, it will have been the technology—necessary and constitutive—that gave the empty idea of mutual respect some content and turned it into a policy that Gutmann and Thompson could actually practice; they can now say, we respect *you* for the following reasons, and we don't respect (instead we tolerate) *you* for the same reasons.

But why not go whole hog and do mutual respect for real; that is, just respect everyone. Well, theoretically you could, and not pass judgment on anyone or anything and leave the sorting out of good and bad, useful and subversive, helpful and dangerous, life affirming and fraught with death (Oliver Wendell Holmes' great phrase) to God and eternity. But then of course you'd have no government, no judiciary, no admissions procedures, no parenting, no Nobel Prizes, no arguments, no giving of reasons, no normative thinking, nothing you would be willing to fight for and certainly nothing you would be willing to die for. In short you would not have any form of organized social life, for organized social life is impossible absent the discriminations a pure regime of mutual respect (should there ever be one and I assure you there won't) would rule out of court. The conclusion seems inescapable: while "mutual respect" names a possible form of human behavior distinguishable from others—you can be known as a generally respectful person rather than as a person given to sharp and hasty judgments—it does not name a program one can carry out independently of an *already-in-place* demarcation of those who are candidates for receiving it and those who are not. And that demarcation, to repeat my main point, is not a limitation on mutual respect; rather, it is the mechanism through which mutual respect acquires an intelligible and doable form. The limitation (or exception) comes first, the abstraction second.

The same argument holds for tolerance. You can certainly be a person who tends to be tolerant of others and who doesn't get upset at seeing or hearing things you think reprehensible; but you can't be just Tolerant with a capital T—tolerant toward everything and in every circumstance no matter what is at stake—without withdrawing from all the acts of judgment that make you a citizen, a legislator, a worker, a parent, an educator, a student, a pastor, the operator of a vehicle, a consumer etc.

That is, for you, and for anyone else, tolerance will always be thought of as having proper and improper objects in relation to a prior and person-constituting sense of what is valuable, vulnerable, worth protecting, worth fearing etc. And, again, the exceptions to tolerance—*that* we simply can't allow without undoing the fabric of our civilization—should not be thought of as diluting a value, but should be recognized as the necessary prior ground in the absence of which that value would be unintelligible and unperformable. Mutual respect and tolerance are usually thought of as overriding or outflanking or rising above substantive judgments: you respect or tolerate someone *despite* your rejection of that person's views. What I am saying is that in the absence of substantive judgments already in place mutual respect and tolerance are shapeless and without directing force as imperatives.

Ditto for freedom of speech. A full regime of free speech—where anything and everything could be said with impunity—would be a regime in which nothing particular could be said, for assertion only has traction—is heard as saying something rather than everything—if it resonates against a background stipulation (not consciously grasped, but constitutive of what consciousness can grasp and therefore of what can be expressed) of what is worth saying, what goes without saying, what needs saying, what it would be brave to say, what it would be harmful to say, etc. It is this background, already in place before a word is spoken, that enables any assertion to have a bite; that is, to be heard as going in this direction rather than that, as doing this job rather than that one. Were there no such background in place, were words just uttered in the context of no pre-conceptions, no vision, no preferences, no expectations built up from the personal and community history of expression, the result would not be assertion, but noise. Totally free speech, rather than being an ideal compromised by exceptions, is a condition (or would be a condition if it ever existed) that renders speech incapable of bearing significance, incapable of mattering. (This is the ideal state in certain religious traditions where union with deity is conceived as doing away with the need for communication—there is no distance either between you and the other or between you and the God you would know—and speech as we humanly practice it is replaced by a universal mantra of praise and by the music of the spheres.)

That is why, despite the rhetoric that surrounds the First Amendment, totally free speech is not what anyone desires. What people desire is the ability to speak freely about things that matter, and, as in the case of tolerance and mutual respect, the decision about what matters and does not matter (which will also be a decision about what deserves protection and what does not) is prior to the emergence of any free speech zone that is then configured in its wake. Free speech in whatever form it takes—and it will take different forms, as the background stipulations of what is worth saying and worth protecting are different; that's what First Amendment debates are about—cannot be threatened by exceptions because it is unthinkable apart from the exceptions that are necessary if speech is to be meaningful, to be more than noise. Once again, the limitations and exceptions come first, and the value they supposedly dilute but in fact lend content to, comes second. It is not that free speech is an illusion; it is, rather, that free speech in order to be a coherent concept requires the constraints thought to be its opposite; that's why it's a good thing that there's no such thing as free speech. (In his essay for this volume Michael Robertson elaborates this and related points in a manner more elegant than anything I have ever managed.)

Pace Eagleton, I am never in the business of denying the existence of valued forms of behavior (although I often suggest in provocative titles and slogans that I am doing just that); rather, I deny that the bare abstraction (tolerance, mutual respect, freedom of speech) can do real work without adding to it the leaven or alloy of the very thing thought to compromise it—intolerance, disrespect, regulation. You can't wake up in the morning (or so I say) and resolve to be "just" tolerant, or resolve to exercise mutual respect, or speak freely. You can, however, resolve to be tolerant with respect to a particular issue (although there will always be issues in relation to which you are quite hard line). You can resolve to extend respect to *this* point of view that you used to deride (although there will still be many points of view you regard as crazy or criminal). You can resolve to speak up on a particular matter (because you think it important to do so, although you don't care whether speech about some other matters is protected or not.) These values (and values they are) do not command a *general* adherence; rather, they are to be inserted (or not; there are times when you think that tolerance, respect and free speech are bad ideas) into particular situations when you judge that they would usefully serve whatever real imperatives impel and inform your actions.

By "real imperatives" I mean the imperatives that follow from substantive moral commitments, like the commitment to redistribute wealth, or the commitment to educate every child (leave no child behind), or the commitment to protect the environment, or the commitment to end violence against women. What make such commitments different from the commitment to be just tolerant or mutually respectful—tolerant or mutually respectful absent the specification of value—is that once you've signed on to them, your course of action is fairly clear; the means may still be debated, but the end has been specified, and you can resolve to work for its realization, a realization that will be empirical and substantive. Those, however, who invoke tolerance or mutual respect (or fairness or equality or neutrality) typically claim to have sidestepped substance in favor of what Thomas Nagel calls a "higher order impartiality," a resolve not to hew to your strongly held moral and political views or try to institutionalize them, but rather to subordinate them to a proceduralism that renders them indistinguishable from the views of your opponents. The advice to be tolerant or mutually respectful is the advice to withdraw from your commitments, to not work for them, to forsake particulars for a general imperative; but since that imperative is empty (that is, of course, the claim) it cannot direct you to do anything, or if it does so direct you it is only because it will have been supplemented—given substance—by the very kind of consideration it claims to have outflanked. In the liberal-rationalist story I argue against, abstract moral imperatives—sometimes called neutral principles—come first, and it is on their foundation that one can erect (and justify) a particular agenda. In the story I tell, particular substantive agendas—sometimes called policies—come first and the vocabulary of abstraction can then be called in for rhetorical and political service as needed. Again, the argument is not that tolerance, mutual respect, or free speech are bad things or nothings, just that they are not the kind of things you can inscribe on your banner and then follow without a strong dose of the substantive particularity they disdain. They don't give you marching orders and therefore, as I often say, you can't "do" them.

Neither can you do contingency or adhocness, the favored abstract values or principles of antifoundationalism and postmodernism. The vocabulary of contingency is part and parcel of the critique of essentialist notions of gender, politics, race, history, culture, truth, the self, agency, consciousness, and so on. In place of the "master narratives" of unified selves who prosecute determinate agendas in the service of well-defined moral and political aspirations and in the name of immutable truths, antifoundationalism and postmodernism substitute multiple and self-divided narratives of fissured and hybrid selves who act out of motives they cannot know and produce effects (far in excess of any intention) they cannot recognize or acknowledge or control. Now, I cannot speak for all those who deploy words like fluidity, adhoccery, dispersion, fragmentary, contingency open-endedness, dissemination and so on, but when I use them I intend them to be descriptive rather than prescriptive. (Michael Robertson: "Fish's project . . . is descriptive; it is neither destructive nor prescriptive.") That is, I am not advising people to act in an adhoc or contingent way (I don't even know what that would mean); I am saying that if you study the way decisions are made and the relationship of those decisions to effects both anticipated and unanticipated, what you will find are not design and straight-line patterns of cause and effect, but contingency, chance, accident, serendipity, and surprise. I am not saying that those who participated in the events (academic and historical) that I discuss set out to "perform" contingency, adhoccery, and so on—again whatever could that mean?—but that those and related words accurately describe the career of their efforts and experiences.

In the writings I have published, the best illustration of this point is the essay "Transmuting the Lump," which asks and answers the question, how did it come to pass that between 1942 and 1972 the last two books of *Paradise Lost* went from being dismissed (by C.S. Lewis) as an "untransmuted lump of futurity" to being celebrated as the very center of the poem's meaning and art? How did that happen? How did dross become gold? Part of the answer surely is that scholars made arguments in opposition to Lewis' pronouncement and that (at least some of) those arguments were persuasive. What I am interested in, however, is the set of background assumptions and disciplinary conditions that made it possible for those arguments first to be framed and second to be heard. To this end, I rehearse, among other things, the rise of spatial thinking in philosophy and art, a change in the mode of criticism from praise and blame to the demonstration that every rift is loaded with ore, the pressures (conceptual and material) exerted by World War II, and most importantly, the fact that the rehabilitation of books XI and XII had become a more or less official project of the Milton industry. Those who participated in that project did not think of themselves as doing so, and neither (with the exception of G. Wilson Knight) did they see themselves in battle against the Axis powers; nor did they self-consciously embrace the new vogue of spatial thinking (although a few did). Rather, they just set out to tell what they took to be the truth about books XI and XII and to support the assertion of that truth with what they took to be indisputable and objective evidence.

They were not wrong to do so; indeed, they would have been wrong to do anything else because that was the business they were in (telling the truth about literary works). In writing the essay, however, I was in another business, not the normative business of assessing their arguments, but the *sociological* business of describing how some of those arguments gained traction for reasons not always related to their strength and weakness and played a part in overturning one standard view of the matter and replacing it with another. In offering that description, I was saying nothing about the intentions of those who made the arguments and I certainly did not identify those intentions with the effects I described. It is those effects that, in my account, merited adjectives like contingent, rhetorical, serendipitous. Those adjectives did not name motives they consciously or unconsciously had. They did not set out to be contingent (a literally unimaginable aspiration); contingency, in the sense of not governed by rational design, was just what befell their efforts.

This is a point Reed Dasenbrock misses when he takes me to task for saying that the victory of the civil rights movement was "not a victory of a set of principles," but "the accomplishment of politics rather than theory," a matter of "one vocabulary [falling] into [dis]favor and disuse while another stepped into the place it had formerly occupied." Dasenbrock objects that "it certainly didn't feel that way to any of the participants" who "regarded it as a victory for the principles of morality and justice," and, moreover, he adds, "the language used at the time wasn't contingent or specific in the postmodern fashion" but was the language of the "strong universalism characteristic of the discourse of moralism: discrimination is wrong; we are equal in the sight of God." But I wasn't claiming either that the participants were using the language of contingency or that it was their wish or plan to be contingent. I was just saying that contingency and related words accurately describe the process by which the universalist moral declarations in which they firmly believed took hold and won the day. After all, people had argued before that discrimination was wrong and that we are all equal in the sight of God, and not very much had happened. The question is why did those arguments succeed in the 1960s and 1970s? Part of my answer is given in a long paragraph (which takes up the space between the two statements Dasenbrock attacks) citing the convergence of factors—precisely parallel structurally to the factors that enabled the rehabilitation of books XI and XII of *Paradise Lost*—that prepared the ground for the flowering of the civil rights movement, factors like the popularity of the television program *Roots* and the decision of one man (Branch Rickey) to break the color line in baseball. This convergence was not designed (designing it was not in the minds of those who were contributors to it); it was, in short, contingent, and one can describe it as contingent without retroactively projecting contingency into anyone's intention. It is no contradiction at all to acknowledge that what impelled the civil rights movement was a strong, non-contingent, universalist conviction of the rightness of the cause and at the same time to argue that the success of that cause was attributable to forces other than or in addition to the force of that conviction. One should not conflate the question "what were they trying to do?" and the question "how is it that they managed to do it?" The answer to the first question is that they were trying to right a wrong as defined not by local but by universal standards. The answer to the second question requires an elaborate account of the sociological and political (and contingent) circumstances within which their efforts bore fruit, and these circumstances were not universal (a circumstance by definition cannot be universal), but local. While truth claims are always universal, the justification of truth claims is always local; therefore the "localism" of one's explanatory account is entirely compatible with the universalism of one's aspirations. It is simply a mistake to think (as Dasenbrock seems to) that an analysis of an event from a socio-political perspective substitutes the concerns and interests of that perspective for the concerns and interests of the actors and makes them into cynics or Machievels. (The same mistake was made by some readers of my Sokal op-ed essay who didn't get the point when I argued that sociologists of science were not in competition with science or bent on diminishing its achievements, but were offering an account of the emergence of those achievements. The fact that the scientists themselves would not recognize their motives or their activities in that account proves only that science and sociology are different forms of inquiry and that when the latter takes the former as is its object of study the result will be meaningful and interesting to sociologists, not scientists.)

It is because he fails to see the distinction between finding contingency and adhoccery in the way events unfold and urging contingency and adhoccery as a way of life, as a *program*, that Dasenbrock finds a contradiction in my work between "the language of morality" and "the language of contingency and adhoccery invoked throughout." There is no contradiction. The two languages are not applied to the same phenomena or offered as answers to the same question. When I use the language of morality, it is to prefer substantive agendas with desired specific outcomes (the alleviation of poverty, the protection of the wetlands) to so-called neutral principles (tolerance, fairness, impartiality) that disdain specific outcomes and demand fidelity to their contentless selves. (Dasenbrock sees no difference between the two because, he says, both are justified by rhetoric and tactics; the difference, however, lies not in the justification—which will always be tactical and rhetorical—but in the claims of being substantive on the one hand and of having transcended substance on the other.) When I use the language of contingency, it is to describe both the untidy process by which substantive agendas get accepted and institutionalized and the similarly untidy process by which some or other substantive agenda (like civil rights) has had conferred on it the label of right and true.

I do not mean by this that right and true are the outcomes of rhetoric and politics (true is true and right is right, not just for me or my group or my generation but for everyone at all times) but that the reigning sense or public justification of what is true and right is the outcome of rhetoric and politics, of the successful strategic deployment of disputable arguments (what else could it be?). I do not, as Dasenbrock asserts, "engage in a critique of ethical universals." I engage in a critique of justificatory universals, and I do so (to repeat a point made earlier) because while truth claims are universal, their justification cannot be. This applies to my own truth claims as well as anyone else's; they too must make their way (or not) via the mechanisms and contingencies of public debate, but nothing in my account of those contingencies bars me from making those claims. I do not give up the right to say how "things really are" as a consequence of believing that my ability to back up what I say will depend on forces I cannot control and may not even recognize. In a formulation I have often used, it is perfectly consistent to declare "I believe X to be absolutely, non-contingently, true" and to declare also that it will be a matter of contingency whether or not the truths I strongly and unequivocally affirm prove persuasive to others. (Witness the present occasion.)

My stance on the non-contingency of truth claims may be obscured by the fact that in my theoretical writing (as opposed to my writing about seventeenth-century literature) I am usually not engaged in making truth claims (it has often been complained that someone reading me will have no idea of where I stand on the substantive matters I use as examples), with the exception, of course, of the claim, which I certainly believe to be true, that justification is always local not universal. That is where my interest lies—in the tracing out of the routes by which descriptions, accounts, and interpretations enter the conversation, make their way to the center, hold sway for a while, are challenged, and (perhaps) dislodged. And this brings me to the concept of the "interpretive community" and what I mean by it, a question taken up by several of the contributors to this volume.

Interpretive communities are not hard to find and I found reference to one in this morning's (July 20, 2003) *New York Times*. A major story detailed the failure of hip-hop mogul Russell Simmons to broker a bill that would have repealed or softened New York's drug-sentencing laws, laws that lead to long periods of incarceration for relatively minor offences. Simmons thought he had a deal and a handshake from the Governor, but as it turned out opposition, both philosophical and tactical (some legislators who shared his views resented his access to the Governor and key legislative leaders), quickly surfaced and in the end nothing substantial was accomplished. One lobbyist commented, "People who are new to the Albany culture . . . are inexperienced at reading the political tea leaves," and a long-time student of that culture remarked, "He wanted to do the right thing, and he came into a world with which he was not familiar, and at the end of the day did not produce a result because he did not know that world." Or as I might put it, because the practices and decorums of a particular interpretive community were not part of the structure of his consciousness, he did not see what was there to be seen and mis-stepped; and it would be possible, were one of a mind, to follow this judgment with an analysis, first, of the "ropes" and "rules of thumb" that Simmons didn't know (not know "of," but know in the sense that knowledge of them organized any situation for him, immediately and without self-conscious reflection), and, second, of the "performed ignorance"—the things he did and didn't do—that contributed to his failure.

That would be an "interpretive community" analysis; for it would begin by identifying the (in this case professional/political) space within which what I have called "competent actors" perform and it would then proceed (1) to inventory the resources (internalized understandings of protocols, obligatory routines, trumping arguments, tactical pitfalls, etc.) that community members bring with them (not as tools externally held, but as dispositions to notice and attend), and (2) to trace out the routes by which, enabled (and constrained) by those resources, they prosecuted a task (like getting a bill through the legislature) or dealt with a problem. This is exactly the form of my analysis of the critical rehabilitation of books XI and XII of *Paradise Lost*, where the task, never officially announced, was to overturn C.S. Lewis' harsh judgment, and the resources were the standard ways of arguing and marshaling evidence known (again in the deep, internalized, I-don't-have-to-look-around-for-them sense) to every Miltonist. (Needless to say, skillful deployment of those resources does not assure success; always remember the contingencies.)

Martin Stone rehearses some of the problems critics have had with the "interpretive community" idea—how does one identify "the relevant 'community?' " what constitutes a community? can there be different but equally "right" answers for different communities?—and he might have added questions like, aren't we all members of many interpretive communities and doesn't that mean that the fact of membership in one will be an insufficient account of our behavior, and if every splinter group is to be understood as forming an interpretive community isn't it the case that disagreement and agreement rather than being explained are simply re-described in an unhelpful and circular vocabulary? But these and related questions misunderstand the promise of the term, which is neither to *identify* interpretive communities (provide a map or taxonomy of them) nor to specify what is in the mind of individual community members. The concept is not empirical, and therefore available to empirical correction (as in you've misidentified the interpretive community; it's over there, not here); and it is not psychological, and therefore revisable in the wake of reports by members of what they actually think. Indeed an interpretive community is not an entity at all—it's not something awaiting your description—rather it is what emerges in the effort to answer a certain kind of question, like the question how did books XI and XII get to be so good or the question why did Simmons fail? The interpretive community is a device of interrogation, and what it promises and delivers is a method. Once a question has been framed, the interpretive community thesis tells you that in order to answer it you should attend to the relevant background conditions—assumed definitions, notions of evidence, locations of reputable archives, storehouses of legitimate arguments, lists of exemplary achievements, lists of achievements for which one will be rewarded, lists of authoritative practitioners, senses of what we do around here and what it is not our business to do—within which the relevant actors perform.

"Relevant" is the key word, for not all of the conditions and not all of the actors and not all of the actors' interests will be to the point, just those that are pertinent to the task of explaining how something happened or was prevented from happening. Both the membership of the interpretive community and the size of its territory—the items it has scope over—come into view as a consequence of the particular question the concept is called upon to answer. If, for example, you want to know why the term "metaphysical poets" and the critical practices attached to it have virtu-ally disappeared even though they were once at the center of the enterprise of literary criticism, your interpretive community will be made up of those who participated in the debates about what the designation meant, to which poets it applied, by what stylistic devices they were identified, and so on. Your time frame will be the period from Grierson's and Eliot's annointing of the term to the early seventies when its currency began to fade; and your archives will be the journals and books in which the various debates were conducted, the anthologies purporting to fix the canon, and the later anthologies in which that canon had been replaced by another. Your analysis will identify key actors, key moments, formulations that proved compelling, and the contingent and unpredictable ways in which they combined to produce a result that was not inevitable. (Metaphysical poetry could still be a centerpiece of literary study and books XI and XII of *Paradise Lost* could still be in critical limbo.) And, again, none of these—the key actors, the key moments, the relevant archives, the accidents that "took"—will have been available and perspicuous before the question was asked and the notion of an interpretive community was invoked to answer it.

Much of the criticism directed at the interpretive community idea flows from a misconception of the claims I make for it, which are not normative, but sociological. That is, I do not employ it to answer questions like what does *Paradise Lost* mean or is this or that reading of *Paradise Lost* true. I employ it to explain how a particular reading of the poem gained the ascendancy and became the leading candidate (perhaps the entirely triumphant candidate) for the designation of "true one," but I neither identify that institutional success with the emergence of the real meaning or of "the truth," nor do I assert that the question of truth is foreclosed by the judgments the community has produced. (In "Transmuting the Lump," I point out that one could be entirely persuaded by my account of how books XI and XII acquired significance and value and still decide that C.S. Lewis was right to dismiss them.) Thus, when Stone declares, "I do not think that . . . a story about interpretive communities can provide a satisfactory account of meaning," I respond "neither do I." What it can provide is a satisfactory account of how meanings have made their way, and the question of whether or not those meanings were the right ones remains open; an interpretive community analysis cannot answer it or even approach it; it's not that kind of exercise. And when Stone insists that "the question is what the text means, not what other people think it means" and terms the latter a sociological inquiry rather than a normative one, I couldn't agree more. I am at once the literary historian who produced the reading of the critical history of book XI and XII and the classroom instructor who teaches books XI and XII. When I am working in the first mode, I treat meanings and their careers as data for my analysis of how a certain shift in reputation occurred.

When I am working in the second mode, the meanings I put forward are the ones I think to be true (as in, this line means X, not Y). Moreover, my performance in one mode is independent of my performance in the other. My account of how certain meanings become regnant does not commit me to those meanings, only to the account. And the meanings I see as the true ones will be seen by me that way no matter what I have reported about which meanings the interpretive community has anointed. The subtitle of *Is There A Text In This Class?* is "the sources of interpretive *authority*," not "the sources of meaning and truth."

Once the interpretive community notion is understood in this way—as a story about institutional processes and not a story about truth and meaning—many (but not all) of the problems Stone perceives are dissolved. "The problem, for Fish's story, is to see what entitles any of a community's agents to represent (to themselves or to others) that the rule, for example, 'no vehicles in the park' genuinely prohibits such-and-such events, once it is understood that whether one has gotten things right, must ultimately be a question of what the community agrees the rules prohibit." But I don't equate the category of getting things right with community agreement (just as I don't equate "correct judgment" with "that view which the community realizes from among the interpretive possibilities") and, anyway, "agrees" is the wrong verb, for it implies that the community (as I conceive it) is some kind of superagent doing a form of collective work that might include, for example, taking votes. This implication is even stronger when Stone defines an interpretive community as "a community agreeing in its critical judgments." No, agreement might be a (temporary and contingent) feature of a community's landscape at a particular time, but what makes something a community for my purposes is not whether its members agree or disagree, but whether there is an in-place set of assumptions about what the project is (recovering the past, sequencing a gene, interpreting literary works), what the resources are for implementing it, what the obstacles are to its implementation, what past performances are exemplary and tutelary, what workers are currently in the forefront of the effort, what marks one as a participant in the game. Within these assumptions there is plenty of room and opportunity for disagreement; but those who have not internalized them will be able neither to agree nor disagree because they will not have—could not have—a sense of what is at stake. These are not assumptions members self-consciously wield (literary critics don't muse to themselves at the beginning of an exercise, "now what is it that a poem is, or what form does a reading take"), but assumptions that structure their consciousnesses (at least while they are doing community work) and deliver to them the objects of their professional attention. (To be sure, debates about those same assumptions can go on and go on self-consciously, but such debates suspend "ordinary science" and when they are resolved everyday activity resumes.)

The large point is that interpretive community membership is not a positive, aggressive affair, self-consciously performed. Membership is something imputed to you by sociologically inclined types like me, not something you have always in the forefront of your mind (although the topography of your mind will be the effect of membership) or are even aware of. One doesn't commence a task by loudly announcing, "I belong to the guild of historians and therefore . . . or I belong to the guild of anthropologists and therefore. . . . " And surely one does not think of oneself as enacting a theory of community meaning. Rather, one thinks of oneself as interpreting a novel or studying a culture or sequencing a gene. The interpretive community idea, when applied, tells us, if we are interested, what conditions (largely but not exclusively institutional) enable those thoughts and enable too the activities—not monolithic or static but variable, conflicting, and in development—that follow from them.

It is because Stone thinks of interpretive community members as professing a theory that identifies meaning with group consensus that he sees them playing a game of hide and seek with themselves when they move to practice and normative judgments. "For the [interpretive community] story tells agents that in making such judgments—that is, that the rule requires such-and-such no matter what others may think—they are engaging in an illusion" and "it hardy seems clear how the attitudes agents must have in their practical concourse with meanings could be psychologically stable ones" once the theoretical truth about meaning gets around. If the interpretive community idea were in fact a theory of meaning, and if that theory did identify meaning with group consensus, it would indeed take an act of desperate compartmentalization to hold to the idea and still make genuine truth claims about meanings or anything else. But if the interpretive community idea is a device for pinpointing enabling conditions and for bringing to analytical attention the routes by which success and failure occur within those conditions, then someone who thought that the idea pointed to something true about the workings of disciplines could without any tension or sense of strain also think that many other things were true and say so.

Stone's unhappiness with the interpretive community concept is part and parcel of his more general unhappiness with what he calls my "rampant interpretivism," that is, my assertion that interpretive work is *generally* required so that every meaning one perceives or points to is the product of interpretation. Stone finds this development in my thought "disappointing," and wishes that my thesis about interpretation were more "restricted" because it could have then, he says, "told us something genuinely informative" about the different kinds of interpretive activity appropriate to different enterprises or about the times when acts of interpretations were required and the times when they were not, which would correspond to the distinction between plain no-problem meanings and meanings that were doubtful or in dispute, a distinction that is lost if interpretation is a general condition. A similar critique of rampant interpretivism is also made by Michael Bérubé, who finds everything I have written since 1976 marked (or infected) by "the insistence on the ubiquity of interpretation" and the thesis "that every ostensibly obvious "feature" of texts is actually produced by interpretation." This thesis, Bérubé complains, deprives us of the category of objects "that exist independently of anyone's perception of them," and, he adds, there must be some such category if "a small but important set" of objects "are to be understood properly as the kinds of objects they are." (Stone would, I believe, think of that set as quite large.) Bérubé makes his point in part by declaring, "I know of no reader who is willing to dispute that the title of *Is There a Text in This Class?* is *Is There A Text in This Class?*," or, he might have added, that the book has 16 chapters and an introduction and is divided into two parts. Facts like these are not the product of anyone's (or any community's) interpretive activity; they are plain facts, and a reader who disputed them would be dismissed as either tiresomely tendentious or insane, although a reader might intelligibly dispute what I meant by the title or what exactly was divided by the two parts and could certainly dispute the arguments I put forward in the book. With respect to the easy and immediate agreement (or at least on the part of those who know what a title is) about what the title of *Is There A Text In This Class?*" is and about what "a diet coke, please" (one of Stone's examples) means, "no explanation of the possibility of such agreement" should be "on offer"; there should be "no attempt to go deeper than the fact that we do (often enough) agree." Someone who offered such an explanation would be doing something at once superfluous and misleading, providing what is not needed and creating puzzles where there are none. Better, says Stone, that we "return the word 'interpretation' to its ordinary use, whereby interpretation is sometimes needed and sometimes not—it is no longer a general requirement."

Once again I find myself in agreement with an argument mounted against me and inclined to claim it as my own. The point that interpretation is only an interesting and helpful notion if its scope is restricted is exactly the point I make in the preface to *Professional Correctness* when I say that "the thesis of social constructionism can do genuine work only if it is limited, a thesis about some things but not about everything" (viii). And when Stone tries to dissuade me from going any deeper than the everyday "weave of *our lives*" to account for the "normative aspects of signs," he gives back to me the advice I long ago gave Ronald Dworkin when I told him to stop looking for a theory that would shore up the "weak constraints" (his phrase) of practice because the constraints of practice—of the weave of our lives—are not weak and supply everything we need to make sense of signs and have confidence in the sense we make. More recently I say pretty much the same thing to those who wonder how someone persuaded to an antifoundationalist account of fact could continue to believe in the facts of his or her experience: but it is only if we went around actively—as the positive consequence of some theory—believing in fact that some alternative theory could weaken our belief and take away our facts; "in ordinary life, [however], we don't believe in facts; we encounter them" (*The Trouble With Principle*, 303); and when a particular fact is put into question, it will not be because of a general theoretical doubt, but because of a doubt arising from the same context of practice that presented us with the fact we encountered.

So there is plenty of evidence in what I have written to suggest that I already am where Stone and Bérubé (and before them Dennis Patterson) would urge me to go. But there is also plenty of evidence in what I have written to support Stone's and Bérubé's reservations and strictures. I do say the things (like "Interpretation is the only game in town") that they take me to task for, and this brings me to still another guilty plea and a big one: I have too often surrendered to the temptation of making flamboyant statements that are rhetorically effective but misleading at best and downright mistakes (to which I myself at times become captive) at worst. (This tendency is noted and commented on by Wihl, Veeser, Graff, Eagleton, and Robertson, in addition to Stone and Bérubé.) The result is an argument that appears to go in two different directions, depending on whether I am peddling a weak antifoundationalism that asserts the ubiquity of mediation ("everything comes to us under a description") but draws no moral or marching order or negative conclusion about truth from the assertion, or a strong-antifoundationalism in whose wake truth, fact, evidence, conviction and a lot of other things become problems and puzzles. I have usually wanted to do the first, but more than occasionally put things in a way that allowed—no, encouraged—others to read me as doing the second. To a certain extent, it is a matter of how generous a commentator is inclined to be. Stone is consistently generous in his effort to win me over to what he thinks to be my best self. Bérubé takes a dimmer view, as when he writes that I really do "say that you can't draw a line between brute fact and social fact" and am not making "the more modest and defensible claim that distinctions between brute fact and social fact are always drawn by social fact, particularly by those 'interpretive communities' whose job it is to try to understand the physical phenomena of the universe *precisely* as phenomena that live and function independently of interpretive activity." In fact, it is the second more modest (but not uncontroversial) claim that I want to be making, but Bérubé has good reason (which I have given him) for thinking otherwise.

A nice example of the "double game" I play with myself and others is the phrase "in and of itself" as applied to texts or, more generally, signs. I more than occasionally say, as Stone points out, that a text or sign considered "in and of itself" will not yield a meaning and requires an interpretation if meaning is to be imputed to it. Now, there are two ways to understand what I mean—pardon the word, but one has to use it—by such statements. I could mean (a) that before texts are embedded in circumstances—in the form they have in and of themselves—they mean nothing in particular but contain in potential all the possible (and infinite) meanings they might later acquire as a consequence of acts of interpretation. Or I could mean (b) that the very notion of a text in and of itself— apart from or abstracted from the mundane circumstances within which it is intelligible (we shall have to get rid of the "it" here)—is incoherent because for something to be a text is by definition for it to have meaning; a meaningless text or (it amounts to the same thing) a text of infinite meanings, would be a contradiction in terms. I mean (b), but there are many places where I more than suggest (a), and that, as Stone observes, gets me into a lot of trouble. If I imagine a state for texts before they have meaning, I then have to come up with an explanation of how they get it, and it would seem that in the repertoire I usually offer, the agency of meaning—the device that jump starts what Stone calls the "dead matter" of a text—is most likely to be identified with the interpretive community. This would be wrong, for, as I have already said, the interpretive community idea is not a theory of meaning; but if some of my formulations suggest the need for such a theory, the interpretive community will be the handiest available candidate in the neighborhood. If, however, I am arguing not that a text in and of itself is such-and-such, but (as I should be) that there is no such thing as a text in and of itself and that the text, if it is a text, always and already has a meaning, then the need for an explanation and a theory disappears, and I will conclude with Stone "that we have no use for such notions as signs or texts 'in themselves' and "no use for the thought that there must always be an interpretation that fixes a sign's meaning," unless, that is, "we are trying to give a *philosophical account* of the meaning of a text."

A philosophical account would be an account from on high, just the kind of platonizing account I set myself against. Although there is a difference between asserting that a text has a fixed meaning apart from all circumstances and asserting that a text can mean anything at all, the two assertions are still in the same line of work, the work of abstracting from everyday contexts of meaning to some foundational condition (of absolute determinacy or absolute indeterminacy) that is the "real" truth about texts. "One does not get rid of philosophical foundations by denying that there are any," but by seeing that the project of specifying the philosophical foundations of meaning is unnecessary because everyday "straight-on" meaning (as in " a diet coke please") presents no problems such a foundation would be called upon to resolve. (Unless you suspected that "a diet coke, please"was code for something like "detonate the bomb," in which case you would check out your suspicion by empirical means and not by the means of some philosophical foundation.) This is in fact what I did see when I pointed out in *Is There A Text In This Class?* that the position that texts are "characterized by a timeless stability" and the position that texts are characterized by a "timeless instability" are "the same position" because both assume a stage in the life of texts *before* they are contextually encountered, before they have meaning. To be sure, the meaning a text already has may not be perspicuous to everyone, and there can always be a dispute about what that meaning really is; to acknowledge *that* is not, however, to say, as I sometimes did, that a text can always be made to mean something else (which would substitute interpretive will for the project of determining a speaker's or writer's intention), but to say, as I also sometimes did, that it is always possible to be mistaken about the meaning of a text (which preserves the essential idea of there being a meaning), and that there is no independent mechanism—no theoretical foundation—for determining definitively and absolutely and forever what is and is not a mistake.

Some readers may be surprised to hear me talking about the meaning a text (or sign) "has," but that surprise would be the result of the careless formulations into which I have at times seduced myself. Gerry Graff is right when, as a friend of the court, he tones down some of those formulations and rewrites me thus: "we always assume . . . that . . . whatever we refer to exists independent of our interpretive apparatus and in some sense invites us to describe it the way we do. You'd be talking nonsense if you said 'I think this text is a poem by Milton, but, in saying that, I in no way claim that it *really* is a poem by Milton independent of my description of it." I haven't produced that particular bit of nonsense, but I have produced some similar bits, usually when I slide from saying that the properties (of meaning, structure, imagery, and so on) we now see in the objects of our professional attention have been established by that attention—by the constrained and enabling history of interpretive debate—to saying that the objects of our professional attention have no proper shape of their own independent of that debate. To say the first is to pay due respect to the possibility of error and the promise of correction. To say the second is to render notions like error and correction incoherent, and to deprive the very act of reading of its point: "Reading makes no sense unless we assume that it's a matter of discovering what is there" (Graff).

It is time now to move from the guilty pleas and the elaborate efforts of self-defense to things I am not guilty of, either because I didn't do them or because I wasn't interested in doing them. I am not guilty, as Margaret Kohn says I am, of "teaching that we do not need to reflect systematically upon our moral intuitions" when I insist "that theory doesn't matter." First of all, I don't exactly mean that theory doesn't matter (although I do issue that pronouncement in some of my self-indulgent moments); I mean that it doesn't matter in the ways claimed by its advocates, as a guide or stimulus to everyday ordinary behavior. Someone committed to a theoretical position (say, a theory of truth or meaning) will not be enabled *by virtue of that commitment* to answer any question aside from the question of which theoretical position is the right one or perform any action aside from the action of arguing for that position. (Of course, being committed to a theory doesn't bar you from answering extra-theoretical, practical, questions; it just doesn't help you answer them.) Or, as I sometimes put it, theory doesn't travel; it does not do normative work in areas other than the area of its own contestation.

That said, there are all kinds of ways theory can matter, but they are contingent; they will be a function of particular social and political conditions in relation to which a theoretical vocabulary might have a resonance or cachet useful to this or that party. The usefulness of the vocabulary will be the result not of something inherent in it—that is why theory doesn't matter if by "matter" you mean generate agendas or matching orders all by itself—but of the way a particular issue has been framed by partisan agents with an eye on the moment. That is to say, a theoretical vocabulary will not belong by natural right to one party or the other (that is the mistake made by those who see postmodernist arguments as the natural ally of the left and are then discombobulated to see them skillfully deployed by creationists and Holocaust deniers); one need only recall how various theories (of freedom, autonomy, equality and so on) have migrated from one side of the political aisle to the other as first liberals and then conservatives opportunistically appropriate their terms and turn them to a new advantage. So the ways theory matters are innumerable, but they are not necessary—built into theory—and no one or group of them is generalizable; knowing that a theory mattered in a particular way in this or that situation will not be predictive of how it might operate or be made to operate in the next situation.

This argument is a sub-set of the general argument that denies to theory the capacity to do anything except defeat or be defeated by its rivals. One of the things theory cannot do by right—although it can do by accident, contingently—is cause us "to reflect systematically upon our moral intuitions." It is not that systematic reflection is impossible; it is just that theory has no *special* role in bringing it about. Reflection, systematic and not so systematic, happens all the time, and it can be provoked by many things (indeed, by anything), even by the formulations of theory, but no thing, including a theoretical formulation, is uniquely fitted to provoke it. Reflection, in short, is an ordinary piece of behavior— we do it when shopping in the supermarket, when we think about leaving our present job for another, when we decide whom to vote for, when we consider the consequences of staying in bed on a morning. Those who want to link reflection with theory often don't intend by the word these and other mundane actions; they intend something grander, something (in Stone's sense) philosophical, a *general* capacity for stepping back from or suspending the concerns, investments, and perspectives of our in-place "moral intuitions or politico-ethical commitments to a "space of reflection" where we can just reflect on everything we have been and done. Here my message has been consistent and oft delivered: there is no such general space of reflection, but because there are the varieties of reflection that occur within the mundane spaces of our everyday, non- (not anti-) theoretical lives, the absence of a theoretical form of reflection —a form of reflection hostage to no assumptions or interests—takes nothing away from us; it doesn't matter that theory doesn't matter in the way some hope it will matter and others fear it will matter. As I have put it elsewhere, there is nothing theoretically interesting to say about theory.

However, as I have already acknowledged, theory can be very interesting, politically and sociologically, and it is part of the criticism directed at me in some of these essays that I pay too little attention to theory's real world effects, which, contingent though they may be, can nonetheless be significant. (Mailloux: "although there are no necessary, logical connections between practice and theory . . . there are still contingent, rhetorical connections.") This criticism comes in two forms: (1) I am insufficiently aware (even careless) of the effects that my own theoretical (and anti-theoretical) pronouncements have in the precincts where important political and ethical issues, including ones in which I have a stake, are being debated, and (2) I slight the role played by emotions and feelings in the public sphere, limiting myself to the logic of argument and ignoring its affect. There are also two forms of (1), the philosophical and the rhetorical. Dasenbrock pursues the philosophical line when he attributes what he takes to be my "ineffectual[ity] in the public policy arena" (more about this later) to a tension between a strong moralism and an anti-universalist argument that undercuts it. Who is going to listen to me if it's obvious that I am not fully committed to the truth of what I say? I allow my desire to appear theoretically sophisticated to overwhelm my desire to advance a particular substantive agenda, invoking "a conventional system of morality" at the same time that I show myself to be "aware of its limitations." But the limitations I am aware of are the limitations on my ability to persuade others to the moral truths I urge, not limitations on the universal scope of those truths. In short, to repeat the point once again, a commitment to the universality of a truth claim is not incompatible with an acknowledgment that its justification is necessarily local and therefore by no means sure.

Nevertheless, even though I am not involved in the contradiction Dasenbrock rehearses, he thinks I am, and if he thinks I am others less sophisticated than he is no doubt think so too; and this speaks to the danger, and perhaps the ineffectuality, of retailing postmodern or antifoundationalist arguments even in their "weak" version where it is justification and not the claim of truth that is declared local. Surely,

Dasenbrock is right to observe that the language of principle "remains dominant" in the public arena; and this means, one might presume, that another language—one that requires the drawing of nice and difficult distinctions—is likely to be politically disastrous whether it is internally coherent or not. Perhaps, as Mailloux says (his is the rhetorical version of [I]) I miss "the full rhetorical force hovering around the term *postmodernism*" and fail to appreciate the "rhetorical effects of advocating this or that philosophical theory in the public sphere" and the political potency of the "terminology of human rights" and of universalist vocabularies in general.

To this I have a rather complicated response that turns on the difference between the two kinds of work I usually do. More often than not, I am either trying to persuade a small group of readers that my interpretation of Milton or Hobbes or Marvell is the right one, or I am trying to persuade another, but also small, group of readers that my account of interpretation, evidence, and the relationship between theory and practice is the right one. In this mode, I am entirely focused on the logic (or illogic) of arguments and interpretations, and I am not interested in the way those arguments and interpretations might play out in the public sphere because the relevant public is made up of my professional colleagues. By hewing to this narrow focus, I open myself up to two criticisms. The first is that the professional sphere I would confine myself to cannot be so confined because it does not exist in isolation and is in fact constituted, made possible as an area of inquiry, by the larger forces and investments of society as a whole. To this I usually respond, yes, every activity is enabled by conditions exterior to it, but those conditions are the answer to another question—how did it come to be that such and such a field of inquiry happened to emerge and have the shape it does?—as opposed to the questions that arise within the field as constituted: what does this line mean or what makes an interpretation authoritative or what is the difference between being authoritative and being true? Acknowledging that no discipline can finally be self- originating or self-sustaining doesn't mean that questions asked within its admittedly revisable and permeable boundaries are without sense.

If the first criticism is that you can't do it (confine yourself to disciplinary matters), the second criticism is that you shouldn't do it, for isn't someone who chooses to operate within those boundaries without looking outside them for either materials or consequences merely spinning his wheels and defaulting on the obligation of an intellectual to fashion "tools for improving our shared world" (Kohn)? To this I respond (in every sentence of *Professional Correctness* and in many columns for the *Chronicle of Higher Education*) that tasks, academic and otherwise, only retain their distinctiveness if they are sharply defined so that those who take them up know pretty much (there are always borders being pushed out and contracted) what the job is and so that others will look to them whenever there is a call for that particular job to be done. No one is forced to be a literary critic or a student of epistemology, but if that is the line of work you have chosen, you should stick to it and not try to expand it to the point where it loses its shape and you lose your sense of purpose, having exchanged its saving narrowness for the heady (but impossible) purpose of doing everything. Do your job, don't try to do someone else's job (for which you won't have the qualifications anyway), and don't let anyone else do your job. And if you don't want to give a reading of *King Lear* or a critique of Kant's critiques, but want to save the world, get out of the academy and go into politics or social work. (This is an instance of what Veeser calls my "fundamentalism.")

So when Gary Wihl chides me (gently) for "failing to use interpretation as a bridge between textual analysis and publicly shared values" and for remaining too often "in the sterile zone of epistemology" or warns that my works courts "banality unless it can find its purpose within rather more broadly shared debates and public venues," he is descriptively correct. But his is a description of what I want to do, not what I should apologize for doing. Textual analysis and epistemology are what interest me and they offer me no end of projects to undertake. My prosecution of those projects is certainly vulnerable to criticism and challenge, but I don't see why I am vulnerable to the criticism that I should be doing something else or something more. Wihl would have me tie my interests more closely to the larger interest of the public life of a democracy; in fact, he says, "the study of democracy is the true home" of my writings. Not as I see it. The true home of my writings is the collection of disciplines that set the tasks (of interpretation and argument) taken up in them. Others working to intervene in that democracy and turn it in new directions may find something I have written useful and appropriate it for their frankly (and honestly) political purposes, but my purposes remain narrowly academic and disciplinary.

But not always. As Wihl also notes, in recent years (since about 1995) I have been writing for the popular press and for magazines and speaking out on some of the issues of the day. Through "advocacy, rhetoric, coalition building, and public speaking," I am, he says, "stand[ing] up as a public intellectual" and thereby participating directly in the democratic process. (Wihl has a more positive view of my efforts in this vein than do Bérubé and Dasenbrock, and in this he is closer to Veeser.) When I do that kind of work, I do in fact consider the way theoretical arguments, including postmodern arguments, "play" or fail to play in the public sphere. Sometimes, as in the op-ed essay (discussed by Veeser) about the sex conference at SUNY New Palz, I rebuke those who use the vocabulary of theory to avoid confronting empirical, nitty-gritty issues. Sometimes, as in a number of pieces on affirmative action, I explain why proponents of affirmative action should steer clear of engaging in arguments about principle because, as it is now retailed, the "language of universalism" is owned by their opponents; and while it is possible to contest the vocabulary of that language (fairness, autonomy, merit, and the like) and try to wrest it away from those who have fashioned it to fit their agenda, the kind of lengthy analysis required by the effort would be no match in the public sphere for the snappy soundbites available to the opposition. (You can surely make an argument detaching merit from test scores, but will your audience be there at the end?) And sometimes I do take on the tricky task of explaining postmodernism to a popular audience in order to correct a misleading and vitriolic account of its implications, as when Dinesh D'Souza blames postmodernsists and antifoundationlalists for the demise of Western civilization, or when Alan Sokal blames the same folks for the demise of truth and truth-speaking, or when William Bennet blames them for September 11, 2001, or when Deborah Lipstadt and a bunch of other historians blame them for the rise of Holocaust denial. It is in these pieces that I am in the most rhetorical danger, if only because the extravagance of the attacks tends to beget an answering extravagance in the response. (It was a mistake, for example to claim, in my op-ed after September 11, that postmodernism could be a resource for us at this terrible moment; I should have said that postmodenrism had nothing to do, in either a positive or negative way, with what had happened or with planning a course of action in the aftermath.)

The misunderstandings one courts when trying to unpack theoretical arguments and trying to give practical advice at the same time are on display in Michael Bernard-Donals' essay in this volume. Bernard-Donals is writing in response to a piece in which I advise historians combating Holocaust denial against claiming (as they often do) that what is at stake in the controversy is some big philosophical value like truth or the sanctity of fact. If they pitch their arguments at that level, I warn, they will find themselves debating epistemological issues rather than mundane issues of evidence, archives, and testimonies, and they will be in danger of losing the debate if only because they are not epistemologists and can easily be tied in knots by those who have mastered that particular game. The advice, again, is do your job, the one you've been trained to do, and don't try to do a job for which you are not qualified.

Bernard-Donals misunderstands my argument when he has me saying that "the historian's storytelling function pulls the rug out from under any claims he or she might make about having all the facts." I never talk about the historian's storytelling function, and I am uncomfortable with the distinction, hinted at here and developed later in his essay, between what narrative accounts give us and the historical "reality . . . outside the narrative" or between the textual presentation of evidence and "evidence itself." Actually these are two different distinctions. The first distinction, between narrative accounts and reality, does have a sense: Louis Mink's "conviction 'that the past is after all *there*'" is a pre-condition of there being an historical task in the first place; who would undertake it if there were nothing to establish? But the past that is after all there is not there in a way that exerts a directing pressure on those who would reconstruct it. You can't look "there" for guidance; you are seeking guidance from archival and other materials as to where and what "there" is. Moreover, declaring firmly that it is there is not a methodological move—nothing in a way of a next step follows from it—and, at the other end of the process, the assumed "thereness" of the past does not provide us with a mechanism for deciding between competing accounts of what that thereness is. In short, the assumption (to which I cheerfully ascribe) does no work, although it is necessary if the effort to do the work is to be intelligible. The work is done by the usual and ordinary activities of marshaling evidence, making connections, drawing conclusions, etc., and since those activities are carried on within professional protocols and decorums—protocols and decorums given to us by the history of a discipline and not by Reality or God—they are at every point vulnerable to challenge. When a challenge is issued—say, by Holocaust deniers—it will not be met, if it is met, by stamping one's feet and invoking Reality or Truth, but by the same tried and true methods in the historian's repertoire. The mistake, as Graff says, is not in believing in Truth and Reality, but in invoking them "to resolve a dispute when what a true or objective position *is* is itself disputed."

The second distinction, between the textual presentation of evidence and evidence itself, unlike the first, has no sense at all. Evidence is by definition the product of discourse (Hobbes: "Where speech is not, there is neither Truth nor Falsehood"); evidence is what we educe in our efforts to establish the lineaments of the past that is after all there; that past exists before and independently of our representations of it; evidence, the heart and soul of those representations, does not. Bernard-Donals needs a Reality that does methodological work and evidence that is available in a non-textual form because he wants to be able to combat Holocaust deniers with something more powerful and conclusive than the ordinary giving of reasons in the course of debate; for he knows, as the deniers know (this is what keeps them going) that reasons can always be challenged and that any argument, no matter how fully documented, is "based on yet another reconstruction of evidence . . . and is itself susceptible to the same doubt as any other argument." (That's why my advice is don't let the endless agon of argument go on if you are in a position to stop it as mainstream historians are, at least in the disciplinary precincts they control.) He wants to say to the David Irvings of this world, "look, here is the evidence; here is a Reality you can't distort"; and so much does he want this that he is willing to diminish the significance of his own discipline by declaring that historical work is "constrained by reality, which . . . is 'beyond the modes of narrative.'" It is certainly true both that there is something beyond or, rather, prior to the modes of narrative—call it Reality if you will— and that it is our aim, as historians or anthropologists or physicists, to apprehend it; but invoking "it" is not a move in the evidence game; all the testing and concluding and challenging and revising goes on *within* the discourses—modes of narrative and description—developed by human beings to consider this or that question. The point is precisely parallel to one made earlier: just as truth claims are universal but justification of truth claims local, so is Reality prior to the modes of narrative, but the specification of Reality a matter only of narrative modes. The limits of representation are not the limits of what is, but what is is only available to us in representational form. One can gesture to Reality or to the ineffable or to evidence itself or to the undistorted event, but such a gesture is like invoking the name of God: it has great force for believers, but it doesn't have much force in the public sphere where reasons are given and debated. (How can you debate Reality?)

Now, there is more than one public sphere, and as Bernard-Donals notes (and here he joins company with Wihl, Kohn, and Mailloux), I pretty much confine myself to the public sphere of the academy; it is in relation to what goes on in that sphere that I maintain that the battle against deniers has already been won. But, he asks, what about the "real people"—survivors, relatives of survivors, friends of relatives of survivors—who are hurt by denial? What happens in the enclosed world of academic historians doesn't reach them or is lost on them, and at any rate, it does not mitigate their real pain. And what about the deniers whose intention it is to produce that pain—produce "a damage"—rather than to engage in rational argument, no matter what their protestation to the contrary? The answer to this second question is given at length in the essay Bernard-Donals critiques: if you find that deniers aren't really playing the giving of reasons and evidence game, don't let them play it; send them packing with all the authority at your disposal. To the first question—what about the pain?—I have no answer, and I don't see why I should be expected to have one. I'm not denying the pain or downplaying its significance. I just have nothing helpful or relevant to say about it. The Holocaust is an enormous topic, but its enormity does not oblige someone who writes about it from a limited perspective—in this case the perspective of academic debates and membership in History departments—to consider every question it raises. If you want to read about pain, trauma, memory, mourning and forgetting, there are plenty of people who will accommodate you, but I'm not one of them. That's not what I do.

Nor, as Gary Olson and Lynn Worsham observe, do I say very much about emotions, painful or otherwise. "Fish never explicitly addresses the role of emotion in epistemology or rhetoric." Olson's and Worhsam's account of the way emotions are related to beliefs and convictions shows why. They speak of "an ideoaffective system," an "affective mapping of the individual psyche that arguably begins before birth" and continues to develop "over the course of an individual's lifespan" and results in an "emotional disposition [that] tends to shape all subsequent experience"; and they contend further that this emotional disposition, rather than standing aside from the system of belief and conviction, is part and parcel of it. Beliefs, they say, "always have affective valences, and therefore "the 'content' of one's belief about the world . . . is in large part affective and it is linked to the 'content' of their beliefs in an intricate 'lattice' or 'web' . . . whose component parts (emotion and belief) are mutually constitutive of what we typically mean by 'individual identity.'" They conclude that "rationality not only takes place 'in the light of our beliefs' . . . but also in the color, so to speak, of our emotions."

I am quite willing to entertain the idea that underlying our beliefs is an "affective valence" that is deeper and more durable and less susceptible to change than they are. I can also see how such an "ideoaffective system" might be a key determinant of individual identity. (I think immediately of Hobbes who confessed to having a naturally fearful nature and who devised an intricate and reasoned political structure based on fear.) But I have no real interest in individual identity, and, indeed, individual identity is a casualty of my theorizing and my textual analyses, both of which are concerned with the life of institutions and tend to turn individuals into an extension of that life. (That is how far I am from the "subjectivist position" Bernard Donals attributes to me.) Olson and Worsham think that the seed of their argument is in mine because of my use of words like "heartfelt" to describe the firmness of the convictions that structure consciousness; but all I mean by heartfelt is strong, or without reservation, as opposed to convictions (not really the word) that are closer to opinions, as in "I kind of believe that, but I'm not sure and I wouldn't stake very much on it." It's not that my vocabulary could never be linked to the vocabulary of emotion and affect; it could well be, but it's not I who is going to do it. (This has been true ever since the early days of reader response criticism which in my hands was a cognitive not a psychologistic enterprise.)

Evan Watkins is concerned with something else I don't do, and in this instance I must agree that it is something I perhaps should have been doing. Watkins faults me for focusing exclusively on the "immanent intelligibility" of particular disciplines (Law, English, History), and thereby ignoring the intelligibility—also institution specific, but the institution is much larger and arguably more important to our welfare and flourishing—of the relationships between disciplines: "Fish seems singularly uninterested in positional relations among disciplines or in the claims disciplines make on each other within their institutional structure." It is this lack of interest, he says, that has prevented me from seeing that "the *position* of English in the university . . . has been changing in a number of ways," and from seeing too that these changes play out "through the labyrinthine complex of the academic institution with its currencies of FTEs and SCHs and its channels of committees and administrative hierarchies." And since that institution is a public one (even when it is private), it "exists in an immense network of connection to all kinds of 'outsides'" and a refusal to engage with that network, and to remain cabined (and cocooned) in the pleasures of one's disciplinary tasks, "is also the refusal to do the politics that matter first and most immediately for both our students and ourselves."

That is, of course, the politics I do—or try to do; the verdict isn't in yet—every day in my capacity as a dean. Watkins takes note of this and says generously that my "practice in these matters is far better than [my] epistemology." I am not so sure that the epistemology must be left behind.

The practice of deaning is necessarily involved with the labyrinthine network Watkins alludes to; budgets, legislative pressures, the competition between disciplines, the waxing and waning disciplines—no dean could or should avoid such matters or fail to think hard and long about them. But is this the obligation of every academic? Not according to professional administrators (a class to which I now belong) who are likely to think (and perhaps say) that members of English and other departments should do their jobs and let us do ours. What Watkins urges me to is a more capacious understanding of what the distinctive task is and of what is at stake in prosecuting it. I can agree with him and with his contention that attention must be paid to the "material resources required to sustain the 'intelligibility' of a distinct disciplinary set of practices" without thinking that in order to do so I must renounce (as opposed to expand) the arguments of *Professional Correctness*. Nevertheless, he is right to say that to date I have not paid that attention, and that my narrowness has its price, a point made also by Mailloux when he urges me and other theorists "to attend to how the rhetoric of academic theorizing travels across different cultural domains."

At the beginning of his essay Watkins notes that when *Professional Correctness* was first published, many readers found it "so out of step with emergent intellectual directions" that the book seemed "to mark an end to Fish's representative status." Eight years later he comes back to the book and finds it "disturbingly relevant," which suggests that in his view at least I have not yet outlived my time. Hap Veeser, who also takes note of my turn to administration, is less sanguine. He has more than due praise for my fundamentalism—by which he means my contention that everyone, including self-identified multiculturalists, is a uniculturist at heart, an argument that leads to or has its source in a disdain for "ambivalence and self-doubt"—and he demonstrates how this "monism" informs all of my writings (is my ideoaffective signature) from the account of Milton as an intolerant Puritan zealot to my urging that academics give up the dubious pleasures of reflecting endlessly on many-sidedness, hybridity, and their own "split subjectivity" for the more legitimate pleasures of actually getting something done. But while Veeser believes that my "yearning for continuity and . . . faith in a unified, uninterrupted history are reassuring" to readers who might be put off by my "somewhat less conventional views" (he sees a political utility where Eagleton sees a "tame conservatism" masked by a supposedly radical epistemology), he finds that same yearning and its issue in an "anticosmopolitan intolerance for ambiguity" undermining my ability to function effectively in the very academic precincts that have for so long been my home. "With ambivalence and hybridity moving to to the center stage of academic humanities research, a continuist and organicist view of history and narrative will no longer advance the debate." This "discredited historicism" may be a "ticket into the popular press," but "from the point of view of specialists who are developing new ways of writing subaltern and alternative histories, that is exactly where Fish and his outmoded historicism belong." So once again, in 2004, I am apparently out of step.

Any response to this judgment is sure to be defensive; no one wants to think of himself as "past it." But the judgment is not mine to make (time will tell) and I will confine myself to explaining why I am not "more welcoming" to these (no longer so) new forms of analysis. First, I find them incredibly dull, which is not to say that those who produce them are dull—they are often quite brilliant—but that I fail to see either the interest or the payoff, in part because the payoff (at least analytically) is always the same—the discovery of hybridity, double consciousness, and divided loyalties where unity was formerly thought to be. I am reminded of the heyday of the New Historicism when every article and book revealed the interdependence of political and cultural work or demonstrated that power was distributed to all agents in a network rather than being concentrated in the hands of a few or showed that forms of resistance were available even to the apparently downtrodden. Okay, I get it, so what's next? Usually what's next is some *political* payoff, some program that follows from the fact of hybridity or double-consciousness. But that is (to my ears) just another version of the mistake of thinking that a technique of analysis can be made into a technology of political action. Hybridity and split-subjectivity may be descriptively rich labels for what our lives are like—many of us have multiple contexts of self-identification, religious, economic, ethnic, sexual, institutional—but I don't see how they can be made into an agenda, as in let's *do* hybridity or split subjectivities.

What one can do, however, is move from the awareness of a particular instance of split subjectivity—I am an historian, but I am also gay and a Catholic and born in Puerto Rico—to a correspondingly particular course of action: let's inquire into the Church's efforts to comes to terms with homosexuality both within its ranks and in the society at large, and let's try to map the ways in which those efforts have intersected with or been impeded by various social, economic and political realities, national and international, beyond the Church's control. (No doubt someone is at this very moment pursuing just such a project and with infinitely more sophistication than my formulation of it would allow.) Plenty of doubleness, hybridty, multiple motives, and ambivalence there to be sure; but the analysis or account that finally emerges will not perform doubleness or hybridity or ambivalence; although doubleness and hybridity will be what it uncovers and ambivalence might be a component of its conclusions. Rather, it will assert something specific (if nuanced), and its authors will believe that something to be true and believe alternative accounts to be false; that is, they will, like everyone else, be fundamentalists, although their preferred vocabulary will indicate a fervent desire to scorn and escape that condition. Now, it is possible that persons with divided loyalties and multiple sites of self-identification will decide that academic work does not give sufficient scope to that part of their beings to which they feel most drawn. They will complain that the academy tends to turn all issues and concerns into grist for its rationalist mill, and they will be right, which means not that the academy should remake itself into an instrument more immediately political and trans-forming, but that they should forsake the academy and go into a line of work more directly in touch with what they consider urgent and essential. Not that they will do this just because I tell them to. Veeser may be right to say that this is their time; and it may be that their (apparent) capacious-ness will prove more attractive than my (apparent) narrowness. But if that capaciousness is tied, as I think it is, to unrealistic political ambitions—the same ambitions once held out for theory in general and now consid-ered by almost all to have been disappointed and dashed—my time may come again, even if I am no longer around to enjoy it.

A few final words. First let me acknowledge and apologize for the uneven treatment these uniformly excellent essays have received. My angle of entry into the conversation they form led me down some paths and away from some others, and differences in the amount of space I devote to the various contributions should not be read as differences of admiration and respect. I particularly regret having said relatively little about the es-says—by Graff, Mailloux, Robertson, and Wihl—with which I largely agree.

Second, let me express my appreciation to Gary Olson and Lynn Worsham for the immense labor of organizing this volume and seeing it through to publication. They are, I know, very busy people with plenty of scholarly and administrative tasks to perform. They needn't have done this, just as those they drew into the enterprise needn't have participated, but I am grateful that they did.

And finally, let me say how much I look forward to holding the finished book in my hand, not only when it emerges into the world (although that will be a particular pleasure), but years from now when, if I continue to be lucky, an old man will sit up late at night looking back at a professional life and wondering what it was all about.

Contributors

Michael Bernard-Donals is Professor of English and Jewish Studies at the University of Wisconsin at Madison, where he teaches courses on rhetorical and critical theory and representations of the Holocaust. He is coauthor (with Richard Glejzer) of *Between Witness and Testimony: The Holocaust and the Limits of Representation* (SUNY P, 2001) and co-editor of *Witnessing the Disaster: Essays on Representations of the Holocaust* (Wisconsin UP, 2002). He is completing a book on Jewish memory in the wake of the Shoah.

Michael Bérubé is Paterno Family Professor in Literature at Penn State University. He is currently editing a collection entitled *Aesthetics and Cultural Studies* (Blackwell), and he still teaches Fish's essays, early and late.

Reed Way Dasenbrock is Professor of English and Dean of the College of Arts and Sciences at the University of New Mexico. Educated at McGill, Oxford, and Johns Hopkins, he taught at New Mexico State University from 1981 to 2001. His books include two published by Johns Hopkins UP: *Imitating the Italians: Wyatt, Spenser, Synge, Pound, Joyce* (1991) and *The Literary Vorticism of Ezra Pound and Wyndam Lewis: Towards the Condition of Painting* (1985). His most recent book, *Truth and Consequences: Intentions, Conventions, and The New Thematics*, discusses the work of his former teacher, Stanley Fish, at length.

Terry Eagleton is the Thomas Warton Professor of English Literature at Oxford. His most recent books include *Scholars and Rebels in Nineteenth Century Ireland* (Blackwell, 1999) and a memoir, *The Gatekeeper*

(2002). He is Professor of Cultural Theory and John Rylands Fellow at the University of Manchester.

Stanley Fish is Dean of Liberal Arts and Sciences at the University of Illinois at Chicago.

Gerald Graff is Professor of English and Education at the University of Illinois at Chicago, where he serves as Associate Dean of Curriculum and Instruction in the College of Arts and Sciences, reporting directly to Dean Stanley Fish. He is author of *Professing Literature: An Institutional History* (U of Chicago P, 1987), *Beyond the Culture Wars: How Teaching the Conflicts Can Revitalize American Education* (W.W. Norton, 1992), and *Clueless in Academe: How Schooling Obscures the Life of the Mind* (Yale UP, 2003).

Margaret Kohn is Assistant Professor of Political Science at the University of Florida. Her research on radical democracy, political space, and civil society has appeared in such journals as *Political Theory*, *Polity*, *Dissent*, and *Constellations*. Her book, *Radical Space*, will be published by Cornell University Press in the fall of 2002.

Steven Mailloux is Chancellor's Professor of Rhetoric at the University of California at Irvine, where he teaches rhetoric, critical theory, and cultural studies. His books include three published by Cornell University Press: *Interpretive Conventions* (1982), *Rhetorical Power* (1989), and *Reception Histories: Rhetoric, Pragmatism, and American Cultural Politics* (1998). He is currently working on a book tentatively titled *Rhetorical Paths of Thought*.

Gary A. Olson is Professor of English at the University of South Florida, where he serves as Interim Associate Vice President for Academic Affairs (chief academic officer) at the St. Petersburg campus. His most recent book is *Justifying Belief: Stanley Fish and the Work of Rhetoric* (SUNY P, 2002).

Michael Robertson teaches law at the University of Otago, New Zealand. Besides writing on the jurisprudential aspects of Fish's work, he has published articles on property theory and on critical legal studies. His publications include "Picking Positivism Apart: Stanley Fish on Epistemology and Law" (*Southern California Interdisciplinary Law Journal*,

1999), "The Limits of Liberal Rights: Stanley Fish on Freedom of Religion" (*Otago Law Review*, 2002), and "What Am I Doing? Stanley Fish on the Possibility of Legal Theory" in Legal Theory (forthcoming, 2002).

Martin Stone is Professor of Law and Associate Professor of Philosophy at Duke University, where he also teaches in the Graduate Program in Literature. His recent publications include "The Significance of Doing and Suffering" in G. Postema, ed., *Philosophy and the Law of Torts* (Cambridge UP, 2001) and "Wittgenstein on Deconstruction" in A. Crary and R. Read, eds., *The New Wittgenstein* (Routledge, 2000).

H. Aram Veeser is Associate Professor of English at City College, CUNY. He is editor of four books, including *The New Historicism, Confessions of the Critics*, and *The Stanley Fish Reader*. He has written for *The Nation* magazine.

Evan Watkins is Professor of English at the University of California at Davis. He is the author of numerous works on cultural studies, critical theory, educational politics, and literacy studies. His most recent book is *Everyday Exchanges: Marketwork and Capitalist Common Sense* (Stanford UP, 1998).

Gary S. Wihl is Dean of Humanities and Moody Foundation Professor of Humanities at Rice University. He is the author of two books published by Yale University Press: *Ruskin and the Rhetoric of Infallibility* (1985) and *The Contingency of Theory* (1994). He is currently completing a book on liberalism and literature that includes chapters on George Eliot, Walt Whitman, Judith Shklar, and E. L. Doctorow.

Lynn Worsham is Professor of English at the University of South Florida, where she edits *JAC*, an award-winning journal publishing scholarship on rhetoric, culture, politics, and literacy. Her books include *Race, Rhetoric, and the Postcolonial* (SUNY P, 1999; with Gary Olson).

Index

303